HERE IS YOUR
COMPLIMENTARY

Examination
Copy

Capers-Maddox:
IMAGES AND IMAGINATION

$8.50

We believe you will find the book well
suited to the needs of your course and will
want to consider it for adoption.

THE RONALD PRESS COMPANY
15 East 26th St., New York 10, N.Y.

ROBERTA M. CAPERS is Professor and Chairman of the Department of Art at Tulane University. She previously held positions as Instructor and as Assistant Dean of Education at the Metropolitan Museum of Art; Director of Education and later Acting Director of the Museum of Art of the Rhode Island School of Design; Visiting Lecturer at Wheaton College; and Associate Professor at Indiana University. She has been a Director of the College Art Association and has served as its secretary.

JERROLD MADDOX, Assistant Professor of Art at the University of Kentucky, received his M.F.A. from Indiana University. He was previously Assistant Professor of Humanistic Studies at Monteith College, Wayne State University. Professor Maddox is a well-known painter, having been exhibited at the Museum of Modern Art and in one-man shows. He is also the author of several articles in his field.

Images and Imagination

an introduction to art

Roberta M. Capers
Tulane University

Jerrold Maddox
University of Kentucky

THE RONALD PRESS COMPANY · NEW YORK

Library of Congress Catalog Card Number: 65–11698

PRINTED IN THE UNITED STATES OF AMERICA

Preface

THIS book is addressed primarily to the beginner, whether he be a college freshman, an art student with hopes of becoming a professional painter or sculptor, or a student of the humanities or sciences with a curiosity about the spiritual and creative activities of human beings, an interest in the world of the senses and of the spirit.

In a letter to a friend, George Eliot had this to say of aesthetic education: "I think aesthetic teaching is the highest of all teaching, because it deals with life in the highest complexity. But if it ceases to be aesthetic, if it lapses anywhere from the picture to the diagram, it becomes the most offensive of all teaching." In this book we have done our best to avoid the diagram. We are far too aware of the irrational element in all art to rely solely on rational means to arrive at its understanding. For instance, we offer no theory of color although we recognize that a terminology with which one can think precisely about the artist's use of color can be of service. In the list of further reading that follows the chapter on "The Painter's Means," books are recommended in which the matter of color is fully explored.

In the fullest aesthetic response to a work of art there should be a great deal of imaginative re-creation, and for this reason, it has always seemed to the authors that a book on art appreciation should include the point of view of the practicing artist as well as that of the non-artist. The present text has, therefore, been divided into two parts: Part I, "Art as Experience," has been written by a viewer of art; Part II, "An Artist Looks at Art," by a painter. We are confident that in this division the basic unity of approach is apparent.

The authors had the privilege of studying both formally and informally under the late Professor John Alford, of sharing his personal "dialogues with works of art." The basic ideas of this book, where they are in any sense new, had their source in the vigorous inquiry and discriminating but always warm responsiveness of his relation with the arts. His was the approach of a poet, a philosopher, and a painter.

The authors wish to express their gratitude to three persons in particular who have taken time from busy professional lives to read individual chapters: to Dr. J. A. Hadfield, formerly Director of The Tavistock Clinic in London, who read the section on dream imagery and made valuable suggestions; to Professor Dorothy Seago, Chairman of the Department of Psychology at Newcomb College, who has gone over the whole of Chapter 3 with a searching eye, clarifying the terminology and helping to adjust the related but diverse fields of aesthetics and psychology; and to Dr. Charles Parkhurst who read the entire manuscript with painstaking care and made excellent suggestions for its improvement.

There are two people who, in a most practical way, are largely responsible for this volume, for their patience in constant revision and retyping has known no limits. To Mrs. Edith May and Miss Josephine Reid, who typed the manuscript, our warmest thanks.

We are also grateful to the artists, museums, collectors, and church officials who have allowed us to reproduce the works for which they are responsible.

ROBERTA M. CAPERS
JERROLD MADDOX

Foreword

THERE is nothing so like a human being as that work of his mind and hand and heart, a work of art. We use the word "heart" advisedly, because our language endows that organ with functions that are central to the subject of this book. In our language—which is to say, in our thought—the heart is the seat of the affections and passions, of the will. We are stout-hearted or faint-hearted. One man may be described as all head and no heart; another as tender-hearted, and so on. These phrases have meaning, and, by the same token, it is meaningful to describe art as the work of an artist's heart, because he puts into it so much beyond what is rational (of the mind); so much that transcends craft and technique (of the hand); so much of feeling and emotion, of his life's blood. Here the metaphors of language and of science meet.

To understand a work of art is as difficult as to understand the complexities of human personality, and as rewarding. And just as we accept the need to see another human being in many situations, to take time to explore his mind, and just as we find this an endlessly fascinating study, so with a work of art.

This book is based on the assumption that art, like human beings, takes time to reveal itself and only does so in response to friendly, searching inquiry. One learns to listen to and to watch people; one must learn to look at and, in a sense, to listen to a work of art with an open, undemanding awareness, for the sake of seeing and understanding, not, at the start, in order to make judgments. Evaluative judgments come inevitably as a by-product of understanding. One seeks understanding, and discrimination comes of necessity. We make choices among works of art as we do among people.

Ananda K. Coomaraswamy once remarked that "the artist is not a special kind of person but each person is a special kind of artist." This is the second assumption on which our book is written. This fact accounts in part for the fascination the study of art holds for us, because its variety is directly relative to the variousness among artists. Furthermore, if one looks on oneself not simply as a layman, a stranger in the enchanted world of art, but at least potentially as a "special kind of artist," then one enters the fellowship in a modest way. The fully responsive viewer re-creates the painting or the sculpture if only for himself.

To discover for oneself the special kind of artist one is can be exciting. If you will take up brush or pencil or clay or wax and try for yourself, even though the results may be disappointing, you will find the process illuminating. Your perceptions will be sharpened, your responses enriched. But while this helps, it is not essential. There are clues to be found as much in one's responses to other men's art as in doing it oneself. One of the purposes of this book is to help you to find such clues.

In a lecture on the "Dignity of Man," Pico della Mirandola, philosopher and man of letters of the Renaissance, asked why it was that the Ancients had considered man "of all creatures of the world's stage" the most worthy of wonder. He then proceeded to answer his own question. Having told how "the Highest Father, God the Master-builder, had by the laws of His esoteric wisdom fabricated this house, this world which we see, a very superb temple for the Godhead," he goes on to say, "with the work finished, the Artisan desired that there be someone to reckon up the ratio and proportion of such a big work, to love its beauty, and to wonder at its greatness. Accordingly, now that all things had been completed, . . . He lastly considered creating Man." This contemplator whose function was not only to love and wonder at the beauty of the world, but also to "reckon up its ratio and proportion," that is, to inquire into the laws of its being, was placed at the center of the world from which point he "might more conveniently look around and see whatsoever is in the world."

Thus, according to Pico, God originally laid upon Man the triple duty of wonder, love, and inquiry. But man has always, since leaving Eden, been so occupied with practical matters that these divinely ordained responsibilities have become relegated to specialists: the duty of wonder and love to poets, artists, theologians, and lovers; the duty of inquiry, to philosophers and scientists. And yet even the specialists share in some degree each other's functions: the artist celebrates the beauty of the world, but in so doing, "reckons up its ratio and proportion," while behind all scientific investigation lies the element of wonder.

The capacity for wonder and love is in no way the exclusive possession of the artist. All children have it in large measure; the artist never loses it. But for most of us, aesthetic response to experience for its own sake gradually becomes dulled. It loses its sharp impact as we learn to ask of every color and texture, sound and shape, "What must I do about this, of what use is this to me?" In the arts lies the corrective, the reminder that nothing is commonplace except as we make it so; that when we cease to exercise what Pico called our duty of love and wonder we relinquish our high place only a little lower than the angels, and we acquiesce in mediocrity.

R. M. C.

Contents

I. Art as Experience

ix

II. The Artist Looks at Art

I. ART AS
EXPERIENCE

1. Bruegel's Land of Cockaigne

The Initial Response to the Painting

THE way to learn to read is to read. While the construction of the language, the prosody as it were, may be unfamiliar, the vocabulary which comes out of the artist's experience as a human being is already known. This, in large degree, is shared with him. Just as we all construct with words a world of consciousness parallel to but different from the objective world we live in, so the artist uses his symbolic forms to construct a world analogous to but different from the world he knows through his senses. These other worlds lie close at hand, ours for the entering.

Let us begin our study of art not with generalities and critical theories, not with an analysis of the structure of the language, but with a single work "written" in the language of lines, shapes, colors, images, and ideas. In this first chapter we shall ask you to take a long, leisurely look at a painting by the sixteenth-century Flemish painter Pieter Bruegel the Elder (Pl. I). We shall try to show you the painting in detail and to explain as far as possible the interest it has for us and the pleasure with which we respond to it. In later chapters the artist-author of this book will examine other works more technically, but for the moment we shall approach the painting as viewers or users of art.

Gertrude Stein is credited with once having asked, "How can I tell what I think 'till I hear what I say?" This cogent query can be varied slightly to fit the problem of seeing a picture: How can you really tell what you see until you hear what you say about it? So, tell yourself now what you see in this painting by Pieter Bruegel

3

the Elder. The order of perceiving and the sequence of "awareness" will be your own and will differ from everyone else's. This is right and proper; in fact, it is essential that you look at the picture in your own way, with the responses that are natural to you. It is fatal to understanding to try to have the "correct" reaction to a work of art, or to respond to it in what you believe to be the acceptable manner.

You will presently be given a kind of guided tour through the *Land of Cockaigne*, but let us assume that you have arrived before the scheduled hour and have time to make your own exploratory tour first. The following suggestions may help you in looking. What did you see when you first looked at the reproduction of the painting? What was your initial impression? Did you have any feeling about it, or were you chiefly curious about the subject? Now, as you look again, how are the main objects arranged? What is the general form of the picture? The details are rather extraordinary; why not proceed through the entire picture making a kind of annotated inventory of what you find? The annotations will be your own comments on how things affect you, what they remind you of, and what overtones of meaning they have for you. It is a tendency to which most of us are prone to stop far short of a complete inventory of the contents of a picture; we think we leave out details because they seem unimportant, but actually we fail to see them. Try to see everything, important or unimportant: identifiable objects and their relations to one another; colors, lights, darks; lines, solid masses, shapes; soft, smooth, or rough textures; empty spaces, near foregrounds, distant backgrounds—everything. Long before your "inventory" is complete you will have formed a pretty clear idea of the nature of the *Land of Cockaigne*. You will also have found that the picture has assumed an unmistakable identity of its own, a formal shape and character independent of the separate details and yet made up of them.

At this point you will do well to close the book and try to reconstruct the picture from memory. The major formal character, the organization, will come out clearly, while the background and details will tend to recede. This form is certainly central to the artist's purpose and should prove a clue to his theme, to the central meaning that it was his intention to convey.

All this is not to suggest that to grasp the central theme of an artist's work (if, as in this painting, it has a theme that can be verbally stated) is the one goal of our efforts at understanding. It may be the ultimate goal, but one undertakes the journey quite as much for the pleasures to be encountered along the way as for the satis-

BRUEGEL. *Land of Cockaigne.*

(c. 1525–1569; Flemish.)
Panel, 20½″ × 30¾″.
Alte Pinakothek, Munich.

Pl. I.

faction of reaching the end. So, now, before the tour starts, turn again to the *Land of Cockaigne* and look at it idly with no purpose other than that of amusement. In this less purposeful looking, you may very well see things you missed earlier.

The Detailed Inventory

If you have really looked at the Bruegel picture, what you will now be shown will seem the merest skeleton. It may, however, serve to point up the significance of some of the things you have seen in your own exploration, and will serve as a point of departure for further inquiry.

A small corner of the out-of-doors occupies four-fifths of Bruegel's picture with a glimpse beyond of a hilly coastline and a quiet bay. We look down on three lumpish men sprawled beneath a tree around whose trunk is a circular table loaded with food. The three men, arranged like the spokes of a wheel, with the centered tree as the axle, dominate the picture. A man to our right, who wears a rose-colored jerkin and breeches, has spread out his fur-lined coat beneath him, laid aside book and papers, and, with legs spread wide and hands under his head, is staring upward, wide-eyed and empty-faced. He may be hoping to catch on his tongue the last drop from the overturned wine flask at the edge of the table. His sprawling posture seems out of keeping with the handsome clothes he wears, which certainly suggest a well-to-do gentleman, as his book suggests a scholar. The next man, probably a farmer, is fast asleep with his flail beneath him; while the third, a knight in chain mail and red breeches, his lance and steel gauntlet beside him, is comfortably asleep on what may be a red cushion or, possibly, the curved inner side of his shield. A fourth figure, perhaps another knight since he wears a helmet and gauntlets, rests his arms comfortably on a red cushion and peers up from beneath a low shed on the roof of which is an array of pies or cakes. In an engraving after the painting one can see a roasted bird which appears to be flying directly into the soldier's open mouth.[1]

A fence of woven sausages marks the top of the slope on which the sleepers lie. On a white napkin, spread out as a picnic table cloth, is a pewter dish on which a roast goose is settling itself, ready for the carver; and beyond, a fat little pig trots by with a knife stuck conveniently in its side, and one slice already cut from its

[1] For further discussion of the engraving, see page 8.

BRUEGEL. Detail of the *Land of Cockaigne*.

Alte Pinakothek, Munich.

Fig. 1-1.

back. The cactus plant at the right edge of the picture seems to have leaves made of pastry, and in the middle foreground of the picture, an egg, probably soft boiled, with a wooden handled knife stuck into the open shell, walks off on two legs in the same direction as the pig.

Beyond and below the sausage fence and shrubs clinging to the edge of the bank is the blue-gray water of an arm of the sea on which can be made out a small boat near at hand and a larger one in the distance. Curiously putty-colored and lavender hills, creased and folded, form an irregular coastline, while above the nearest inlet a very puzzling incident is in progress. A figure in a blue shirt and red trousers, with a large wooden spoon in one hand, has apparently emerged, head first, from a hole in the face of the hill and is attempting to cross the inlet with the help of a tree growing on the bank nearer us.

The Subject of the Painting

We have not identified everything and certainly not explained *anything* in this curious picture, but perhaps we have seen enough to have arrived at some understanding of the subject. Cockaigne is obviously a country where there is no shortage of food; where all classes of society abandon the tools of their calling—the scholar-gentleman his books, the farmer his flail, the knight his lance—and comfortably give themselves up to the pleasures of eating, drinking, and sleeping. Food is everywhere at hand, and no one need lift a finger to get it. Such a land of well-fed idleness exists in the folklore of many peoples; an American name for it is the Big Rock Candy Mountains where, among other delights,

> There's a lake of stew, and of whiskey too,
> And you paddle all around in a big canoe . . . .

Pieter Bruegel (c. 1525–1569) lived in the Netherlands where this lazy man's paradise is called *Luilekkerland,* or "lazy-and-licker-ish land" as it has been translated by an authority on Dutch language and culture. According to Prof. Barnouw, "They say it cannot be reached unless you eat your way through the *Rystenbryberg,* the Rice Pudding Mountain." So this is what the little man with the wooden spoon has been up to. Judging from his precarious position, one doubts whether the painter intends him to survive the final perilous lap of his journey into *Luilekkerland.* In our language we have a metaphor rather closely related to this, but evincing a slightly different taste: we speak of someone who has the luck to "live off the fat of the land."

The Netherlanders also have a proverb about the folly of "thatching one's house with tarts," an obvious case of the misuse of good materials. This Bruegel has illustrated in the shed at the left of the picture. It must have been an image that appealed strongly to his sense of the absurd for he had used it in the same literal manner in a picture painted eight years earlier in which he illustrated almost a hundred Flemish proverbs within one village. In the earlier

BRUEGEL. Detail of the *Land of Cockaigne.*
Alte Pinakothek, Munich.
Fig. 1–2.

picture the tarts, or pies, are hopelessly out of reach of anyone without a ladder, and bear more than a slight resemblance to the "pie in the sky, bye and bye" of which the nineteenth-century American worker sang ironically.

An engraving of the *Land of Cockaigne* was published by Hieronymus Cock and inscribed *P Bruegel inventor*. While it follows the painting as we know it very closely (the engraving was apparently made after the wooden panel of the picture had been cut down at the top and at the left), there are certain minor differences between the print and the painting, particularly in the distant view of a town that appears in the print.

The interest for us, however, lies in the fact that at the foot of the print appear rhymed verses in Dutch, that may be translated as follows:

All ye who are lazy and gluttonous, be ye peasant, soldier or scholar, get to *Luilekkerland* and taste there all sorts of things without any labor. The fences are of sausages, the houses covered with cakes; capons and chickens fly around ready roasted.

This is very close to the version popular in England during the Middle Ages which described the rivers as flowing with wine, houses built of candy, streets paved with pastry, while "buttered larks fell from the sky." It is also close to the poem "Schlaraffenland" by the sixteenth-century German poet, Hans Sachs, who matches image for image Bruegel's ambulatory edibles like the pig and the boiled egg, the roast capon, and the sausage fence. Bruegel was certainly familiar with the popular version, but it seems likely that he also knew it in more literary forms where it took on the edge of satire. A thirteenth-century English poem, "The Land of Cockaigne," is a satire on monastic life, and while there is no reference to monasticism in Bruegel's picture, there is more than a hint of satire in his treatment particularly of the military and of the gentry. The one is made to look ridiculous, especially in the little figure under the shed, and the other awkward, both very tender points with these classes of society. The peasant gets off rather better, for while he is certainly overly fat, who can deny the right of a man who works hard to eat well and then to sleep? There is a solemn, tongue-in-cheek literalness in the way Bruegel translates the metaphors of the roof thatched with tarts and the rice pudding mountain into visible, tangible reality. He does precisely what we all do in dreams: he takes a figure of speech and turns it into an image of reality.

The Formal Structure

The real vehicle of his satire lies in the form of his painting, in the organization of his images. Let us look at the painting again. As we made our initial "inventory" of its contents, you may have noticed that there was a marked progression or sequence in our listing, one almost dictated by the picture itself: the scholar-gentleman whose body descends from the center to the lower right; the farmer turned to our left, his body extending from the tree toward the lower left corner of the picture; the knight's body directly opposite the scholar's, but turning slightly clockwise around the tree. The white napkin echoes the white shirt of the farmer and sets up, with his body, a secondary diagonal axis crossing that of the other two figures. These form the radii of an unseen, but no less felt, circle on the ground which is echoed and made explicit by the smaller circle on the table above.

At first glance nothing could seem more static than these three prone figures that lie so heavily on the earth. There is, however, an implied movement, clockwise around the tree. One finds it first in the sweeping curve of the fur-lined coat from below the calf of the scholar's left leg down toward the frame of the picture. Not appreciably slowed by the counter movement of the biped egg, it is picked up again in the obtuse angle of the flail and in the leftward curve of the farmer's body. The long arm of the flail carries on to the lance, and the curve of the knight's body adds momentum despite a second counter movement in his backward turned face. The line of the bank leads us down to the little pig and almost back to our starting point.

But while the pig is clearly going away, we feel compelled to stay with the clockwise movement. The painter makes doubly sure of this by his use of a device with which we shall become very familiar in our discussion of pictorial organization (Chapter 2), that of echoing one element with another similar to it in some way. Our eyes tend to pick up repetition of any sort, apparently as part of the process of perception. Having noted with some surprise the dark-handled knife stuck in the side of the pig, our eyes go next to the similarly dark value of the scholar's left shoe; from it to the second shoe and to the curved area of black broadcloth coat showing under the furs, which points on toward the egg shell where the knife, at least, continues the clockwise direction. A knife has by nature of its use a definite directional character, from handle to blade. Both knives, in the pig and in the egg, point in the main direction that our attention is to travel.

This is the dominant movement in the painting, clockwise around the trunk of the tree. But there is another directional movement from upper left to lower right, stated most firmly in the major diagonal axis of the picture set up by the bodies of the scholar and the two knights. There can be no doubt of the direction of movement along this axis: it is determined first by the fact that the picture is closed at its upper left end and the little figure under the shed faces along the diagonal; and second, by the contrast between the "open" line between the scholar's two feet and the "closed" echoing line of the lance near the other end of the axis. Finally, the direction so determinedly taken by the pig and by the egg makes explicit what would otherwise only be suggested, that while there *is* a way out of this glutton's paradise, the human beings are curiously tethered, unable to leave if they would.

A marked characteristic of the figures, in fact of all the parts of the painting, is that each remains separate from the others and complete in itself. The lower part of the knight under the shed is lost in shadow, and the hind legs of the pig are hidden behind the bank, but with these exceptions, each figure is fully accounted for and in such a way that we sense it very completely, that is, with all our relevant sensory equipment. The fact that there is never confusion between the figures and the background gives further emphatic importance to the figures. The body of the scholar has a geometric simplicity of form. It takes the shape of a St. Andrew's cross whose two diagonal members intersect between the ribs of the figure. Within this geometry, however, is a most convincingly described man of flesh and blood. Look at the legs, the bulging calves, the knees so fat as to be scarcely distinguishable from the thighs above; and the great paunch over which the handsome clothes barely meet. As one looks at the scholar, one is forced to feel in one's own body the ominous sense of having overeaten, of being most uncomfortably "full."

The peasant's body does not differ much from the scholar's in size and weight; only in position. While the scholar still hopes to catch one more drop of wine, though he is beyond getting it for himself, the farmer's position is one of complete relaxation. Where the geometry of the first figure creates a tense balance between its two crossing cylinders (the left arm a continuation of the right leg, and the right arm of the left leg), every curve of the next figure spells rest. Bruegel does more than describe the way a sleeping man *looks*: he makes us *feel* in our own bodies the comfort of getting

ART AS EXPERIENCE

BRUEGEL. Detail of the *Land of Cockaigne.*

Alte Pinakothek, Munich.

Fig. 1–3.

as close as possible to even a rather hard bit of earth before losing all consciousness in sleep.

Bruegel presents his main characters in terms both of their visible shapes and of our tactual-muscular sensations. By "tactual-muscular" sensations are meant both those that come to us through the simple act of touching or stroking a surface, such as fur, its texture; and the sense of solidity that we gain by using our muscles, by pushing or lifting a heavy object. (If you will imagine yourself trying to shove the sleeping farmer to one side, your imaginary sensation will be tactual-muscular.)

There is, however, another aspect of our own experience that Bruegel calls on: our sense of bodily position in relation to the pull of gravity. In the semicircular canals of our ears, and in our muscles, tendons, and joints, we have sensory receptors whose function it is to keep us oriented in space and in relation to the earth. Somehow— and it is impossible to say just how—Bruegel awakens in us bodily sensations of tense and of relaxed muscles, of the heaviness of fatigue and the heaviness of having overeaten. While he does not neglect to describe the look of this fabulous land, there is no question that the painter is concerned primarily with conveying the massive solidity and material "reality" of things rather than the more immaterial, visible delights of the landscape setting in which his parable is placed.

The Theme

This brings us to the basic question of what, in addition to illustrating a popular Utopia, is the painter trying to convey? You will recall that we were very early struck by the wheel-like configuration of the main parts of the picture. The three men serve as the spokes, and we have seen how the wheel seems to move around the axle of the tree. Bruegel has described types of men, not individuals, endowing them with appetites and physical characteristics that unite them to all men while he insists that we recognize them as our brothers by reminding us that we too have felt as they feel. He says, in effect, that not one class of society but all classes, not one man but all men, are unutterably lazy and greedy. But he goes further. He does not for a moment suggest that after a short nap these men will awake and return refreshed to their proper tasks. It is made quite clear that they will wake only to eat again—plenty awaits them—and that their lives will consist forever of a round of eating, sleeping, and eating again. They are caught as helpless spokes in the wheel of their own gluttony and sloth, doomed to go around in an endless circle over which they no longer have any control.

In Bruegel's day, gluttony was looked on as a deadly sin; it was a form of self-indulgence that worked hardship on others. In an economy of scarcity, if one man overeats, another is apt to go hungry. An awareness of this fact Bruegel could assume in his audience. It is characteristic of this painter that he should re-examine such a concept and interpret it in the light of his own experience and of his own values. Thus his picture of gluttony is purposely set in the mythical land of plenty where the social implications of the sin are removed. Bruegel is then free to portray the vices of gluttony and sloth not in theological terms, but in terms of the individual who is caught in their self-destroying grip. It is further characteristic of this sixteenth-century humanist-painter that while the morality play is performed with generalized actors standing for classes of society, it is ultimately with the individual that he is concerned.

The setting of his "morality play" Bruegel makes as sensuously agreeable as space and his main purpose permit. He records his own delight in blue distances over water, and notes with loving care the characteristic light banding of the dark violet bark of the cherry tree. (This particular cherry tree bears fruit that resembles *brioches*, but this is just one of the vagaries of Cockaigne.) While Bruegel deals with generalized images of men, he allows himself free rein when it comes to describing the few particulars of nature called for by the subject. The line with which he describes the contours of each figure is a firm, uncompromising boundary, clearly setting out the shape and solidity of each, with all the definiteness of a clear-cut, conceptual image; but when he turns to a description of the shrubbery and of the tree whose branches pierce the rice pudding mountain, his line becomes a living thing, full of the unexpected irregularities that nature offers. In describing what he sees, the artist suggests; in setting before us the images of his conceptual ideas, he defines. The color of the three men's clothing is again generalized: one feels that each is the color that it should be, inherent in the dye of its material. But grass, which in the same system of mental imagery ought by rights to be green, varies from a pale unnatural green through various tones of warm brown to rose, while the hills are putty-colored and lavender with a pervasive, rosy bloom.

The painter's primary intention seems to have been to make his theme as credible as possible by making us feel the bodies of his actors as though they were our own. Sloth and gluttony are sins of the body first; therefore we are made to feel them in a bodily rather than a visual way. But the image of a turning wheel with which the painter presses home his point can only be understood as a thing seen. Here he must appeal to our eyes, and the whole structure of the picture must be grasped visually.

In the central image of a turning wheel whose spokes are human beings, lies the statement of the painter's theme. It may be summed up as the proposition that although man has every opportunity to realize the fullness of life, set down as he is in the midst of an abundant and beautiful nature and endowed with capacities beyond those of other living creatures (witness the scholar's book, the farmer's flail, even the lance of the soldier—all artifacts beyond the ingenuity of other animals), he falls victim to his own weakness, his own sins—in this case, sloth and greed. More briefly, the sins of the flesh fetter and imprison the mind and the body of man.

Representation and Abstraction

The great French painter Henri Matisse (1869–1954) once made the statement that art arises from one of two impulses felt by the artist: the first is to share with others something of the quality of experience; the second is the desire to make an icon, a holy thing. The first leads generally to representation; the second, to some sort or degree of abstraction. We shall come back to these terms *representation* and *abstraction* presently, but for the moment let us see how, if at all, the statement applies to our picture. Bruegel shares the quality of his own sensory experience with us both in the figures of his main theme and in what little we can see of their setting. Is there also something of the icon? Not perhaps in the sense of a "holy thing," but is not our gluttons' wheel an icon, the image of an idea? Bruegel uses an abstract, geometric form to convey his meaning to us, and it is characteristic of the painter that the form he uses is one that has had a long life in human history both practical and symbolic. It is a form with which we are all familiar, not intellectually as we know geometric figures; it is not simply a circle, but a wheel, the circling of whose spokes is intimately bound up with the life of everyone. There is certainly a connection between Matisse's icon and Bruegel's wheel, but it is not entirely clear. What then, did Matisse mean by an icon?

The Greek word *icon* has the meaning of *image* or *representation*, and it is clear that Matisse must have had in mind something other than this. Since he went on to say that the impulse to make an icon leads to abstraction, we can guess that he had in mind the Christian, Greek, and Byzantine religious images which we generally describe as *abstract* (Fig. 1–4). The word *abstract* is one for which we shall have use in later chapters so we may as well come to terms with it at once.

Among Webster's several definitions of the verb *to abstract* the most significant for our purpose is this: "to select or separate; to epitomize or reduce to a summary." The adjective also has various meanings, the most useful to us being: "general, not concrete; as an abstract subject." The verb *to abstract* is made up of two Latin

Madonna and Child.

(c. 520 A.D.)
Mosaic, San Apollinare Nuovo, Ravenna.
Photo: Alinari-Art Reference Bureau.

Fig. 1–4.

PIETRO LORENZETTI. Detail of
*Madonna and Child with St.
Francis and St. John the
Evangelist.*

(fl. 1320–1345; Italian.)
Fresco, left transept, lower church,
   San Francesco, Assisi.

Photo: Alinari-Art Reference Bureau.

Fig. 1–5.

words: *abs*, meaning *from*, and *trahere*, to draw. So an abstract or abstraction is something *drawn out from*. In the mosaic (Fig. 1–4) the essential meaning of the image of the Mother of God holding her divine Child has been drawn out, *abstracted*, from the likeness of a mother and baby; it has been given a form which expresses dignity, is remote and more than human; it has indeed become a "holy thing." The Byzantine artist has epitomized the abstract qualities of maternity, of love, and of divinity instead of describing the Virgin Mary with Jesus simply as a loving mother with her baby. In Pietro Lorenzetti's painting (Fig. 1–5) there is much more description of observable behavior and of human qualities though the painter's purpose is still clearly to convey a sense of divinity in human form. But in Andrea Mantegna's *Mother and Child* (Fig. 1–6) the artist's purpose has changed and the emphasis is now on the observable, perceptual image with which the painter is familiar.

MANTEGNA. *Mother and Child.*

(1431–1506; Italian.)
Engraving, 13⅝″ × 10⅚″.
Courtesy of the Trustees, The British Museum, London.

Fig. 1–6.

RUBENS. *Hélène Fourment and Her Children Clara, Johanna, and Franz.*

(1577–1640; Flemish.)
Panel, 44½" × 32¼".
The Louvre, Paris.

Fig. 1–7.

In Matisse's words, Mantegna is sharing with us his sense of the quality of perceptual experience, and if, in the human relationship of mother and baby he finds something divine, and shares this with us, he has arrived at a statement of divinity not by a process of abstraction but of description. Rubens in the portrait of his wife and children (Fig. 1–7) carries this even further away from the general toward a very particular, very special instance.

In order fully to understand the use of the word *abstraction* in art criticism we must go a step beyond Webster in another direction from that indicated by the "drawing out of essential meaning."

ART AS EXPERIENCE

MONDRIAN. *Composition.*

(1872–1944; Dutch.)
Oil on canvas, 15⅞″ × 12⅝″.

Collection, The Museum of Modern Art,
    New York.
Gift of Philip C. Johnson.

Fig. 1–8.

To take a very simple example, while an apple is concrete, its redness is abstract, as is its sweetness or roundness. Furthermore, one may pick two apples from a tree and one from the ground and have enough to supply each of three children, the whole procedure being quite objective and concrete. But the transaction can be translated into a simple statement of relationships: $2 + 1 = 3$, which is, of course, a complete abstraction expressed in abstract symbols. It is this matter of *relationships* that is further significant for a study of the arts, and we speak of the *arrangement* of the parts within a work of art as its *abstract form;* the non-representational elements, we call abstract.

In a work of completely abstract art like Piet Mondrian's *Composition* (Fig. 1–8) there are no images of things seen, felt, or handled, but *only* relationships between areas, squares and rectangles, and quantities of "redness," "blackness," white, and yellow. But in every work of art the abstract elements exist; the parts are related to each other; there is some sort of organization. In our painting by Bruegel, not only is the wheel the abstract form within which the visible, tangible figures are related; but the relations between the figures and the space enclosed within the frame, the directional relationships which we have discussed at some length, the relation of one color to another, and finally, and not least important, the relation of the idea of human sin to the subjugation of the human will— all these are abstract elements of the picture. Abstraction in art is, then, not a phenomenon peculiar to the twentieth century; it is the structure, the inner form of all art.

Suggestions for Further Reading

The following books are all useful for accounts of Bruegel's life and particularly for further examples of his work.

DELEVOY, R. L. *Bruegel: Historical and Critical Study.* S. Gilbert, Trans. Geneva: S. Skira, 1959.

GLÜCK, G. *Pieter Bruegel the Elder.* E. B. Shaw, Trans. Paris: Hyperion Press, 1937.

GROSSMAN, F. *Bruegel, the Paintings.* London: Phaidon Press, 1955.

HUXLEY, A., and JEAN VIDEPOCHE (pseud.). *The Elder Pieter Bruegel.* New York: Willey Book Co., 1938.

2. Form and Meaning

Practical and Aesthetic Artifacts

Before pursuing further the matter of abstract form introduced at the end of the previous chapter, let us digress briefly in order to widen the subject of our inquiry. A book which purports to introduce its readers to an understanding of art should certainly not postpone indefinitely the question, "What is art, this thing we are trying to understand?" Art is many things, and it cannot usefully be compressed into a single definition. On the other hand, the question should very properly be asked and may be answered discursively if not succinctly.

Because the word *art* is so various and so thoroughly imbued with emotional and aesthetic overtones, it will be useful to start with a thoroughly unemotional, quite colorless word which will provide us with a sound but cautious approach to its more prestigious relative. This word is *artifact*. The Bruegel painting we have been considering, this page of text, the house, the bridge, the highway intersection, these are all artifacts—literally, things made by skill.

The purpose and function of an artifact may be practical, as in the case of a teapot, which acts as a means to another end, that of pouring tea. Or the purpose and function may be aesthetic, as in the case of a picture or a piece of sculpture or of jewelry. Such aesthetic artifacts, as distinguished from practical, are ends in themselves, serving no other purpose than to be enjoyed (used) for their own sake. They "ask" only that we adopt an aesthetic attitude toward them, an attitude of open, disinterested awareness. (The meaning in which we use the word *aesthetic* becomes quite clear if one thinks of its opposite, *anaesthetic*.) An artifact that functions aesthetically appeals through our un-anaesthetized senses to our mind and our feelings. A work of so-called fine art is simply an artifact whose purpose and function are aesthetic and which meets certain acceptable standards of quality.

Human beings are not the only makers of artifacts. A bird's nest, a spider's web, the beautiful though rather fearful cone of a hornet's nest are all artifacts into whose design, over the generations, has gone a high degree of constructive imagination and whose making has required great skill. These forms have been developed as the most efficient solution to practical problems posed by the conditions and habits of the lives of their makers: birds, spiders, hornets.

The purpose of an artifact lies with its maker, the artist; its function or use lies with the finished object and is primarily the concern of the user. The success or value of the artifact will depend on how well it works, on how closely its design is adapted to its purpose, and is in direct proportion to the skill and integrity of its maker and to the appropriateness and durability of its materials. The standard by which one judges an artifact is not, "Do I like it?" but "Does it work well?" We shall assume that works of so-called fine art are simply artifacts with special purposes and functions, and will apply to them as to their practical counterparts the same standard: "Does it work?" However, this at once presents a difficulty, since the artist's purpose in making an aesthetic artifact is not always self-evident. Take, for example, the little bronze by the contemporary English sculptor Henry Moore (Fig. 2–1). It is intended like all aesthetic artifacts to exist as an end in itself, for what its form and orderly structure can convey of meaning and pleasure. It appeals to our mind and feelings, and, furthermore, it speaks differently to each of us. Some find in its full-length figure within a kind of bronze sheath a suggestion of the dead sheltered in earth; others, an analogy to the child in its mother's womb; others see it as a plant form, a jack-in-the-pulpit, perhaps. Some respond primarily to the sensuous feel of the form and find no other meaning in it. Henry Moore himself calls his bronze by the non-commital title of *Interior–Exterior*, but seems not to mind when it is read by others as an image of the life and death cycle. The precise meaning in verbal terms is wholly unimportant. What matters is that the little bronze has a vital and meaningful form. It exists on its own terms.

While most of our artifact-environment is primarily practical in purpose, it functions not only practically but also aesthetically. That is, it affects us pleasantly or unpleasantly; it excites our inter-

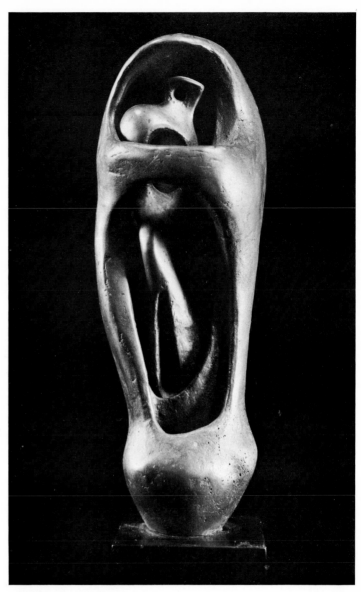

Moore. *Interior–Exterior.*
(1898–   ; English.)
Bronze, H. 8¼″.
Private Collection, New Orleans.

Fig. 2–1.

est, or dulls our senses with its ugly monotony. There are certain objects, like a mousetrap or a toothbrush, which may command our moderate admiration by dint of their efficiency, but otherwise are strictly and exclusively practical. Others have had a certain amount of decorative enrichment added, like rhinestones on a pair of ladies' glasses, and can be described as having been designed with a primarily practical purpose but with a secondary aesthetic purpose. Whether they function well or badly aesthetically is a matter of taste.

However, many artifacts whose purpose is practical have a formal beauty which is a by-product of the designer's solution of his practical problem rather than the result of an aesthetic purpose or intention. This is true of many "tools" which have achieved their formal design through years of development, through years of constant modification toward an ever better solution of the practical purpose. This is also true of some—not all—of our great highway intersections. It is doubtful whether the engineers who design them take into account the pleasure we may have in looking down at them from the air. Even on the ground the beauty of the pattern, as experienced by someone who might be called a participant rather than an observer, seems to be inherent in the sweeping curves and in their intricately efficient relation to one another. While the designer's purpose was probably almost exclusively practical, the complex artifact resulting from the solution of the traffic problem is capable of giving considerable pleasure to anyone who will adopt an aesthetic attitude toward it.

In the case of artifacts whose primary purpose is practical, unless that practical purpose is well-fulfilled, that is, unless the object functions well practically, it will not function well aesthetically. If the highway intersection does not work, if traffic snarls and accidents occur, all its handsome pattern is valueless. The Victorian teacup illustrated (Fig. 2–2) is of a pretty green color, rather attractively decorated with vines in raised relief. But when one tries to hold a full cup of tea, one's fingers are sharply pricked by the embossings on the lower curve of the handle, which is also far too small for

Victorian Tea Cup.
Private Collection, New Orleans.
Fig. 2–2.

Victorian Tea Pot.
Private Collection, New Orleans.
Fig. 2–3.

comfort and security. The designer's efforts to make his cup pleasing to look at ruined it for practical use, and once having experienced the discomfort of trying to drink from the teacup, one can no longer find it visually agreeable.

On the other hand, ornament can be applied successfully to the surface of a practical artifact. The silver teapot illustrated (Fig. 2–3) has been decorated in such a way as to enhance one's pleasure both in looking at the teapot and in pouring tea from it. Notice the smoothness of the inside of the handle, the decorative thumb stop on the upper, outer curve, and the two ivory collars which serve both to insulate the handle and to frame it. The aesthetic function of artifacts designed primarily for a practical purpose is largely decorative, but also, in varying degree, expressive. When the English owner of the silver service of which this teapot is a part went to Hong Kong as its Anglican Episcopal bishop, he had the original silver knob replaced by a little figure of a Chinese Mandarin, an admirable case of ornament which is both decorative and expressive, a polite bow to the bishop's Chinese friends. The teapot is intended to be agreeable both to own and to use; its designer's aesthetic purpose was probably as important as his practical.

Decorative Quality

Decorative quality arises from an ordered variety of sensory stimuli. Too much order in artifacts, as in life, becomes monotonous. On the other hand, too much variety becomes chaotic. One's perception of the character of the whole artifact is confused and therefore unsatisfying. We are all familiar with the wallpaper or the rug in which "too much is going on," in which one's attention is never able to rest on any coherent pattern or organization of the whole, because the various parts are all so insistently demanding.

Ordered variety may be inherent in the nature of the material used, in the grain of a fine wood, for instance; or it may arise from the effect of light on a polished surface such as silver, or from the varying relations between the dimensions of the object, such as the relations between the diameter of the mouth of the Greek oil jug shown in Fig. 2–6 and that of the neck, of the belly at its widest, of the stem, and of the foot. Proportion is a matter of ordered relationships. The proportions of the oil jug and of the wine cup in Fig. 2–7 are decoratively pleasing; those of too many jugs and cups available today are dull and uninteresting.

As we have seen, decorative quality can be added in the form of applied ornament. The material of which the oil jug was made was a rather uninteresting reddish clay, so a "slip," or wash, of white clay was laid over it to make a more pleasing background. The ornamental bands of palmettes around the neck, and the solid base of black were added as a frame—an element whose purpose is to provide order—for the little scene of a child with his toy cart taking leave of his mother as he prepares to board Charon's boat and be ferried across the river Styx.

Practical and Aesthetic Functions of Artifacts

This type of pottery jug was originally designed for the primarily practical purpose of containing and pouring oil; it was an ancient oil cruet. It is important that oil should flow slowly from its container; thus the jug was provided with a narrow neck. On the other hand, it is difficult to fill a narrow-necked jug, so the mouth of the jug was shaped like a funnel. The dimensions and shape of the body must have been arrived at partly in the interests of convenient handling and of stability, and partly with an eye to decorative satisfaction, while the foot was made large enough to provide a firm base, but not so large as to dwarf the body of the pot. The resulting jug undoubtedly functioned most satisfactorily in the household of many a Greek family, but it gradually came to serve another purpose besides that for which it was designed. Its form was apparently considered so beautiful that it became customary to place oil jugs on the graves of the dead. This led in the course of time to the practice of making special, funeral oil jugs appropriately decorated with such scenes of leave-taking as the one illustrated here. Funeral vases are occasionally decorated with scenes of mourners at a grave on which they have placed offerings of similar jugs. Thus, an artifact originally intended to function in a practical way, and carefully designed for that purpose, functioned also so well aesthetically that its aesthetic function finally took first place, and the jugs were made for their symbolic and decorative value alone.

A well-designed house not only provides protection from the weather and from burglars, but also allows its owner to take pride in it as a thing of beauty, as a handsome addition to the community. The proportions of the John Brown house in Providence, Rhode Island (Fig. 2–4) are good; the relations between window openings and plain wall spaces provide the ordered variety that we find visually pleasing; the balance of vertical and horizontal accents is agreeable. Though simple, the house is undeniably handsome. But it also performs an expressive function: it speaks of stability and integrity (good qualities in the home of the head of a great shipping business); of "elegance," so dear to the heart of the late eighteenth century when the house was built; and in almost equal proportions, of expansive hospitality, and of security and privacy. As it approaches its second centennial, the house is structurally sound, and with minor adaptations to modern methods of heating and of lighting, is eminently satisfactory to live in. It still functions well both practically and aesthetically. In the field of architecture the two functions are almost equally important, and the two purposes weigh simultaneously in the mind of the architect.

John Brown House.
Providence, Rhode Island, 1786.
Joseph Brown, architect.
Courtesy of the Rhode Island Historical Society.

Fig. 2–4.

The engineer is traditionally associated with practical purposes, and the artifacts that he produces are certainly primarily practical in purpose and in function, but as we have already seen in the case of the highway intersection, their aesthetic function is not to be overlooked. The designer of the George Washington Bridge (Fig. 2–5), which spans the Hudson River not far from the northern tip of Manhattan Island, was primarily concerned with the construction of a safe highway across the river. As far as the ordinary citizen and

ART AS EXPERIENCE

George Washington Bridge.
Entrance; view toward southwest.
Hudson River, New York.
Othmar Ammann, engineer-designer.
Photo: The Port of New York Authority.

Fig. 2–5.

motorist knows, the bridge fulfills its practical function perfectly; but in addition to this, the pattern of its great pylons and arcs against the sky is a memorable one, and carries an expressive meaning that is hard to define. It probably means something different to every person who has ever approached it down the parkway from the north, and to every resident of upper Manhattan who has lived with its great image of effortless strength framed in his windows. For some the bridge stands as a symbol of man's mastery over space.

Form and Expression

What makes the bridge memorable? What gives it the power to transcend its practical use and to become a symbol? The answer is, its form. The bridge has no appreciable quality of color or texture of materials, and except at night when its spare form is transformed by the addition of lights, its shape is simply outlined in dark against light. What does seem to have meaning is the marching rhythm of the repeated verticals leading up to the two great arched pylons; the tremendous arc swung between these two highest points and the lesser arcs that rise from each land-based terminal to join their giant brother at the top and speed him on his way; and finally, the flatter curve of the roadway which rises very slowly to touch the great arc at its lowest point and then, as slowly, descends to earth. It is as though the roadway, the most obviously practical feature of the whole design, symbolized the horizon of earth itself, deviating little from the horizontal plane on which we live and move.

In such a way one may see the form of the bridge, the formal structure in which the artist's design took shape. The fact that this form was dictated by technical considerations does not in any way detract from the success with which the bridge performs its aesthetic function, in which decoration and expression are combined in proportions differing with each observer and even with the moods of one.

And so we find ourselves back at the point where the previous chapter closed, with a consideration of *form*, but our initial use of the term has been broadened to include not only its aesthetic but also its practical function.

As the term is used in art criticism, form may denote one of two things: it is the sum of all the internal relations of a work of art or an artifact, and it also is used to refer to the total, external character of the work. To put it another way, *form is based on some kind of ordered structure, a set of relationships, but it also denotes the totality, the unity of the whole.* The word *composition* has a somewhat similar meaning. It puts the emphasis on the act of organization rather than on the resultant wholeness.

Order, Form, and Pattern

The most basic factor of what we call order is simply recognizable repetition. We spend our lives in a context both of natural and man-made repetitive order: the sun rises and sets, day in and day out; the seasons follow each other in a sequence that repeats itself year after year. Some form of predictable order is an absolute essential to human life, and within it we plan and live out our lives, taking it very much for granted until it is suddenly upset. A newspaper strike that deprives us of our daily paper, a hurricane that puts all the power lines out of "order," are probably only a little less disturbing to us today than was an eclipse of the sun before man learned to predict with certainty not only its occurrence, but also the reassuring return of light to the darkened world. Strikes and hurricanes, man-made and natural upsets of the ordered routines of our lives, are disturbing or terrifying or merely annoying to us in proportion to our investment (financial or emotional) in the order that is disrupted.

Natural order is evident in a more or less repetitive likeness of forms that provides a basis for orderly classification, so that while we recognize the difference between a maple and a pine tree, we also see the similarity that makes it possible to classify both as trees in contrast to the quite different forms of a lettuce or a parsley plant.

We speak of forms of literature: of prose and poetry, of poetic forms, of the epic or the sonnet; or of forms of government: a democracy, a dictatorship; and what is implied is a likeness of inherent structure among examples which enables us to classify them. We call a fourteen-line poem a sonnet only if we recognize its structure as a complex whole with a recognizable rhyme scheme in which rhymes are repeated in a special kind of order.

When we speak of *order* we tend to mean a *recognizable repetition of elements;* when we speak of *form* we tend to mean the *wholeness* or *unity* of *an orderly, sometimes complex structure.*

The word *form* is frequently used, however, with little or perhaps no conscious reference to complexity, though it is rarely if ever used without reference to distinct unity. If we think of the form of a circle or of an egg, it is probably the object-as-a-whole that we have in mind, rather than any of its parts and their relations to the whole. And even if we recognize the form and respond to it as a unity with an internal structure, neither our recognition nor our aesthetic response need depend on a knowledge or recognition of what the structural relations are. We do not need to understand the geometry of ovoids nor the theory of melody to recognize that an egg and a tune have form. Nevertheless, if the forms of the egg and the tune are examined, both are found to possess an orderly structure involving internal repetitive elements. For instance, the curved surfaces of the egg are symmetrical: they repeat one another about a central axis, from whatever side the egg is examined. The form of the tune is due to the repetition of harmonic intervals or sequences of notes, arranged in an order of tones, or rising and falling pitch. The structure of some primitive music consists of an order of tones in which separate and distinguishable notes do not occur. The music of drums and other percussion instruments may, on the other hand, consist of a repetition of a single sound, without change of tone, but in a repetitive order of time. In any case the repetitive order is basic to the form of the music; repetition is involved.

We sometimes speak of "patterns of behavior," and again repetition is involved. *Pattern* is another word which has meanings approximating those of order and form, and which is also basic to an understanding of the nature of aesthetic artifacts. The oil jug shown in Fig. 2–6 is decorated around its shoulder with a pattern called a Greek fret which serves as an upper border of the space in which the scene of Charon's boat is placed. As it is commonly used by those concerned with material design, pattern signifies an orderly repetition of a visual unit over a surface. In a wider sense, it signifies any model which may be copied, the idea of repetition being introduced in the act of copying. Home dress-makers use paper patterns, and the models from which tools or parts of machines are reproduced are referred to as patterns.

Repetition is at the root of all three terms—*form, order,* and *pattern*—and some kind of repetition of the elements of an artifact is essential to our ability to grasp it as a form. But just as we need not be conscious of the elements repeated or of the manner of their repetition to recognize and respond to a natural form like a tree or an egg, so we need not at once recognize or follow the complexities of an aesthetic form in order to grasp it, to respond to its aesthetic meaning, to have it *work*.

Delight in repetition and a rudimentary sense of form make themselves known very early in our lives and remain with us whether or not we consciously cultivate them. As Sir Herbert Read once pointed out, the impulse to put the clock in the middle of the mantelpiece or parsley around the cold mutton is innate in all of us.

No one who has had any experience with children needs to be reminded of how very early the delight in repetition appears. Imitative play of all sorts is a form of repetition; constant demands for the re-reading of a favorite story or recitations again and again of nursery rhymes which cannot possibly make sense to a three-year-old are repetitive orders that the child finds pleasurable in themselves, that is, of aesthetic value. Books of Mother Goose rhymes

Lekythos, or Oil Jug.

(Early fifth century B. C.; Greek.)
H. 12½″.

*The Metropolitan Museum of Art,
New York.*

Fig. 2–6.

are, of course, generally illustrated, but the child delights in the repeated sounds and rhythms before he begins to look at the pictures (or before they are shown to him) and certainly long before the series of fantastic images that follow each other through "Hey diddle diddle, the cat and the fiddle" can possibly have any kind of meaning for him.

The desire for the unity of forms also puts in a very early appearance, as one realizes from a child's unassisted play with blocks. They are placed "repetitiously" one above the other making a splendid form until they collapse. The idea that it is a house or a tower is generally introduced by an adult or by another child. The forms that the child makes are frequently balanced, sometimes arranged in patterns or in a sequence of shape or color. The same principles of organization that one finds in adult art and artifacts put in an early though tentative appearance, usually obscured by a mass of apparently quite haphazard experimentation.

Repetition is also basic in technical pursuits which, according to Prof. Boas, are in part responsible for the artistic impulse among primitive people.[1] In almost any purposive activity repetition is essential. It seems probable that primitive man's aesthetic pleasure in the woven pattern of his seed basket was a mixture of pride in the practical success of his activity and pleasure in the rhythmic movements or technical gestures that produced the basket.

Vitality

But questions arise: What kind and how much repetition is desirable? When is it meaningful and agreeable, and at what point does it become monotonous? Why is one form alive and another lifeless? These are difficult questions.

What are the requirements and the nature of these forms that seem to us beautiful, or moving, or both? There are many theories of aesthetic value, many criteria of judgment. The theory advanced here, which owes much to others (though it is simpler than most), might be described as a biological theory: what we require in life we demand of art. The character and some of the requirements of the human body and mind are transferred to those products of the human hand and heart and mind that we call art, and we judge works of art by criteria derived from these biological factors.

Our bodies are complex but highly ordered organisms; a true work of art also has this dual character of vital order. Physically we require balance and stability and a sense of assurance that we know our way about in the space that surrounds us. We are made ill when either by unaccustomed motion—in a ship, a plane, or a car—or by disease of the inner ear, our orientation to space and to the pull of gravity is upset. The discomfort we feel when a picture hangs crookedly on the wall and the minor, but real satisfaction we feel in straightening it, making it level, are the simplest instances of the way in which we transfer this physical requirement to the area of aesthetic preference.

[1] Franz Boas, *Primitive Art* (New York: Dover Publications, Inc., 1955), p. 349.

ART AS EXPERIENCE

Certainly the aesthetic principles of harmony, balanced opposition, proportion, and sequence of movement all have their analogies in the complex structure of the human body. Furthermore, there are certain rules of order to which the body conforms in its relations with the outside world that also find an echo in a work of art. Jean Charlot, in an illuminating article,[2] finds the ultimate source of aesthetic order in the nature of our physical circumstances and in the rhythmic character of our lives.

Two main laws, horizontal and vertical—are strung implacably straight: the plumbline of gravity that each of us carries inside himself as if it were a physical conscience, so to speak, ready to reproach man his least attempt at obliquity; and another law, made visible in water levels, that checks from a whole ocean to the content of a cocktail glass. Between the prongs of this compass, set at right angles to each other, man lives cautiously, as if they were the jaws of the dragon that was an essential prop of mediaeval mysteries. A third law, equally faceless, is one of rhythm, meaning for us mostly the clocked beat of the heart and meticulous intake of breath. . . .

In a work of art the clear statement of the horizontal–vertical relationship expresses security, serenity, quiet; the obscuring of this relationship or its alteration, what Charlot calls the "least attempt at obliquity," immediately upsets the equilibrium and suggests uncertainty, mystery, change, or excitement, depending on the context. The *Last Supper* by Leonardo and the same subject treated by Tintoretto illustrate this well. (Figs. 2–10 and 2–11.) Too much emphasis on the horizontal–vertical relationship, too continuous and regular a repetition of equivalent elements make for monotony, for the lifeless character of most kitchen linoleum. Too little of the requisite factors of order, too much variety and unpredictability in the pattern lead to chaos in which we lose our way and all aesthetic value vanishes in the confusion.

In our dealings with others and with the world outside ourselves, some sort of dependable order is, as we have already noted, essential, but so is the element of surprise, of uncertainty. We need the unexpected deviation from order to remind us that we are alive. The analogy is again very close. A work of art must be ordered in structure but it must also live; and living involves deviations from the norm, a sense of movement and, above all, of tension. The elements are held in a tense equilibrium not by inertia, but by the will of the artist.

[2] Jean Charlot, "Nature and the Art of Josef Albers," *College Art Journal*, Vol. XV, p. 194; Spring, 1956.

What Is Art?

There are many definitions of art, many diverse explanations of its function in human life. But a broad area of agreement exists in this matter of order: art involves some kind of order, and, to be meaningful, its ordered forms must have a life of their own. Nor is the vitality of a work of art necessarily a reflection of what is generally thought of as reality. As the philosopher Irwin Edman has put it, "Art with its language of realization may be a way the metaphysician has forgotten, not to describe but to utter reality." And again, "The arts do not tell us *about* or abstract *from;* they exhibit the *what,* the quality itself." [3]

In the balance of this chapter and in subsequent chapters we shall examine artifacts, whether practical or aesthetic or both, in an effort to arrive at some understanding of the order and vitality that make them meaningful, that make them qualify as art.

The Voyage of Dionysos

Let us start with a fine example of a minor art, one of those practical artifacts whose purpose is almost equally aesthetic, an instance of decoration at its best. The painted decoration of the wine cup or kylix in Fig. 2–7 was the work of a Greek painter Exekias, in the latter part of the sixth century B. C. The form of the cup is satisfying to look at as well as to handle, and one learns from the experts that the lip is so subtly adjusted to its function that there is not the slightest danger of spilling the wine. The proportions of foot to body, and of the slender stem to the swelling bowl seem precisely as they should be to give the cup an air of light equilibrium.

The interior is treated as a framed circular picture showing Dionysos, the Greek god of wine, sailing over the sea in a ship whose mast is twined with grapevines hung with heavy clusters of grapes. It was said that the god of the vintage had once voyaged far and wide teaching the peoples of the world the culture of the grape, and presumably the delights of wine. In Exekias' picture the sea is symbolically indicated by a school of dolphins accompanying the god on his voyage. The movement of the ship as it seems to slip smoothly through invisible water is expressed by the beautiful lines of the hull; the prow and stern are carved like the nose and tail of a dolphin.

The form of the picture, like that of the cup it decorates, is curvilinear: its repetitive order is composed of curved lines and images

---

[3] Irwin Edman, *Arts and the Man* (New York: Mentor Books, 1949), pp. 134, 135.

The Voyage of Dionysos.

Inside of a kylix painted by Exekias.
(Mid-sixth century B. C.; Greek.)
D. 14½″.

Staatliche Antikensammlungen, Munich.

Fig. 2–7.

that reflect each other in a fascinating but irregular pattern. No two lines, no two dolphins, are identical. The water line of the ship's hull is echoed by the shorter one of its deck. The bending yardarm, from which the rectangular dipping lug is hung, repeats, but in reverse, the curves of the hull, which duplicate each other on either side of the reclining figure of Dionysos. The shorter, more abrupt curves or humps of his knees and chest are repeated with variations in the four branches of the grapevine as well as in the bodies of the seven dolphins.

The mast, which is stepped a little forward of the center of the boat, leans slightly back toward the right. The junction of the mast with the deck is the center of the picture but is placed just below the center of the cup so that the mast does not coincide with a radius of the cup's circle. The expressive effect of this is to suggest the greater expanse of sky above than of sea beneath and gives the boat a certain stability; but decoratively it supplies the variation from the exact order that is needed to give the picture life. The slanting mast, the taut halliards, and the wind-filled sail all serve expressively to speed the ancient voyager on his way.

It is instructive to experiment with a rearrangement of the elements in such a composition as this where each image is separate and movable. Imagine the ship placed so that its deck would coincide roughly with the horizontal diameter of the circle; put the mast just off the vertical. Can you see the life ebbing out of the design? Try to persuade the dolphins to swim in single file, regularly spaced, and in one direction from a little above the stern, under the hull, and up to a point just above the prow; the procession would be more orderly, but would lose its vitality. The arrangement made by Exekias gives a wonderful sense of the sportiveness of the fish; they are not going anywhere in particular; they are swimming for the fun of swimming. The more orderly form would destroy this effect entirely and would at the same time give the pattern a mechanical instead of a vital character, besides being contrary to the nature of dolphins. And yet, now that the dolphins have been moved about a little, look again at the rather subtle order that does exist. Behind Dionysos, three dolphins swim along with the ship; ahead, three swim around the prow and back toward the ship's stern. These six make a balanced opposition of groups of three. But a seventh dolphin joins with one from each of the two groups to make a third triad, and he decides the issue of direction by swimming left. A seventh bunch of grapes also hangs to the left of the central axis of the picture. Thus the odd fish and the odd fruit add their weight to the direction of the sailor himself to carry the ship over the "wine dark sea." Since this particular boat was usually seen through the wine the cup was intended to contain, Homer's description seems peculiarly apt.

Bellini's *Madonna Adoring the Sleeping Child*

Giovanni Bellini's *Madonna Adoring the Sleeping Child* (Fig. 2–8) is in quite another category. Instead of a piece of decorated pottery intended for festive, if practical use, this little altarpiece, only just over two feet high, was intended as an aid to devotion. The Madonna is shown half-length against a landscape, praying over her sleeping Child who lies with His head on a velvet cushion, His body on what appears to be a marble wall. Whether it is a wall, a table, or a slab is for the moment of no great consequence; what matters is that on its firm, horizontal base the sleeping Child lies secure. Behind it the mother is shown to the waist; her fingertips are lightly pressed together in prayer; her shoulders are level with the horizon of the landscape, and her lovely head is silhouetted against a pale sky. The form of the whole is compact and stable; the mood, one of stillness.

The simplicity of the form, however, contains within itself a very expressive linear pattern. As one looks at the picture in the contemplative, leisurely way demanded by its subject, his attention goes first from the praying hands up to the face of Mary, and following her gaze, down again to the Child. The sturdiness of the infant, relaxed in sleep, is firmly contained within contours along whose lines the eye travels from the round little head on the pillow to the feet, and back again to the curls against His mother's sleeve. The pillow lifts the Child's head and raises the body into a slightly diagonal variant of the horizontality of the wall, yet the little body remains aesthetically a part of the base of the picture, its support.

From this base a tall rectangle rises bounded by the lines of the Virgin's cloak to the right and left of her wrists and extending in the folds of her veil to the top of her head. The eye tends to travel up one side of this area and down the other, sometimes crossing over at the neckline of her dress, or following the oval of her face and chin. Or it travels up one forearm and wrist to the beautiful gesture of prayer, and down the other arm toward the child again. Or it makes brief side excursions into the repeated curves of the folds of Mary's cloak as they fall over her left shoulder defining the curves of her breast and the firm shoulder under the drapery. As one looks

BELLINI. *Madonna Adoring the Sleeping Child.*

(c. 1430–1516; Italian.)
Tempera on wood panel, 28½″ × 18¼″.
*The Metropolitan Museum of Art,
   New York.
The Theodore M. Davis Collection.
Bequest of Theodore M. Davis, 1915.*

Fig. 2–8.

away and then back to the picture, new relationships are forever appearing: for instance, the eye follows the curve of Mary's right cheek from eye to chin, then to the tips of her fingers and down her right hand and arm. A similarly broken curve balances this one from the left cheek to the left hand and arm. But one can go on almost indefinitely finding orders within order and complexities within the seeming simplicity of the total form.

The picture's center is neither the face of the mother nor the body of the Child, nor even the praying hands, but rather it moves slowly up and down a "line" between the mother and the Child she is watching over. The subject of the picture is the *Madonna Adoring the Sleeping Child,* but the theme is adoration, a living, loving relationship.

At the risk of detracting, at least temporarily, from the aesthetic wholeness of the picture by a mechanical reduction of its complexity, try to look at the composition as an inverted T the base of which is the Child's body and the wall on which it lies, and the stem, the upright rectangle that ends in the curving line of the veil over the Madonna's head. Notice that the vertical line is braced from either side by the short diagonals of the Virgin's arms. This is the core of the structure, the firm armature around which the roughly pyramidal form of composition takes shape.

Charlot's two implacable conditions of existence are here made very clear in the marble slab or wall, whose formal function is to provide a stable base but whose expressive function is probably to carry a premonition of the sepulchre; and in the axis of the Madonna's body embodying in itself the pull of gravity. We respond to the stability of this relationship even while our attention moves up and down the central axis, or makes side excursions into the landscape at the back where a winding road lures us away only to curve into a hill that leads directly back to the Madonna's shoulder. And what of that other law, the rhythmic pulse of life? It is felt in the balanced repeat of line against line, now in sequence, now in opposition; in drapery folds which are repeated with variations, no two identical; in the balanced opposition of the praying hands.

The colors are much paler now than was Bellini's original intention, and the light blue sky has taken on a greenish tone, but the rather muted harmonies are consistent with the mood of the painting. The lines have lost nothing of their clarity and are beautiful in their own right even as they perform their roles of defining contours and leading the movement. But it is in the unity of the whole that the meaning of the painting lies, in the unity of the form that encloses the mother and her divine Child in a magic circle of love. Within this unity, however, there is separateness; within the apparent security, anxiety. The Child lies not on His mother's lap but apart, on a marble slab suggestive of the chill of death. The mother's face even in its calm passivity holds some awareness of the sorrow that lies ahead.

El Greco's *Adoration of the Shepherds*

It seems possible that the purpose behind El Greco's painting of the *Adoration of the Shepherds* (Fig. 2–9) was not primarily to tell the story but rather to express the artist's sense of the mystery of "the word made flesh." The theme of the picture is not so much adoration as wonder, though adoration follows. Instead of illustrating the verses from the Gospel of St. Luke with the familiar accessories of stable and manger, El Greco takes St. Luke's words, "shepherds were keeping watch over their flocks by night," and fills his picture space with darkness at the center of which a white light radiates from the Child. It brilliantly illuminates the breast and face of Mary who lifts the white cloth as if to reveal the baby to the wondering gaze of St. Joseph, two shepherds, and two women. Like the flickering light of a fire, this miraculous light plays over the inner surfaces of the figures setting up rhythmic movements as one lighted area responds to another from side to side and forward and back with a constant upward trend. The roughly shaped diamond at whose heart the Christ Child lies is not smoothly contained: St. Joseph's yellow cloak falls in a fold toward the lower corner of the painting outside the "diamond"; his right hand and the right hand of the girl in white at the left extend beyond its imaginary edges as does the right foot of the kneeling shepherd. But still the form is recognizable, with its base the shepherd's crook and its apex the crowning cluster of cherubs who hover high above the Child. On their scroll is inscribed "Glory to God in the highest—we praise Thee, we bless Thee."

Our reading of the picture would not be complete if we failed to notice the animals. St. Joseph's donkey, sleepy after his journey from Nazareth to Bethlehem, is just visible behind the standing shepherd. The red-brown ox whose manger supplied the Christ Child's first crib is hidden except for his head with great curved horns lifted between the shepherd's knee and the Child. Finally, a lamb on whom the full light falls, his legs tied for ease in carrying, lies just below the head of the ox and above the shepherd's crook.

EL GRECO. *Adoration of the Shepherds.*

(1541–1614; Spanish.)
Oil on canvas, 64½″ × 42″.

*The Metropolitan Museum of Art,
    New York.*

Rogers Fund, 1905.

Fig. 2–9.

The position of the lamb almost on the central axis of the painting, with the cherubs at the top and the Christ Child at the midpoint, suggests a double significance. The trussed legs may also be in preparation for sacrifice. The lamb probably represents both the shepherd's gift to the newborn, and the divine gift to humanity, the lamb of God, a kind of symbolic repetition or translation.

There are instances of formal repetition as well. St. Joseph, at the right, half rises from his seat as he spreads his hands in a gesture of bewilderment. Opposite and balancing Joseph, but slightly nearer the picture plane, a tall shepherd kneels with arms crossed over his breast, quietly paying homage to divinity. His gesture is closed in contrast to Joseph's partially, or hesitantly, open one. Behind him another shepherd leans eagerly toward the Baby, his hands clasped in prayer (another closed gesture), while behind him a girl in white flings her arms rapturously wide. The third figure in this upper group, the woman displaying her bare hand and arm, is probably the midwife whose hand, according to legend, had been withered because she doubted Mary's virginity, and was made whole again by contact with the Baby's swaddling clothes. To the right, behind Mary and Joseph, the space opens out to show in the far distance the tiny figure of a shepherd, his flock huddled at his feet. With outstretched arms he receives the "tidings of great joy" while the black sky is shot with flashes of light.

One can read the pattern of gestures in more than one way. Perhaps one sees it as a cadenced line from Joseph to the girl in white forming a U-shaped frame around Mary and Jesus. Beginning with Joseph and moving clockwise the gestures are partially open, wholly closed, partially closed, and wholly open. Or one can read across the center of the picture in a major diagonal at the midpoint of which the Christ Child lies, with His mother Mary and the kneeling shepherd repeating each other in reverse on either side like the curves of parentheses: she uncovers the miracle for all to see; he kneels in recognition of divinity come down to earth.

Or one can read across the picture following the gesture with variations, from the slow puzzled bewilderment of Joseph, to the ecstatic joy of the girl in white, and finally to that echo from the distant fields in which the gesture becomes one of joyful acceptance of glad tidings.

The unity of El Greco's painting depends on rhythmic relations of lights and shadows, on their disposal around the magnetic center which is the Christ Child, and on the opposing and echoing gestures of the figures which are readily translated into variations on the central theme of wonder. As we have already seen, the light plays havoc with individual shapes (note the distorted bare legs of the shepherd), and yet the suggestion of substance remains, though unemphasized.

Here is none of the clarity of statement that we found in the coherent structure and dominant horizontal–vertical relationship of Bellini's *Madonna Adoring the Sleeping Child* (Fig. 2–8). Bellini's figures are clearly defined and modeled; the images are very tactile, giving one a strong sense of the solidity of the Child's little body and the strength of the young mother. The group is seen as a unit within its firm outlines, while the landscape remains a background. The Madonna is not so much *in* the landscape as in front of it. Space is described but not felt all around the figures.

El Greco's figures take form only as they catch the light. His space is a shadowy indefiniteness, convincing because it is occupied by flesh-and-blood people, only partially illumined by a divine light. The images are for the most part visual and kinetic, and they take their places in relation to each other and to the Child in the almost haphazard way of people crowding about a point of common interest.

The only references to the horizontal ground of the painting are in the reclining infant and in a cross beam of the vault whose function in the painting is to keep the vault arch from seeming to fly out into space. Horizontality, "down to earthness," is no part of the theme of this painting. Verticality is another matter, though again the vertical lines are few and not insistent. The only straight edges are those of the pier behind Mary, but these play an important role (as we can see if we try to remove them). They pluck the cord of gravity for us. Vertical movement there is, but it is upward and has a flame-like character. Nothing is more mysterious than a fire in which the individual shapes are always recognizable as flames, but never are any two alike.

As in the Bellini, the theme of the painting moves up and down along the central axis which has as its terminals the lamb of sacrifice symbolizing Christ's death, and the crowning group of cherubs suggesting His ultimate return to heaven. At the midpoint lies the Baby who is both human and divine. The rejoicing girl at the left and the distant shepherd look and gesture up toward heaven; all the rest gaze down on the Baby who is just beginning His life on earth.

LEONARDO DA VINCI. *Last Supper.*

(1452–1519; Italian.)
Oil on plaster.
Refectory, Santa Maria delle Grazie,
 Milan.
Photo: Pinacoteca di Brera'm.

Fig. 2–10.

Two Paintings of the Last Supper

We turn now to two paintings representing the subject of the
Last Supper, the occasion when, as they sat together at their meal,
Jesus said to His disciples that one among them would betray Him,
and when He broke bread and giving it to them said, "Take . . .
eat . . . this is my body which is given for you. . . ."

In Leonardo's *Last Supper* (Fig. 2–10) the disciples are placed
on either side of Christ, six to the right, six to the left, in four groups
of three, each group differing from the next in internal arrangement.
The order is at once recognizable but not insistent; it allows us
almost unconsciously to count the twelve, to know immediately who
these men are and what the occasion. But it is the variety among
them of gesture, of position, and of facial expression that we notice
most; the variousness of response to Christ's fateful words, "One
among you shall betray me," that makes Leonardo's *Last Supper*

ART AS EXPERIENCE

Tintoretto. *Last Supper.*

(1518–1594; Italian.)
Oil on canvas, 143⅞″ × 224″.
San Giorgio Maggiore, Venice.
Photo: Alinari-Art Reference Bureau.

Fig. 2–11.

the most compelling interpretation of the theme that we have. It is a greater work than Tintoretto's painting of a century later (Fig. 2–11). There the variety so far exceeds the order that one feels oneself taking part in an exciting, perhaps terrifying event, in which a number of other people not easily identifiable also participate, and in which all sorts of irrelevancies of movement and of lighting make the whole theatrical rather than dramatic. Leonardo's painting is not only the record of the institution of a sacrament with the ordered solemnity that clothes the celebration of the Eucharist; it is also a great human drama. Leonardo has pictured the outward and visible signs of the struggle going on within each one of the twelve disciples as he questions the meaning of Jesus' words.

It has been suggested that it is the variousness of response to Christ's words among the disciples that makes Leonardo's painting the most compelling interpretation of the theme. But this is a gross oversimplification. Never was the variety of individuality, both human and formal, so subtly contrasted with structural clarity and simplicity. The clearly balanced form with all the stability and permanence it expresses is the vehicle of the institution of the sacrament of the Mass. On the other hand, the human drama played out on Leonardo's austere stage pulses with the immediacy of life itself. The twelve profoundly disturbed men gathered about the quiet figure of their Master carry the meaning of the picture in concrete, human terms. The dark, marching rectangles of the wall hangings leading back to the lighted windows; the long line of the refectory table and the coffered ceiling whose lighted rafters repeat the taut horizontality of the scene, make a cube of space within whose clear geometry the tense tumult of human emotions seems all the more confused and troubled.

Nor is the order of the painting confined to the enclosure and measurement of space. Each group of three disciples bears a relation to a group on the opposite side of Christ; both terminal groups are arranged so that their heads are level with each other and with the group opposite, while in each, one man has risen and is leaning forward. Notice, however, that it is not in each case the man at the end of the table who has risen to his feet. While one looks fixedly toward Christ, the other gestures toward Him but looks in the other direction while speaking eagerly to his companions. Leonardo stops short of exact balance, of precise opposition; these terminal groups do not exactly repeat each other in reverse. He depends more on psychological tensions to hold the four groups together, on their relation to the quiet figure in the center, rather than on a formality of balance. The two inner groups also balance each other in a dissimilar opposition: the left-hand group with Judas drawing back, his arm on the table, is concave; the right is convex.

Only the quiet figure of Christ is without human counterpart, but He too takes His place against the three windows as a part of a triad, one of light. The calm gesture of His hands is repeated in the wider arc of the curved gable above His head. Structurally this gable has no clear reason for being, but aesthetically it crowns the figure of Christ and brings the whole centripetal movement of the painting to a full stop.

In contrast to the quiet clarity and coherence of Leonardo's painting, Tintoretto's (Fig. 2–11) is darkly mysterious, theatrically lighted, and full of action which at times, as in the figure of the man in the lower right corner, seems exaggerated and meaningless. The major movement recedes along the diagonal of the table, beginning and ending in obscurity. A little beyond the midpoint of this diagonal, just above the physical center of the picture, Christ offers bread to the disciple next to Him. A second movement, crossing the first, descends sharply from the hanging lamp to the somewhat irrelevant but attractive group of the crouching maidservant, the posturing man, and the dog who investigates a large basket in the foreground.

Across the table and a little back from the figure of Christ, Judas sits alone, singled out from the others of the twelve both by his position and by the fact that he alone has no haloed light about his head. The other disciples are quite as differentiated one from another as are Leonardo's, but their movements seem curiously less motivated from within than in response to the pictorial demands of the composition. Their reactions to Jesus' words and action are so various that they are difficult to sort out and comprehend.

Two women, one perhaps Christ's mother Mary, hover behind the table to the left, and a mysterious "cloud of witnesses" is dimly seen above their heads in the light from the lamp. At the other side of the picture another group of angels seems to be flying into the space above the table.

Five figures at the right lead one's eye from the foreground in a wide arc to the shadowy regions at the back of the room. These figures would have been irrelevant to Leonardo's purpose of representing the institution of the Mass, but Tintoretto's purpose seems rather to have been to dramatize the event by contrasting its sacramental significance with the commonplaces of an ordinary meal.

Jesus had sent two disciples ahead to prepare a room in the house of a man whom they would recognize because he would be bearing a pitcher of water. In this man's guest-chamber they were to make ready the Passover. The room in Tintoretto's painting is vast: suitable for a king's banqueting hall. The artist appears to confuse his purpose: he gives to the event of the Last Supper the usual accessories of food, drink, servants, even a little dog; but he also supplies it with heavenly visitors, and sets the stage in the midst of a vast, indefinite space that at once removes the event from an everyday context. Unlike El Greco, who substitutes for an ordinary setting a frankly symbolic and suggestive use of space and architecture, Tintoretto offers both reality and symbol, making neither really convincing.

In Tintoretto's painting there is none of the structural clarity of Leonardo's; there is hardly a reference to the basic vertical–horizontal relationship that plays so important a role both in the Bellini and in the Leonardo. The plane of Tintoretto's floor has a tendency to tilt upward toward the inner part of the picture, and the faint echoes of the picture plane (the horizontal front of the picture space), which can be found in the table-end and in the floor tiles, lack the firm insistence they are given by Leonardo. The one strong vertical, the cord on which the lamp hangs, supports the only sharply defined horizontal, the upper edge of the lamp. The isolation of this one small image of equilibrium, silhouetted in the lamplight and hung between heaven and earth, may have had more significance for the painter than is clear to us.

The almost continuous recession from the picture plane into deep, indefinite space is held in tension by the diagonal of the long table and filled with pulsating life by the rhythm of brilliant highlights and dark shadows. We have seen light and shadow used in a similar way by El Greco, who was a younger contemporary of Tintoretto and much influenced by the older man's work. But where El Greco expressed in terms of light and shadow the theme of divine mystery, Tintoretto used light and its rhythmic contrasts to heighten the tension and to give a feverish vitality to the painting.

In El Greco's *Adoration of the Shepherds,* the Christ Child lies somewhat below the physical center of the painting; in Tintoretto's *Last Supper,* the figure of Christ is above the center; and in Leonardo's *Last Supper,* while Christ's head is above the center, the major part of the pyramid formed by His head, shoulders, and outstretched arms is considerably below the center. We are all familiar with the fact that the lower our own center of gravity, or that of any bulky, heavy object, the greater will be its stability, the easier its equilibrium. The psychological center of a work of art, its center of attention, has a similar aesthetic function: a higher center increases the tension needed to maintain equilibrium, a lower one gives a sense of repose.

It has become amply clear in the course of the discussion of Leonardo's and Tintoretto's paintings of the Last Supper that Leonardo's is held to be the finer picture. Since it is the purpose of this book to assist the reader in arriving at value judgments of his own, it is important to face the issue squarely and to make explicit the already implied grounds for this judgment.

Let us take first the matter of the painter's purpose. We feel reasonably sure that we understand what Leonardo's purpose was:

to fuse in one form the dramatic record of an occasion involving human treachery, betrayal, love, and bewilderment, with the institution of the central sacrament of the Church. It is a purpose whose human and cultural richness is immense; it has a real grandeur of scale. We are not so sure of Tintoretto's purpose. Perhaps it was to present in as dramatic a way as possible the historical event, enriching it with supernatural attendants and staging it with theatrical lighting and action calculated to heighten the tensions and raise the pitch of excitement. The difficulty is that the important theme of Judas' treachery and of the announcement to the disciples of impending tragedy is lost in sheer theatre. While we can never be entirely sure of his intention, it seems from our very uncertainty that the painter has not been wholly successful in achieving it. His picture does not "work" as well as it might.

Second is the matter of order and vitality; we are probably agreed that both paintings are generously endowed with these two prime requisites. While the order is certainly clearer in the Leonardo than in the Tintoretto, there may be more vitality in the Tintoretto—though it is of a feverish nature. The two paintings exemplify clearly the styles of the end of the fifteenth and the end of the sixteenth centuries. But even allowing for the late sixteenth century's preference for a degree of unclarity, for suggestion rather than definition of forms, for strong contrasts of light and dark instead of an even distribution of light, and especially for movement and a state of becoming against static balance expressive of a state of being, Tintoretto still seems not to have produced an aesthetic unity from which nothing can be removed and within which nothing can be changed without damaging the whole. It is not a wholly effective form.

Subject and Theme in Landscape

A useful distinction can be made between the subject of a work of art and its theme; between the "material" with which the artist works—a religious subject, a portrait, a landscape—and what he has to say about this material. The subject, if one can be identified, is the artist's starting point; the theme is the expressive content of the finished work embodying both the artist's feeling and that of the viewer who responds to the work. When two or more examples of an identical or similar subject are compared, the differences in theme quickly become apparent, and in these differences one learns something of the preferences and habits of mind both of the artists concerned and of the times in which they lived.

In contrasting the two paintings of the Last Supper by Leonardo and Tintoretto we have arrived at differences in theme. A very different comparison can be made among four landscapes although in only one is landscape as such the ostensible subject. Turn for a moment to Masaccio's *Tribute Money* (Fig. 4–21), to Perugino's *Handing of the Keys to Peter* (Fig. 4–22), to El Greco's *View of Toledo* (Fig. 4–23), and to Rembrandt's *Christ Crucified Between the Two Thieves* (Figs. 10–18 and 10–19), and ask yourself what is the role of the landscape, and how does the painter feel about landscape in each? For instance, take the horizon line to which we referred above; where does it occur in each picture? More important, what is the effect on you of the position of the horizon? For some, a high horizon like the one in the *View of Toledo* evokes a strong feeling of tension, or sometimes of expectancy, while a relatively low one, as in the Perugino or in Vermeer's *View of Delft* (Pl. IIa), carries overtones of relaxation and of calm. On the other hand, Goya in his print of *The Giant* (Fig. 4–25) produces a special kind of tension by giving us a low horizon whose normal calm he then proceeds to shatter by placing his giant on the edge of limitless space, brooding among the stars. Consider also the effect of the lack of an horizon, as in Rembrandt's *Christ Crucified* (Figs. 10–18 and 10–19). The horizon is, however, only one element in the aesthetic totality of a landscape, and it is in the total form, in the unity of all the elements that one must seek the artist's theme.

Subject and Theme in Portraiture

Portraiture is an area of subject matter which, as one might suppose, waxes and wanes in popularity in accordance with the importance of the role the patron plays in the instigation of art. In the Renaissance, the interest in human personality and the importance of the individual in the social scene led to a development of portraiture unparalleled since Roman times. Antonio Pollaiuolo's *Man in Red* (Fig. 2–12) is presented as the embodiment of human power. His is an arrogant self-confidence; he has an air of rejecting intimacy. The clarity with which his figure is silhouetted against the void of negative space about him tends to present him as a type, as a mental image of "the man of the Renaissance." While the portrait is unmistakably a likeness, the theme is a very general one: the self-confident assurance of a man who believes that he has a

POLLAIUOLO. *Man in Red.*

(c. 1432–1498; Italian.)
Oil on wood, 21¼″ × 15⅞″.
National Gallery of Art, Washington.
Mellon Collection, 1937.

Fig. 2–12.

god-given right to use and enjoy the world in which he finds himself. (Pico della Mirandola a generation later was to make this theme explicit in his essay on the "Dignity of Man.")

In sharp contrast to Pollaiuolo's *Man in Red,* is Leonardo's *Mona Lisa* (Fig. 2–13), probably the most famous and possibly the most distinguished of all portraits. The stable, almost geometric form of the half-length figure, the clarity of its simple shape within the gentle but definite contours, its strongly tangible reality—all these are belied by the mystery that pervades the image, a mystery that derives not, as one might suppose, from the suggestion of a smile in the quiet mouth or in the actually smiling eyes, but from the painter's masterly use of half-light and shadows. One remembers that Leonardo in his Notebooks advised the aspiring painter to look for the beauty of women as they stand half-shadowed in doorways during a rain.

LEONARDO DA VINCI. *Mona Lisa.*

(1452–1519; Italian.)
Panel, 30½″ × 20⅞″.
The Louvre, Paris.

Fig. 2–13.

One is tempted to see both in the personality of the lady and in the style of the painter a cogent answer to all questions about character in life and in art. No sooner have we a working pattern, a mental schema or form that seems to fit and to explain things, than the artist slips out of the pigeonhole; the work of art (whether on canvas or that major work of art which is a human personality) refuses to be explained. One then starts the search all over again, and new forms, new images appear. The portrait of *Mona Lisa* is the paradigm of the classical style of portraiture at the beginning of the sixteenth century: a stable pyramid, a clearly defined volume set in measurable, if somewhat romantically conceived space. And yet the theme of this clear image is the opposite of clarity. It might well be termed the ultimate mystery of human personality. It is of these tensions between statement and intimation that art is made.

Subject and Theme in Bruegel and Renoir

One more comparison of two paintings of similar subject and unlike theme will serve to make the distinction clear and also to bring us back to the starting point of our inquiry. Compare the painting by Renoir of *The Luncheon of the Boating Party at Bougival* (Fig. 2–14) with Bruegel's *Land of Cockaigne* (Pl. I). These two have in common only one thing, and it is in the area of subject matter: both paintings represent people who have been eating and drinking. Bruegel's theme and Renoir's theme are utterly different.

We have already seen that while Bruegel describes the fabulous *Land of Cockaigne* in fascinating detail, his primary concern is to point a moral. In order to do so, he simplifies and generalizes the visual image of the sleeping gluttons, emphasizing their strongly tactile quality, and bringing to mind vivid bodily images of heavy sleep. He puts into his picture a maximum of meaning which takes time and attention to read and reflect on. The images are independent, discrete, but related to each other. Bruegel's purpose is essentially dogmatic; his style is clear, concise, and admirably suited to his purpose.

Renoir is a painter who delights to celebrate the beauties of this world, not analytically as the Renaissance artist did, but descriptively presenting the richness of sensuous imagery for its own sake, available to us at a glance.

A dozen or more young men and girls have finished their lunch on a veranda or balcony under a gay yellow and orange striped awning supported on poles which echo in a darker tone the blue-

RENOIR. *The Luncheon of the Boating Party at Bougival.*

(1841–1919; French.)
Oil on canvas, 51″ × 68″.
The Phillips Collection, Washington.

Fig. 2–14.

green of the foliage. A white table cloth is rumpled into blue shadows. The girl nearest us, who is talking to her small moppet of a dog, is dressed in blue with a yellow straw hat bedecked with orange calendulas. The men's white shirts are also shadowed with blue, and the yellow straw hat of the young man in the foreground has a sky-blue band. On the table is a clutter of agreeable objects, nothing clearly defined, but one notices grapes and peaches and other varicolored but unidentifiable fruits, crusty bread, pleasant shapes of wine glasses and of green-blue bottles not quite empty of wine. A golden light permeates the picture suggesting the warmth of a sunny day and a general holiday mood. In contrast with the Bruegel painting where each figure is self-contained within its own firm outlines, these figures are almost fluid in shape, free to move about within the secure corner of the world whose light and warmth they share.

There is little conversation; no one appears to be saying anything of importance, and no one pays much attention to anyone else. But the mood of the group is unmistakable. This is a picture of light-hearted gaiety and well-being. Its theme is a hymn to joy, to the good things of life, of companionship, of sun and air and food and drink.

Suggestions for Further Reading

BOAS, F. *Primitive Art.* New York: Dover Publications, Inc., 1955.
   A basic text on the origins of art.
SWINDLER, M. H. *Ancient Painting.* New Haven: Yale University Press, 1929.
   Still the best comprehensive text in this field.

In the field of aesthetic and art criticism:
CLARK, SIR KENNETH. *Looking at Pictures.* New York: Holt, Rinehart and Winston, Inc., 1960.
   A masterly presentation of the approach to pictures advocated in this text.
CLARK, SIR KENNETH. *The Nude: A Study in Ideal Form.* New York: Pantheon Books, 1953. (Bollingen Series XXV.) (Also a Doubleday Anchor Book, A 168; Garden City, N. Y.: Doubleday and Co., 1959.)
   A classic of art criticism.
EDMAN, I. *Arts and the Man.* New York: Mentor Books, 1949.
   One of the best discussions of "What is art."
FEININGER, A. *The Anatomy of Nature.* New York: Crown Publishers, Inc., 1956.
   The order and vitality of nature set forth in photographs of the highest quality with commentary of equally high standard.
FERGUSON, G. *Signs and Symbols in Christian Art.* New York: Oxford University Press, 1961. (A Hesperides Book, HS 1.)
   Useful for the understanding of the explicit meaning of Christian art; a handbook for the identification of subject matter, this book deals specifically with subject rather than theme.
READ, SIR HERBERT. *The Meaning of Art.* London: Penguin Books, Ltd. (Also available as a Pelican Book, PB 213.)
   Excellent elementary text.

In the field of more sophisticated aesthetics:
FOCILLON, H. *The Life of Forms in Art.* New York: Wittenborn, Schultz, 1949.
FRY, R. *Vision and Design.* London: Chatto and Windus, 1920.

KEPES, G. *The Language of Vision.* Chicago: Paul Theobald, 1944.

LANGER, S. *Philosophy in a New Key; a Study in the Symbolism of Reason, Rite and Art.* New York: Mentor Books, 1948. (M 25.)

MOHOLY-NAGY, L. *The New Vision: Fundamentals of Design-Painting, Sculpture, Architecture.* Chicago: Paul Theobald, 1947.

READ, SIR HERBERT. *Icon and Idea.* Cambridge, Mass.: Harvard University Press, 1955.

THOMPSON, SIR D'ARCY W. *On Growth and Form,* abridged ed. J. T. Bonner, Ed. Cambridge: Cambridge University Press, 1961.

3. Images of Reality and of Fantasy

What Are Images?

THE poet organizes words into forms which convey richer, more complex meanings than the words alone carry, and with these ordered, verbal forms he conjures images that are the substance of poetry. The artist, whose medium is not audible but visible and tangible, is also concerned with images. Without images we cannot imagine, we cannot remember, we cannot think.

What then are images? As we use the term in art criticism it connotes more than is suggested by any of the various dictionary definitions: a representation, a similitude of any person or thing; an idea; a metaphor. The artist's images partake of all these but are not limited to any one. The artist creates an imaginary world parallel to and deriving from the world of objective reality but never exactly reflecting it. The character of his images derives from the character of his experience, whether sensory, emotional, rational.

In order to understand the complex nature of creative images— and that of course is what this book is about—it will be useful to look closely at their origins in perceptual experience: to consider briefly the physical equipment with which we receive sensory data, and the various kinds of sensory experience through which the artist, like everyone else, stores his mind with the materials of thought and of feeling.

Perception

How do we come to know what we know? How do we acquire the store of images and of ideas that make up our reality? For our purposes we shall think of images as akin to ideas which have their ultimate roots in sense perceptions, but which vary in accordance with the purpose to which the mind puts them.

Perception is the whole process of awareness resulting from the stimulation of one or more of our receptors. These are located in the eyes, ears, nose, tongue, skin, muscles, and internal organs. As we are stimulated the symbolic process is set up, and we give to the sensation meaning which is based on past, remembered sensations. Also simultaneously, we respond to the sensory stimulus affectively, that is, pleasantly or unpleasantly, with emotion such as excitement or boredom, or in any of innumerable other ways.

The receptors are classified according to the type of information they bring us: *proprioceptors* and *interoceptors* give us sensory information on our own bodies; *exteroceptors* inform us of the external world. To avoid the sheer bulk of the two terms *proprioceptive* and *interoceptive* we shall often use the less precise but clear term *bodily* to describe the sensations that lead directly to a sense of self. The terms *bodily* and *exteroceptive* can be applied as well to the images deriving from sensory stimuli as to the sensations themselves, and as well to the creative images of art and of dreams as to the direct percepts of experience. In the Bruegel painting discussed earlier, the visual beauty of the landscape, with its soft haziness of distance and its sharp definition of forms in the foreground, is exteroceptive in sensory character. The tree with its loaded table, the little pie-thatched hut, and the figures of the men, are both visual and tactual in character—they are *exteroceptive*. But Bruegel appealed strongly to our remembered, proprioceptive and interoceptive experience when he painted his three gluttons sleeping so heavily on the ground.

The proprioceptors are located in the semicircular canals and vestibules of our ears, and in the muscles and tendons of our bodies. The first are sensitive to bodily position and to rotation, the second to the varying positions and to the stresses and strains of the various parts of our bodies. When bodily movement is involved, while still proprioceptive, the sensation is often described as kinaesthetic. However, the absence of movement may be as vividly felt as its presence, as for instance when, in the grip of terror, we feel "rooted to the ground."

ART AS EXPERIENCE

The interoceptors are perhaps even more responsible for our self-awareness than the proprioceptors. The interoceptors are in the viscera and their close relation with emotion can best be indicated by the metaphors of our language: "My heart was in my mouth," or "My heart sank"—movement in either direction being highly unpleasant; "butterflies in my stomach." The familiar feeling of levitation which plays an important role in dream imagery and in that of art has its counterpart in metaphorical language. We have all felt as though we were "walking on air." It is hard to be sure whether this last "image" is *proprioceptive* or *interoceptive,* or both. The distinction really does not matter and brings us back to the convenient term *bodily* to refer to sensory qualities which are either proprioceptive or interoceptive or both.

Bodily sensations are apt to be overlooked when they bring us information only of a normal state of affairs; if we are right side up, moving easily about over the surface of the earth without abrupt changes of position or direction, we tend to think of other things. If we are conscious of any feeling it may be a rather vague sense of well-being, though this may be connected with our thoughts rather than with our bodily behavior. But if the usual pattern is suddenly altered; if a hitherto smooth flight suddenly becomes "bumpy" or an elevator seems to drop out from under, leaving us to follow as best we may; or if, after great exertion, excessive fatigue makes us welcome a horizontal position as the greatest possible good, then all these bodily sensations take on special meaning.

In contrast to the information we get from our proprioceptors and interoceptors about ourselves, the exteroceptors tell us of the outside world. Hearing, sight, taste, smell, and touch are all exteroceptors. Man's progress in exploring the nature of reality was vastly accelerated when he invented the telescope and the microscope, both means of increasing the reach of vision, while the telephone, radio, and television extend enormously our exteroceptive range.

For our knowledge of the world immediately surrounding us, and in dealing with it, we frequently "handle" it; we depend very largely on our sense of touch. The hand is our most valuable tactual receptor, and the history of civilization was, for millennia, bound up with the slow development of tools by which the reach of the human arm and hand could be extended. While there is a saying that "seeing is believing," vision leads us more often into error than does touch, particularly when exteroceptive evidence of touch is reinforced by evidence derived from bodily movement. The familiar example comes to mind of the child who can "see" the railroad tracks come together at no very great distance, but no matter how far he walks, he can never achieve the desired feat of bestriding them, one foot on each rail.

Touch requires contact with the object about which information is wanted, an obvious limitation. Furthermore, contact alone is not sufficient if we want something more than knowledge of a surface. Mere contact, as when we touch a surface gently, or move our fingers lightly over it, allows us to identify texture, but to this must be added some involvement of the muscles, some pressure, if we are to learn whether the surface bounds a solid object.

A homely example will make the point clear. Look at a bag filled with purchases from a supermarket, and, relying on vision alone, gauge the size of the parcel and note the kind of container. If you then touch its surface you confirm your visual impression of its being a paper bag. But only when you use the muscles of your hands and arms to grasp and lift the parcel, bringing into action your proprioceptors as well, can you tell whether beneath the lettuce showing at the top of the bag are cartons of dry cereal, quite light, or possibly canned goods, decidedly heavy.

Bodily, Tactile, and Visual Images

To divide sensory experience into exteroceptive and bodily, to separate sharply information about the world outside ourselves from evidence of our own ability to handle it is, like so many generalizations, useful but misleading. No one type of sensory experience is ever isolated. Tactual experience is rarely, at least when it is active rather than passive, purely exteroceptive. The experience of touch is rarely without muscular involvement. We do not make a practice of going around touching or stroking the objects in our world, chiefly because texture alone is of no great practical significance to us. The word "handle" immediately implies muscular movement, and to handle an object leads to proprioceptive experience as well as exteroceptive; we gauge weight in relation to our own strength and automatically test ourselves against this portion of the world of external reality.

Consider the difference between touching and being touched, between scratching and being scratched, or grasping and being grasped. The passive experience may be purely tactual, though it may result in proprioceptive sensations with varying effects of pleasure and pain. The active experience involves our proprioceptors and is an intermediary between our bodies and the external world.

ART AS EXPERIENCE

For purposes of aesthetic enjoyment of works of art, particularly of sculpture, it is this active kind of tactual–muscular response that is involved.

Visual sensations unsupported by touch and by muscular, bodily sensations, and uninterpreted in terms of past experience, present themselves as shapes of varying size. They may also change under our gaze, and then we see movement. Imagine looking from a window, and seeing large shapes that present themselves as green in various values of light and dark and various kinds of hue—blue-green, green, and yellow-green; some shapes are gray flecked with gold and green; some are square and some triangular; others are blue and still others are white. The white shapes move and as they shift position the blue shapes enlarge in one part of the field of vision and diminish in another.

In the foregoing, the symbolic process of naming shapes such as grass, trees, stone buildings, clouds, and sky has been carefully avoided. There has been no interpretation of the colors, shapes, and sizes in terms of space, though it has required an effort for the author not to say, "In the foreground the green grass is long and unkempt; behind the stone garage the horse-chestnut tree guards the entrance to a path which leads up the hill to where the tall pines stand black against the sky." Here the symbolic process is clearly at work, and the interpretation is subjective—in terms of previous experience of moving about in this or in a similar area, and acquiring an understanding of the spatial relations which now the purely visual image is sufficient to recall.

As with space, which is the result of interpretation of visual evidence in terms of motor experience, so with texture and solidity—their perception is the result of interpretation in terms of tactual experience. Gray stone buildings with dark green slate roofs present two very different textures even though seen at a distance of thirty feet. The mottled gray and yellow stone is rough, while even more vivid, perhaps because less pleasant, is the recall of the feel of the slimy green roof tiles.

Visual and tactile imagery make up a large part of the store of sensory material on which a painter or sculptor draws: of persons and things outside himself, of their relation to each other and to the indefinite extension around them known as space. If, however, the artist limits himself to recording, however accurately or attractively, exteroceptive images—and the attraction often lies more in the qualities of the object than in the creative image—the resulting artifact image is apt to lack the power to move us or to sustain our interest. Only when the artist becomes to some extent an actor as well as an observer, when his bodily imagination is also involved, do we find ourselves really responding.

The Sensory Character of Artifact Images

Four artifact images of related though not identical subjects will clarify the distinction between exteroceptive and bodily imagery. The first, a figure modeled in clay called *Youth Imploring* (Fig. 3–1) is a wholly non-visual piece of sculpture. It was modeled by a seventeen-year-old girl who was born blind. Therefore, not even dimly remembered visual images entered into its creation. Images of tactile sensations undoubtedly played some part; the girl had probably felt her own body with her hands and stored up memories of how the shapes felt; but this piece of sculpture is primarily a work of bodily imagination, proprioceptive and strongly subjective. The legs of the figure are thin and unimportant; the torso, not much more emphasized. The pronounced shoulders are the seat of muscular strain as the arms reach high above the head in a tense gesture toward a power somewhere above. The hands, which are to the blind so nearly what our eyes are to us, are subjectively exaggerated out of all proportion to the body, and in them lies the climax of the expressive theme.

Max Beckmann, in his *Man in the Dark* (Fig. 3–2), is obviously much less dependent on proprioceptive imagery than is the blind sculptress. But he enlarges and emphasizes the reaching hands and the hesitant feet making us feel participants in the dark rather than observers of the timid groping of the man.

Rubens, on the other hand (Fig. 3–3), draws the image of a blind man as he sees him, describing the way he appears, not the way Rubens imagines blind helplessness to *feel;* while Rembrandt (Fig. 3–4) presents *The Blindness of Tobit* in an image that is both visually convincing and proprioceptively very moving.

Individuals differ enormously in the importance they attach to the various kinds of sensory experience and in the enjoyment they derive from them. To some the delights of the eye—color, light, and the patterns of shapes—will mean most. To others the pleasures of tactility, of varying textures and solidity, will count for more. Still others find in movement, or in bodily action, the greatest satisfaction and interest. These preferences are usually a matter of degree rather than of exclusive preoccupation, and they are to be found as much among artists as among laymen. One of the clues to an artist's

Youth Imploring.

Sculpture by congenitally blind seventeen-year-old girl.

After V. Löwenfeld, Creative and Mental
Growth, *Fig. 39.*
New York: The Macmillan Co.

Fig. 3–1.

BECKMANN. *Man in the Dark.*

(1884–1950; German.)
Bronze, less than life size.
Formerly in the Collection of Curt
  Valentin, New York.

Fig. 3–2.

RUBENS. *Blind Man.*
(1577–1640; Flemish.)
Drawing, 10⅞″ × 16⅜″.
The Albertina Collection, Vienna.

Fig. 3–3.

creative personality, and thus to his personal style, may be found in these preferences which are expressed in a dominant sensory interest.

The late Prof. Viktor Löwenfeld [1] has demonstrated that personalities differ in the reliance they place on one or another kind of sensory experience. He has distinguished between the visual or exteroceptive type and the haptic or bodily type. As an artist, the visual or exteroceptive type is usually an observer (like Rubens in the drawing mentioned above) while the haptic or proprioceptive

[1] Viktor Löwenfeld, *The Nature of Creative Activity*, 2nd ed. (London: Routledge and Kegan Paul, Ltd., 1952).

REMBRANDT. *The Blindness of Tobit.*

(1606–1669; Dutch.)
Etching, 6¼" × 5".
*The Metropolitan Museum of Art,
    New York.*
Dick Fund, 1937.

Fig. 3–4.

and interoceptive artist is a participant, like Beckmann. The exteroceptive tends toward a descriptive and objective style; the bodily, toward a style of subjective expressionism. The giants, such as Leonardo, Michelangelo, and Rembrandt, or Goya, whatever their native constitution, develop to the utmost both the exteroceptive and the bodily imagination.

The Affective Process

The affective process, as we have seen, is closely involved with the proprioceptors and interoceptors. We do not feel in our eyes the acute distress that is simultaneous with the sight of an accident; we feel it in the muscles about the heart and in the throat and mouth ("My heart was in my mouth"). Our spirits may be elated or depressed, we "walk on air" or feel "sunk," and our bodies respond companionably with lightness or heaviness. We find ourselves in the "grip of fear," and all our muscles contract; we feel "rooted to the ground" and are, indeed, helpless to run away. This is well illustrated by Munch in his nightmarish *The Shriek* (Fig. 3–5). We may describe a state of mental confusion by saying, "My head is swimming," or one of chagrin and humiliation by the expression of "feeling small." Figures of speech are telling because, while they often distort the "facts" (one's heart does not literally "turn over"), they are vivid projections of the bodily sensations that are bound up with emotion. In this they are closely related to some of the expressive distortions of art. Bodily sensations and their accompanying affects or feelings are so intimate to ourselves, we identify ourselves so completely with them, that we often substitute for the verb *to feel* the verb *to be:* instead of saying, "I feel tired," we say, "I am tired."

These sensations, being internal, are for the most part only slightly apparent to the external observer. The artist trains himself, consciously or unconsciously, to detect and to read the outward signs, such as they are—the changes in facial expression that result from tiny muscular contractions, and the more visible bodily gestures of posture and movement that communicate to the sensitive observer the inward feelings of the person observed. But the signs are not always enough. They are adequate in direct proportion to the degree to which the artist identifies himself with the emotion to be expressed. If the emotion and therefore the bodily sensations are his own, not those of another, he cannot see the outward effect they produce; he can only feel them inwardly. Yet his artifact image

MUNCH. *The Shriek.*

(1863–1944; Norwegian.)
Lithograph, 13⅞″ × 10″.
Collection, The Museum of Modern Art,
  New York.
Matthew T. Mellon Foundation Fund.

Fig. 3–5.

of emotion must be a visible, external thing. He therefore resorts to what is in effect a projection into visible form of the implicit sensation. It not infrequently takes form as a distortion of the usual visual image.

Some such procedure probably lay behind the creation of Picasso's *Weeping Woman* (Fig. 3–6) or behind the agonized distortion of the mother mourning her dead baby in *Guernica* (Fig. 3–7). The dying horse in *Guernica* is an image in which are combined the exteroceptive appearance of a horse with its mouth stretched wide open (as actually occurs when a horse yawns) and the proprioceptive feeling of a horse screaming in death-agony. It seems likely also that this projection into visible forms of bodily feeling may very well lie behind some of the grotesques of art, accounting in large measure for the dread vitality that gives them their nightmare quality.

Creative Images

We have seen that the material of imagination, as of thought in general, is largely made up of images deriving from and corresponding roughly to sensations. There are direct percepts, which coincide with the presence of the stimulus, and memory images where the sensation is recalled. When we speak of having a mental image of something, it may be that we remember a sensory experience that has occurred, or it may be that we are imagining one. In the latter case it can be called a creative image. There are two major types of creative images: dreams, including daydreams and fantasies which are all creations of the mind but have no existence outside it; and artifact images, also creations of the mind and hand, but here the image is given objective form and can be used as a means of conveying ideas and feelings to others.

Creative images differ from memory images of experience in that they vary in accordance with the purpose, whether conscious or unconscious, of the artist or dreamer, the "imaginer." They vary in the degree to which they correspond with the original sensory experience; one will seem very "real," another "fantastic," another "distorted," and still another "abstract." One will emphasize visual quality, another tactile, another bodily; while another seems to draw impartially on all kinds of sensory experiences.

We turn now to a study of those creative images which for various reasons, not least that they are irrational, can throw most light on the artist's images: the imagery of dreams.

PICASSO. *Weeping Woman.*

(1881–   ; Spanish.)
Oil on canvas, 23¾" × 19¾".
The Roland Penrose Collection, London.

Fig. 3–6.

Picasso. *Guernica.*

(1881–   ; Spanish.)
Oil on canvas, 11′ 6″ × 25′ 8″.
*On extended loan to The Museum of
Modern Art, New York, from the artist.*

Fig. 3–7.

"The artist is not a special kind of person, but every man is a special kind of artist." When the art-historian and philosopher Ananda Coomaraswamy made this statement, he was not supposing that we all make artifacts or artifact-images. Neither did he have in mind the fact that in sleep and in daydreams we all create images that often bear a close resemblance to those of the artist though they have no objective existence outside our own minds. Coomaraswamy was convinced that we are all potential makers of artifact-images; and he would probably have agreed that while our dream imagery does not in any way prove his contention, it does certainly give it added weight.

The Aesthetic Character of Dream Images

In asking you to study the aesthetic character of your dream images, there is a double purpose: to interest you first in a study of your dreams with a view to discovering what "special kind of artist" you may be; and second, in developing a better understand-

REAL AND FANTASTIC IMAGES

ing of your own creative imagery in order that you may become more curious about the images of other people, notably those to be found in works of art.

It has been suggested that the subconscious mind finds images in which to pose a problem the dreamer is facing or refusing to face in his waking life, and even to suggest its solution. As in works of art, the images of a dream are based on experience, but are "rarely exact reproductions." [2] They depend heavily on recall, but the processes of selection, arrangement, distortion, and even abstraction, are very various and sometimes no less effective than in a work of art. Without fully understanding either the purpose or what Freud called the "latent" meaning of a dream, it is possible to be aware of its aesthetic character, to look at it as one does at a work of art.

Try, then, to adopt an aesthetic attitude toward your dreams. As dreamer, you are at once the artist and the critic; your judgments in no way depend on the opinions of others. You may protest that you never dream. Perhaps you dream without remembering, and with a little effort you may begin to recall what you have dreamed. You may also find that your powers of imagery are increased, and that your whole conscious life is considerably enriched by the attention given to these images of your unconscious. Begin by asking yourself certain questions.

1. Are the dreams you remember realistic or fantastic, the images real or distortions of reality?

2. Do you dream in perceptual images or in a simple narrative of events? In other words, do you see and feel the situation in which you find yourself, or do things simply happen? For example, do you remember crossing the grass from one building to another, and was the grass green and soft, or brown and dry? Had it been freshly mown? Or do you only remember crossing the grass instead of following the path?

3. If you dream in perceptual images rather than in verbalized events, what sensory qualities are you aware of?
    a. In the first place, from the evidence of your dreams, do you lean to bodily or to exteroceptive imagery, or do you use both kinds as the character of the dreams may dictate?
    b. If you can recall proprioceptive images, are they the general rule or do strong, bodily images of feeling enter at a particular time, to make a particular point in the dream?

[2] J. A. Hadfield, *Dreams and Nightmares* (London: Penguin Books, Ltd., 1952), Part II, Chapter 4, p. 65 ff. (Also available as a Pelican Book, A 294.)

ART AS EXPERIENCE

c. If the images are largely exteroceptive, are they generally in color? Are you aware of tactile quality, of texture, or of solidity?

4. Are your dreams ever non-objective? In one sense the dream of events might be called non-objective because there are no perceptual images in it. There is, however, another type of dream to which this term out of art criticism can very legitimately be applied, where a bodily feeling is recalled but without any exteroceptive context. Such a dream might equally well be termed abstract, since the sensation or feeling is abstracted from the experience.

5. Finally, if the sensory quality of a dream is marked, or if you suddenly find abstraction and distortion where you are accustomed to realism, can you discover what role they play in the dream? What point do they seem to make? It should be easier for you to answer this last question when it relates to your own images than to answer the same question about Picasso's *Guernica* (Fig. 3–7), because, as the dreamer, you are at once the sender and the receiver of the dream's message. You know how the images make you feel, and you respond to them directly without needing to have them explained. This is important.

These questions have formed the basis for discussions of the aesthetic character of dreams which have been for some years a regular part of a university course in art appreciation. The material that follows is derived from these discussions.

The terms *abstraction, distortion,* and *non-objective* all occur in the questions given above, and it is essential that our use of them be clearly understood.

Abstraction we have already discussed in Chapter 1 (page 14).

Distortion means literally the twisting out of natural shape, a deviation from the normal. We speak of features as distorted by anger or by grief, or of a body distorted by pain or accident, or disease. To a certain extent every artist alters the representation of his own percepts in order to emphasize certain qualities, for the sake of expression, but we only call this distortion, or sometimes abstraction, when we feel our own visual experience to have been outraged or at least denied. The arts are full of exaggerations and of variants on the usual appearance of things. So too are dreams.

The term *non-objective* as used in art criticism is often made synonymous with the term *abstract*. As we have seen, the latter term should be given a broader significance, referring as it does to all the relations within a work of art. *Non-objective* art is also abstract in this sense, but it specifically implies a disregard for concrete objects.

Non-objective art has its analogy in non-objective dreams. The dream of falling, for instance, may occur in an exteroceptive context, such as driving a car over a precipice, but it often occurs without any perceptual context at all. The dream image is then concentrated in the physical, proprioceptive and interoceptive sensation of falling, and may be thought of as non-objective.

When one adopts an aesthetic attitude toward dreams, so much of interest emerges that one hesitates to report "findings" without first making a carefully controlled study. Since this has not been done and since, for our purposes, the value lies more in the study than in its results, certain generalizations will be presented here only as guides, suggestive of the larger study of the artist's images. Five general types of dreams have been distinguished in the course of discussions of the aesthetic character of dream imagery.

1. Dreams of a continuing waking reality. These are dreams that employ plausibly real experiences in which the dreamer acts the leading part. Perhaps the role is a little closer to heart's desire than real life, or the dream clearly fulfills a wish. Such an agreeable, but not very memorable dream was told by a girl who found herself in a station wagon with her parents and her "date" going to play golf at the country club. She noticed the greenness of the grass and her own definite sense of happiness. But the images involved in such dreams may or may not have minor sensory quality, and may or may not be emotionally colored. Neither the sensory quality nor the emotion seems to the dreamer particularly important, and neither is apt even to figure in a first telling of the dream.

2. Dreams of distorted reality. In these the dreamer moves in a real and plausible if unfamiliar context, and one in which the most unlikely events occur. The Land of Cockaigne is, of course, of this type, as is the Wonderland in which Lewis Carroll's Alice sees a white rabbit hurry off to a party forgetting his kid gloves, and a squalling baby turns into a pig in the dreamer's arms. These dreams are apt to have a very strong sensory quality. Think of the bodily sensations in Alice's long and lengthening neck when she had eaten from one "side" of the mushroom; or the "proprioceptive" necessity of putting one foot up the chimney and one arm out of the window as she grew too big for the room in the rabbit's little house. The red and white rose bushes would lose all point if they were not in color, and one cannot think of the fantastic croquet game without having brought vividly to mind the tactile and muscular sensations involved in playing with a flamingo for a mallet and a hedgehog for a ball.

3. Dreams of reality with emotional climax in a strongly sensory or distorted image. Like those in the first group, these dreams seem merely a continuation of waking reality, but the sensory quality and occasional distortion of the usual appearance of an image assume great emotional significance. The emotion is frequently expressed through the isolated use of a single color in an otherwise colorless context, or through a sudden distortion of events or forms in an otherwise real setting. An example of this type will be recounted presently.

4. Non-objective dreams, where the whole significance is concentrated in a single emotional state or in a single sensory image. If the emotion is one of fear or anger it is generally felt in a strongly proprioceptive image, such as that of being pursued without seeing the pursuer, and without being able to move. If the emotion is agreeable, it tends to attach itself as an affect to an exteroceptive image, but one without objective significance. The dreamer, then, instead of participating, contemplates an image of pure sensation. In each case the dream tends to be non-objective in that no recognizable object is represented.

5. Nightmares. It is very generally true that dreams highly charged with emotion tend to be cast in abstract and distorted rather than in realistic imagery. The dreamer-artist pulls out all the stops; he uses strong color, strong contrasts of light and dark, as well as vivid bodily images. Here one finds much that in art would be called distortion, but which, as has already been suggested, is often a projection into a visual image of a proprioceptive feeling, for example, the screaming horse in Picasso's *Guernica* (Fig. 3–7).

The dreams of the first group are often rather pedestrian reconstructions of real life; they divide themselves into two major types. In one, the dreamer has the role of spectator while the events and scenes of the dream are spread out before him. In the other, the dreamer is a participant, often playing the lead. One student reported that he frequently seems to be in a movie theatre with the dream action taking place on a giant screen. In these non-participatory dreams there is rarely much emotion involved. Emotion, closely related as it is to the bodily receptors, seems to demand that we take part in the drama ourselves, and the more usual type of realistic dream is that in which the dreamer plays the leading role, as in James Thurber's *The Secret Life of Walter Mitty*.

Closely related to the dreams of continuing reality are those in which the improbable but desirable comes true. The dream of Jacob's Ladder is a classic example of this type. He saw a "ladder set up on earth, and the top of it reached to heaven, and behold the angels of God ascending and descending on it." Here the image is essentially exteroceptive. It apparently does not occur to Jacob that he might use the ladder himself. The dreamer remains an observer, not a participant. While he sees recognizable shapes, a ladder and angels moving up and down on it, there is no color, and the shapes have a verbal rather than a sensory significance. Jacob's pleasure in the dream apparently comes from its meaning, not from its aesthetic quality.

The presence or absence of sensory quality in dream imagery probably depends largely on the temperament of the dreamer, though most people employ sensory imagery occasionally. Of the dreams reported, those that had particularly memorable affective quality, or emotional tone of some sort, generally contained some sensory images either throughout the dream or as its climax.

A dream of mild, though very exasperating, frustration concentrated the emotion in a proprioceptive feeling instead of in an exteroceptive image. The dream was realistic, not non-objective; the dreamer was forced to play tennis with eggs for tennis balls!

Tactile quality was combined with a strong proprioceptive image of physical effort in a nightmare reported by a student who had spent a summer working in a limestone quarry. Two great blocks of stone were coming toward him on a moving platform and he knew that he must move one of them to one side or be crushed between them.

One more instance of sensory quality used as emotional climax in an otherwise realistic dream may be of interest. The dreamer was, as a child, climbing trees in an orchard with her friends when she saw another child in a distant tree apparently about to drop to the ground. The dreamer knew that there was some danger on the ground beneath her friend, and rushed over to warn her to climb back into the tree. Arrived at the spot, she found that her friend was hanging not by her arms, but by her neck, and around her neck was knotted a bright red scarf. The red was the only visible color in the whole dream, in fact it was the only detail that the dreamer could remember having *seen:* the rest, she insisted, she simply knew. For her the whole point of the dream lay in the red scarf.

In what have been termed non-objective dreams, the sensory quality of the imagery is again closely bound up with the expressive theme of the dream. It is, in fact, the whole dream. There is one which, like the dream of falling, is, in one form or another, rather common. The dreamer sees colored shapes dancing in slow or rapid

ART AS EXPERIENCE

kaleidoscopic patterns before his eyes. The colors, shapes, and sequences seem to the dreamer very beautiful, and watching them he is filled with a sense of complete well-being.

Analysis of the sensory qualities and aesthetic structure of nightmares would make a study in itself, but one example, told by a G. I. returned from war in the Pacific, will serve to illustrate the sometimes abstract character of imagery which carries a maximum of dread. This was a recurrent nightmare. The soldier dreamed that he was alone in a vast space with nothing to fix his eyes on, frantically trying to probe the emptiness for something firm and definite. Gradually, a very distant horizon appeared, and then a tiny red speck on this outer edge of space. At first, he was grateful for the horizon as it seemed somehow to place him, and glad of the speck to fix his eyes on. But the red area slowly became larger and larger, and at last he realized that it was a fiery red ball rolling toward him. As it steadily grew, and as its direction seemed inexorably centered on him, the dreamer's uneasiness gave way to terror, and when the ball finally rolled over him, engulfing him in its fiery furnace, he waked screaming. The dream invariably prefaced an attack of malaria.

In this dream, three "acts" are expressed in images of combined proprioceptive and exteroceptive quality. In act one the artist-dreamer is conscious only of himself, a bodily image, in an uninhabited, unfurnished emptiness, a space so vast that there is literally no place to hide. One need not be subject to agoraphobia to react sympathetically to this image of desolate loneliness. In act two a stabilizing horizon appears. The dreamer has for the first time a companion in the emptiness; the red speck on the horizon is some comfort, and has the color of warmth and security. But the comfort is of short duration. Act three is a crescendo of terror as the red ball changes from a friend to a deadly enemy, its color no longer warm but scorching, a symbol of blood and of death.[3]

What are the images with which the dreamer builds up his terrifying drama? The central one is invisible, only to be felt—the basic bodily image of a self lost in space. There are two exteroceptive images: the horizon which in some degree defines the space though without limiting it or making it much more habitable, and the red ball. The meaning of the only color in the dream, the redness of the ball, changes as the dream progresses. In its first association

[3] Dr. Hadfield, who has very kindly read this chapter of the manuscript, comments that the red color may be the result of the concentration of blood in the retina due to the dreamer's high temperature.

with the sun on the horizon, the redness carries the benign overtones of warmth. But this is illusory: its real meaning in the dream is of a fiery furnace, and in the end, the redness both represents and symbolizes death. In this dream as in the dream of the child hanging by the red scarf the color is both descriptive of actual appearance and emotionally expressive.

Space also shifts its meaning in the malarial nightmare. At first it is a nothingness, an abstract symbol of a danger so intangible and invisible that one cannot possibly cope with it. Later, it becomes actualized as the path along which the rolling ball moves. Then space vanishes, and there are only two images left: the fiery ball and the "self" of the dreamer. Finally, the exteroceptive and the bodily images merge in disaster.

One final comment on the malarial nightmare before we leave it: it is impossible to translate it into verbal, dramatic events. It must be seen and felt to be understood; that is, one must participate empathetically, or the force is lost. Nightmares tend to be expressed in the imagery of the self, for no matter how one may shudder at horrors inflicted on others they cannot be so horrible as those we suffer ourselves.

Imagination

Since for some, waking dreams or fantasies may be more readily accessible to what we may rather pretentiously call "aesthetic analysis" than are the dreams of sleep, they are recommended to the reader's attention. One example may be pertinent. An elderly lady, a retired schoolteacher, as a young woman had taken one of the early doctoral degrees given to women in Physics. She was an enthusiastic but intensely skeptical attender of museum lectures on modern art. Her skepticism was based on an early ingrained conviction that "art must be real," that its function is to hold up a mirror to nature. It should further, though she was loath to admit this, conform to certain standards of beauty that had prevailed in her youth on an Iowa farm.

A lecture on the sources of modern art, in which the subjects of fantasy and of the fantastic and distorted elements in twentieth-century painting and sculpture were touched upon, led Mrs. C. to raise the question of the relevance of daydream imagery. While she rarely remembered her dreams, she had for years amused herself before going to sleep in "imagining" faces and people of every kind and variety. The practice had begun quite accidentally one night when she was young. She found herself recalling with extraordinary vividness the face and figure of an old man who had very much impressed her as she saw him on a trolley car. To her delight she found that she could in imagination watch him reading his paper, talking with his neighbor, and finally getting off the car and walking away. In other words, it was not simply a memory image of the man as she had seen him, but a re-creation of the old man as an active, moving figure. (This was, incidentally, before the days of moving pictures.) Mrs. C. found this rather fun, and another night as she tried to go to sleep she looked about among her memories of the day for more fascinating figures. It had not been a dull day, but she could remember nothing but events. No strong perception of any sort could be recalled. The next time she tried, she could not recall anyone, but an entirely new and very vivid figure did appear. "I presently found that with my eyes half closed but looking into the darkness of my bedroom, I could summon up all sorts and kinds of faces, real and fantastic, cruel or entertaining. I began to be able to determine at the start what I wanted to see, an embodiment of this or that human quality, an angry personality, a terribly frightened one. Sometimes 'my people' were so scary that I had to light a light before I could go to sleep."

When Mrs. C. was urged at this time to attend one of the art classes for adults available in the city where she lived, she scoffed at the idea as quite beyond her abilities. She "couldn't draw a straight line," and so she contented herself with the pursuit of modern art which had piqued her curiosity by meaning so much to others and nothing whatever to her. In her "people" she had a clue to follow. She started looking for others like them among the works that filled the museum galleries. Mrs. C. was no colorist. Her images all came to life in the dark and semi-darkness, and she saw them as though modeled in varying values, in degrees of light-dark. So it was in sculpture and in drawings and prints that she quickly found herself among the brothers and sisters of her own "people."

Not unrelated to Mrs. C.'s image-making is a method of developing the powers of imagination that Leonardo da Vinci recommended to the student of painting.

I cannot forbear to mention among these precepts a new device for study which, although it may seem trivial and almost ludicrous, is nevertheless extremely useful in arousing the mind to various inventions. And this is, when you look at a wall spotted with stains, or with a mixture of stones, if you have to devise some scene, you may discover a resemblance to various landscapes, beautified with mountains, rivers, rocks, trees, plains, wide valleys and hills in varied arrangement; or, again, you may see battles and figures in action; or strange faces and costumes and an endless variety of objects, which you could reduce to complete and well-drawn forms. And these appear on such walls confusedly, like the sound of bells in whose jangle you may find any name or word you choose to imagine.[4]

Leonardo's advice is as useful to us who would enjoy art as to those who aspire to make it. Like the practice of an aesthetic awareness of one's dreams, the habit of looking in the accidental effects of nature, such as cloud formations, or of our artifact environment, for forms and images is a sharpener of vision. The images may be non-objective or, like Leonardo's, representational, but whether or not we ever "reduce [them] to complete and well-drawn forms," they enrich the imagination and make us more sensitive to the forms of art.

Suggestions for Further Reading

CARROLL, LEWIS. *Alice's Adventures in Wonderland.* New York: Pocket Books, Inc., 835.
   One of the classics of dream imagery, exceedingly useful in a study of bodily and visual images.
FREUD, S. *On Creativity and the Unconscious.* Selections with introduction and annotations by B. Nelson. New York: Harper & Row, Publishers, 1958. (Harper Torchbook TB 45.)
HADFIELD, J. A. *Dreams and Nightmares.* London: Penguin Books, Ltd., 1952. (Also available as a Pelican Book, A 294.)
   Very valuable in a study of one's own creative images.
LANGFELD, H. S. *The Aesthetic Attitude.* New York: Harcourt, Brace & World, Inc., 1920.
   Useful in connection with the concept of empathy which is basic to this textbook.
JUNG, C. J. *Psyche and Symbol: A Selection from the Writings of C. J. Jung.* V. S. de Laszlo, Ed. Garden City, N. Y.: Doubleday and Co., 1958. (A Doubleday Anchor Original.)

---

[4] Quoted by Elizabeth G. Holt in *A Documentary History of Art,* Vol. 1 (Garden City, N. Y.: Doubleday and Co.), p. 283. (A Doubleday Anchor book.)

4. The Artist's Images

The painter who draws by practice and judgment of the eye without use of reason is like a mirror which reproduces all objects which are set opposite to it, very similar but without knowledge of the same: he is like a parrot which talks words without understanding.

—Leonardo da Vinci

I believe that the artist cannot find all his forms in nature, but that the most remarkable are revealed to him in his soul . . . .

—Heinrich Heine, quoted by Baudelaire

He who does not imagine in stronger and better lineaments than his perishing and mortal eye can see, does not imagine at all.

—William Blake

Paint what is true and I applaud. But paint what is alive and individual in you and I applaud even more.

—Emile Zola

In the statements quoted above, the central fact is emphasized that art does not merely mirror nature. The creative artifact-image, to use its most precise and prosaic designation, is not the result of a simple transfer, by way of the eye and hand of the artist, of a direct image from nature to the canvas or other vehicle of a work of art, but is the result of one of the most subtly complex and least understood of natural processes. It involves perception and memory, symbolization and feeling, all of which go into the preliminary stage of imagining before technical skill and coordination of eye and hand come into action.

In this chapter we shall note different approaches to the problem: one artist will treat the material of his sensory experience quite objectively while another will seem to have his images "revealed to him in his soul." One artist will generalize on experience, abstracting or drawing out from it images which may bear little relation to the object in nature from which they derive; another will prefer to celebrate the uniqueness of experience and will represent it faithfully. One will delight in things of the eye, another in texture or in substance, both exteroceptive experiences; while still another will ignore outward appearances in order to convey bodily feeling, proprioceptive experience. And finally, in some great traditions of art, the idea that the artist might hold up a mirror to nature is entirely foreign; for 3,000 years in Egypt creative images were not so much revealed in the soul of the artist as constructed in his mind.

Objective and Subjective Imagery

By way of relating this further study of tangible, visible images to that of the ephemeral imagery of dream and fantasy, we shall examine two paintings of the same subject, Christ mocked by soldiers, the one by Manet (Fig. 4–1), the other by Rouault (Fig. 4–2). If they were dreams instead of paintings, where would you place them among the five types we have identified in Chapter 3? In which does the painter best express for you the *feeling* of being ridiculed, spat upon, held up to cruel mockery? In which painting do you feel more the tangible, visible reality of Jesus and of the soldiers? The most important question, since it probably embodies the artists' intentions, is which painting illustrates more vividly for you the words found in the Gospel of St. Matthew, Chapter 27, verses 27–31:

Then the soldiers of the governor took Jesus into the common hall and they gathered unto Him the whole band of soldiers. And they stripped Him and put on Him a scarlet robe. And when they had platted a crown of thorns they put it upon His head, and a reed in His right hand: and they bowed the knee before Him and mocked Him, saying, "Hail, King of the Jews." And they spit upon Him, and took the reed and smote Him on the head. And after that they had mocked Him, they took the robe off from Him, and put His own raiment on Him and led Him away to crucify Him.

If these were dreams instead of paintings, Manet's "dream" would seem to belong essentially with those of a continuing reality; a realistic dream in which the tangible and visible actuality of the figures is strongly emphasized. The painter has re-created for us the solid flesh of the two soldiers, making their arms and chests far more important than their faces. In contrast to the burly strength of these, the naked body of Jesus is softer, the texture and color of the skin gentler; His whole figure is that of a man accustomed to rely on spiritual rather than on physical force. The man at the left kneels with the ease and grace of an athlete, but he might be offering Jesus a cup of water instead of the mocking sceptre. The colors in the painting—azures, russet browns, crimsons, golds—and the textures of skin, hair, cotton, wool, metal, are presented in great sensuous richness. But take each figure out of the known context of the subject and what is left? Covering the rest of the picture, look at each figure separately. The soldier at the right might be the wonderfully realized figure of a partially nude model holding the corner of a piece of drapery in one hand, while he looks rather dully at the spectator. The old man in the helmet and baldric is more interesting and interested, but again we learn nothing of him other than that he is an old man who keeps the hard muscular condition of his prime. The figure of Christ is alone impossible to remove from its context of meaning. It remains an image of patient suffering and of non-resistance, but, alas, one is not particularly moved by His pain. The painting is beautiful in its form and in its sensuous detail of color, texture, and substance, but it is not an image of deep feeling. The artist remains an observer, not an empathetic participant in the drama.

How utterly different is the Rouault; a nightmare, not simply a recollection of painful reality. As in a nightmare the painter has put himself so completely into the body and mind of Jesus, feeling His sufferings so intensely himself, that he has been able to project in proprioceptive imagery the bodily passivity that makes spiritual strength. He does not describe the men as soldiers; under Rouault's brush, they become monsters embodying the very essence of human cruelty.

Rouault's images differ in almost every respect from Manet's and it will be useful to seek the reason in what we can guess of the painters' respective intentions. Manet tells his story in terms of figures taken out of the known objective world, out of his own studio. He clothes his models with a richness of color, texture, and solidity that makes them extraordinarily credible. The sensuous images, visual and tactile, are more significant than the meanings they convey, their symbolic content. Rouault, on the other hand, evokes the feeling of being stripped of one's clothes, spat upon, and mocked, and by involving us as participants in the sufferings of Christ, he brings to

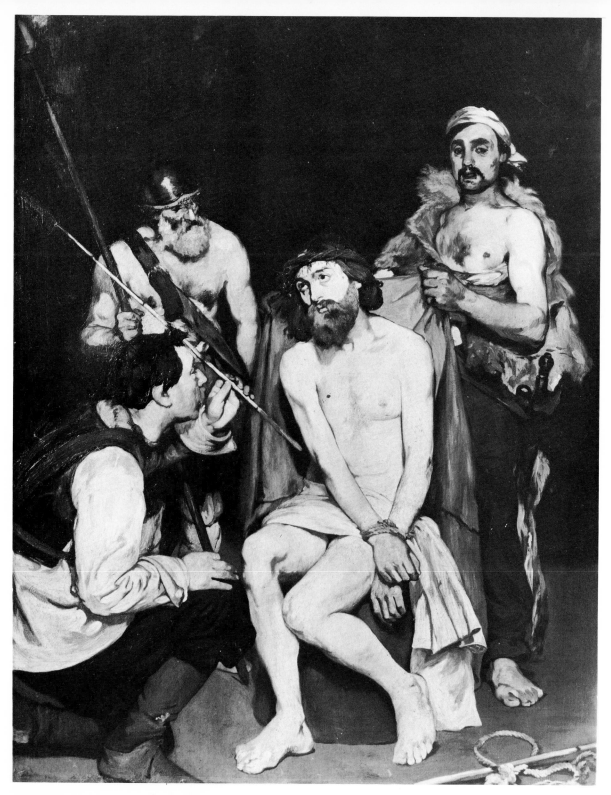

MANET. *Jesus Mocked by the Soldiers.*

(1832–1883; French.)
Oil on canvas, 74″ × 57″.
Courtesy of the Art Institute of Chicago.
James Deering Collection.

Fig. 4–1.

Rouault. *Christ Mocked by Soldiers.*

(1871–1958; French.)
Oil on canvas, 36¼″ × 28½″.

*Collection, The Museum of Modern Art,
    New York.*

Fig. 4–2.

life the passage in the Gospel of St. Matthew. Rouault's painting is composed of subjective images of feeling, while Manet's is an organization of objective images of visual and tactile sensations.

It has been noted in the previous chapter that feeling and emotion have their home in our proprioceptors and our consciousness of them is accompanied by physical sensations. Since our subjective images are generally fused with feeling, they are apt to be strongly proprioceptive in character.

The artist who wishes to render in paint a subjective image of feeling will rely on directly expressive means that can be readily translated into proprioceptive sensation. They may be called abstract-technical devices. While supplying sufficient indication of the forms to make his subject recognizable, Rouault's broad strokes of black are directly expressive of mood. Throughout the painting the color is somber, but it is the downward pull of all the brush strokes, the technical gestures with which the painter creates his images, that carry the heavy freight of feeling. The black areas are not primarily descriptive of the space between Christ's arm and His side, or of the groove between His breasts, or of the shadows beneath His eyes—though our recognition of these physical details counts too; these dark passages exist primarily to convey the heavy sorrow of the body.

To realize the dominant, downward movement of the painting, try to "read" the picture from the knees of Christ up along His thigh and arm to His head. It is like swimming upstream; you are moving against the movement of the painting. The horizontal strokes at the edge of the loin cloth, in the navel, and in the crease of the abdomen; the broad band that marks the lower ribs—all these serve to accent the concavity of the whole figure. From the relatively forward plane at the forehead, back and down through the torso and forward again to the knees, the movement describes the shape of a great C, open and receptive, but tired and resigned. In sharp contrast is the vertical to the left of Christ's face. It can probably be interpreted as the sceptre which was offered Him, or it may be a club in the hand of the soldier. The tensely aggressive figures of the two tormentors emphasize by contrast the passive resignation of Jesus.

No one but Rouault would have imagined the mocking of Christ in just this way. In this painting no test of objective reality is applicable. The painting was as true for the painter as our nightmares are true for us, often painfully so, long after waking, and to feel its truth requires an exercise of our empathetic imagination.

A painting is not necessarily inaccessible to us because its maker has drawn his images from his inner consciousness, but it must be approached by way of our own subjective imagery and frequently through the active participation of our bodily receptors. In this connection consider also Munch's *The Shriek* (Fig. 3–5), El Greco's *View of Toledo* (Fig. 4–23), and Van Gogh's *Starry Night* (Fig. 4–20).

Images of Feeling

In his search for forms with which to express an emotion such as sorrow or mourning, or an idea such as the concept of holiness, the artist has recourse to one of two very different methods. The one is symbolic and abstract; the other is descriptive. The symbolic method is to employ a mental image to stand for the emotion or idea represented. The halo, for instance, stands for holiness or divinity (Figs. 1–4, 2–8), while the cross was a symbol of life in earlier religions long before the death of Jesus made it a symbol of everlasting life to the Christian.

The artist who uses the descriptive method may choose to describe either the object of sorrow, the experience which gave rise to the feeling, as in Jacques Louis David's *Death of Marat* (Fig. 4–3), or the appearance of a person experiencing grief, as in the figures of the Virgin and St. John at the foot of the cross in Grünewald's *Crucifixion* (Fig. 4–4). David's image is more exteroceptive, visual and tactile; Grünewald's more proprioceptive. David is a sympathetic observer; Grünewald almost participates.

Finally, the artist may describe the way it feels in one's own body to be sorrowful, as in Picasso's mother with a dead baby in *Guernica* (Fig. 3–7), or to be in the clutch of terror as in Munch's *The Shriek* (Fig. 3–5). As we have seen, this is apt to involve some degree of abstract symbolization and of distortion, because it is not easy to express in a figure seen from the outside the sinking of the heart or the contraction of the throat muscles that are no less real for being invisible.

In his *Death of Marat,* David has not simply described what he saw; he has simplified both the figure and its setting, leaving out every detail of the room except those most significant and most moving; emphasizing the downward pull of the verticals, stressing the fallen head, the limp arm. In effect, he isolates the physical feeling which describes both the inert heaviness of death and the dejection of living sorrow. He has abstracted from the experience the bodily condition which belongs both to the mourner and to the mourned.

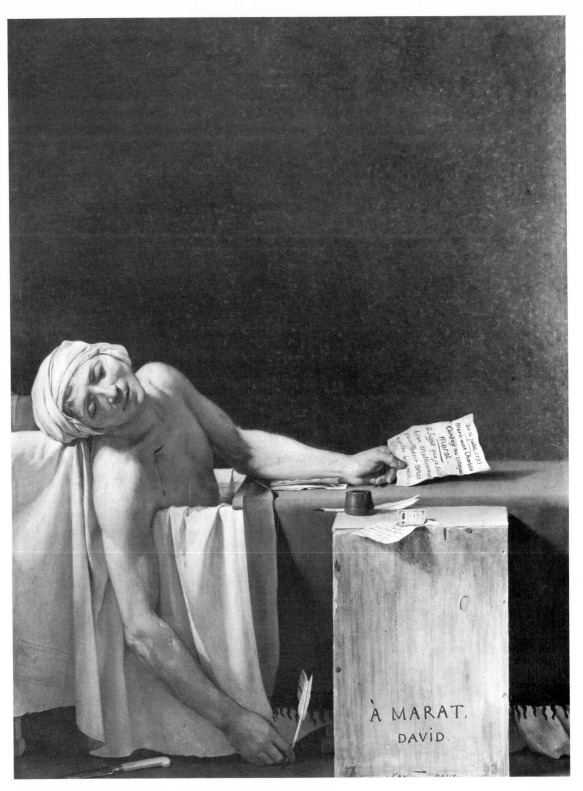

DAVID. *The Death of Marat.*

(1748–1825; French.)
Oil on canvas, 65″ × 50½″.
*Royal Museum of Fine Arts, Copyright
A. C. L., Brussels.*

Fig. 4–3.

Gʀᴜ̈ɴᴇᴡᴀʟᴅ. *Crucifixion.*

(c. 1470–1528; German.)
Panel from the Isenheim Altarpiece.
Over-all dimensions: 16½′ × 26′.
Oil on panel.

Unterlinden Museum, Colmar.

Fig. 4–4.

The great Italian painter Giotto, in the first decade of the fourteenth century, decorated the lower section of a chapel in Padua with allegorical figures of the Virtues and Vices. These he painted in gray stone color (*grisaille*) to look like statues and placed them in simulated niches. Beneath the figure of Justice (Fig. 4–5), Giotto represented the happy life led under a just ruler, while under the tyrant Injustice, people are robbed by highwaymen on the road. The allegorical figure symbolizes the Virtue; the scene describes it as it may be seen. The figures are strongly conceptual; the scenes perceptual.

The allegorical personages in Giotto's Arena Chapel hold their appropriate, identifying attributes: Prudence, a mirror, standing for reflection; Fortitude, a sword for courage. But the painter was not content to depend on the attributes alone: as far as possible he makes the figures embody the virtue or vice they symbolize. Inconstancy, the epitome of unbalance, sits on a rolling disc and flings her arms wide as she falls backward (Fig. 4–6). Hope is a winged figure looking and moving upward. Justice (Fig. 4–5), instead of the usual attribute of a pair of scales, holds in either hand a small tray on which are placed little figures symbolizing Right and Wrong. Right is represented by a tiny, winged figure; Wrong, by a bearded man with arm lifted to strike a blow. With her body in perfect balance, her gaze abstracted, Justice weighs the Right and the Wrong before issuing a verdict.

Giotto has combined the traditional figure of Justice with the image of the weighing of the souls at the Last Judgment, a scene common in medieval art (Fig. 4–7). At Bourges a man's good and evil deeds are weighed against each other. If the good should tip the scales he will go to join the blessed in Heaven. Centuries earlier in scenes of the Egyptian Last Judgment, Osiris presided as judge instead of Christ (Fig. 4–8); the heart of the dead person was weighed in a scale against a feather, the Egyptian symbol of Truth, and the heart which was found "weighed down" by its sins was thrown to a waiting monster, into the "jaws of Hell." If, on the other hand, the heart proved to be as "light as a feather," its owner was judged worthy of eternal life.

Giotto was not, of course, following an Egyptian prototype when he substituted for the rather commercial idea that Good, being more valuable, must weigh more than Evil the basic human and proprioceptive experience that one is "weighed down" by sin. He was consulting his own experience of the bodily sensations that accompany feelings of guilt. While the two little figures held in either hand by

GIOTTO. *Justice.*

(c. 1266–1337; Italian.)
Fresco, Arena Chapel, Padua.
Photo: Alinari-Art Reference Bureau.

Fig. 4–5.

GIOTTO. *Inconstancy.*

(c. 1266–1337; Italian.)
Fresco, Arena Chapel, Padua.
Photo: Alinari-Art Reference Bureau.

Fig. 4–6.

Last Judgment.

Typanum of central portal of west facade.
Thirteenth-century cathedral, Bourges,
   France.

Photo: Archives Photographiques, Paris.

Fig. 4–7.

Judgment of Osiris.

Papyrus of Ani.
Late dynastic.
*Courtesy of the Trustees, The British
    Museum, London.*

Fig. 4–8.

Justice are at the moment level with each other, there can be no
doubt as to the eventual outcome. Arms, wings, and drapery of the
winged figure all suggest an upward movement which will shortly
lift the weight from Justice's right hand. Quite as clearly, the downward movements of the figure in her left hand, the inclination of
the head, the bent right arm, the strong diagonal of the right side of
the little figure, all convey the impending sinking of this side of the
invisible scale.

Not only in the tiny symbolic figures but also in the statuesque
person of Justice herself is the idea embodied. It is implicit in her
frontal position, the backbone vertical to the earth and to the throne
on which she sits, the shoulders parallel to the ground. If one were
to draw horizontal lines through the ears, the shoulders, the hips,

ART AS EXPERIENCE

and the knees, they would all be parallel with the earth's surface, all at right angles to the median line of the figure. The allegorical figure of Justice becomes herself a scale in perfect balance; the weighing, an intellectual and moral, not a mechanical process.

Conceptual and Perceptual Images

We have seen that Giotto presents the idea of Justice in both a conceptual, relatively abstract image, and in a perceptual, descriptive image. There are two opposed types of creative personality that can be distinguished by the emphasis they put on conceptual and on perceptual imagery. The two different approaches may be termed respectively analytical and descriptive. One creative type accepts and enjoys life as he finds it; experience is for him an end in itself. If he reflects on it, "recollects beauty in tranquility," it is not in order to probe beneath the surface but rather to enjoy it for its own sake. If he is a religious person he is apt to take delight in the beauty of the world as God-given, and even to look upon his enjoyment of it as a form of worship. The other type is analytical in approach, reflecting on experience not so much for purposes of enjoyment as for understanding. As an artist, the former type is moved to celebrate sensory experience in descriptive, often quite realistic images; the latter, creative type tends to analyze experience and to reduce it to conceptualized, relatively abstract images.

In the four still life groups illustrated (Figs. 4–9 through 4–12), one finds varying degrees of emphasis on the conceptual and perceptual character of the painters' images. The first is a detail of a state portrait by Holbein of two French ambassadors to the court of Henry VIII. One was a man much interested in navigation and in the geographical explorations which were "news" in the 1530's, while the other, a cleric, was a musician and a patron of music. On the table between them the globe, the lute, the recorders, and the open book of music identify these Frenchmen as cultivated gentlemen whose tastes might well recommend them to the hospitality of the king of England. Hans Holbein gives to each object a clear readability of conceptual meaning. The objects are unmistakable. They are lighted from the upper left, making them appear very solid and substantial, while the clean-cut contours of the instrument make one want both to feel along the ridges of the lute and the crisp edges of its neck, and to hold its body between the hands sensing the enclosed volume. In this painting the images are vividly sensory in character, but with strong symbolic content. *What* they are matters very much.

HOLBEIN. *Still Life.*

(c. 1497–1543; German.)
Detail from *The Ambassadors.*
Over-all dimensions: 6′ 9½″ × 6′ 9″.
Oil on panel.
Reproduced by courtesy of the Trustees,
The National Gallery, London.

Fig. 4–9.

Velasquez. *The House of Martha.*

(1599–1660; Spanish.)
Oil on canvas, 23¼″ × 40¼″.
*Reproduced by courtesy of the Trustees,
    The National Gallery, London.*

Fig. 4–10.

In the Velasquez still life (Fig. 4–10), the insistence on symbolic content is much less strong, and the sensory quality, stronger. The still life is incidental to the story of *Christ in the House of Mary and Martha.* The fish and eggs and the terracotta jug are only a part of the setting, but Velasquez could not refrain from celebrating the special qualities of slippery shapes, of clear white ovals, and of the round dishes and jug. We respond to these shapes and to their textures and recognize their exact appropriateness without stopping to think of their identities.

The paintings by Chardin and Cézanne were intended to stand alone, and here the descriptive and the analytical creative types of artist are clearly differentiated. Chardin, like Velasquez, celebrates

CHARDIN. *Still Life with Goblet and Fruit.*

(1699–1779; French.)
Oil on canvas, 12½″ × 16½″.
Courtesy, Museum of Fine Arts, Boston.

Fig. 4–11.

the sheer sensory quality of the things he represents: the soft gleam
of polished silver, the fitful bloom on the skin of the plums, the matte
surface of the pears contrasting with the glassy transparency of the
grapes, while all the fruits rest firmly on the stone shelf. The light
that make the colors and textures visible, itself becomes a factor in
the totality of the painting; the unity has a kind of inevitable rightness which makes any other arrangement seem unthinkable. Char-

ART AS EXPERIENCE

Vermeer. *View of Delft from Rotterdam Canal.*

(1632–1675; Dutch.)
Oil on canvas, 38½″ ×46¼″.
Mauritshuis, The Hague.

Pl. IIa.

MONET. *The Zuiderkerk (South Church) at Amsterdam: Looking Up the Groenburgwal.*

(1840–1926; French.)
Oil on canvas, 21½″ × 25¾″.
Philadelphia Museum of Art.
W. P. Wilstach Collection.

Pl. IIb.

din takes these things at their face value and loves them for what they offer of simple sensory richness of color and texture and shape.

Cézanne, on the other hand, keeps us at a slight distance from the fruit he paints; we are not allowed to love them as familiars of our own world. He finds in the apples as they spill out onto the table symbols of a geometric order that lies beneath the surface appearance of things. Chardin describes, but with a poet-painter's eye for the exact tone and shape and texture that will conjure up purple plums, yellow pears, and green-white grapes. Cézanne ana-

CÉZANNE. *Still Life with Basket of Apples.*

(1839–1906; French.)
Oil on canvas, 25¾″ × 32″.
Courtesy of the Art Institute of Chicago.
Helen Birch Bartlett Memorial Collection.

Fig. 4–12.

RENOIR. *Three Bathers.*

(1841–1919; French.)
Oil on canvas, 21½″ × 25⅞″.
The Cleveland Museum of Art.
Purchase from the J. H. Wade Fund.

Fig. 4–13.

lyzes the forms of the fruit, relating them to more general perma-
nencies. Chardin's images are highly perceptual; Cézanne's are
conceptual but not as Holbein's are. Where Holbein is content to
identify perceptual experience, classifying its images as a globe and
a lute, Cézanne relates the perception to an abstract order.

The same distinction is well-represented in the comparison of Renoir's *Three Bathers* (Fig. 4–13) and Cézanne's *Great Bathers* (Fig. 4–14). Renoir's delight is in sensory quality, in the way "flesh takes the light," as he once said, in the textures and rich curves of the forms. Cézanne, by slightly distorting the figures, forces us to see them not as nudes but almost as architectural members of a great structure that he builds, a kind of temple in which organic life becomes disciplined in the service of abstract order.

CÉZANNE. *Great Bathers.*

(1839–1906; French.)
Oil on canvas, 82″ × 99″.
Philadelphia Museum of Art.
W. P. Wilstach Collection.

It has been pointed out that perception is accompanied by the assigning of meaning based on previous experience to the direct sensation. This process of symbolization plays a more important role in the image-making of some periods of art than of others, and of one artist than of another. An artist's sketches and studies may be much more records of sensation than of the meaning attached to the sensation. (See Chapter 10.) Historically there was a very slow movement toward the exploitation of sensory quality for its own sake from about 1550 to 1860, when it finally became dignified as part of the doctrine of "art for art's sake." The Impressionists, whose name derived from a painting by Claude Monet of a harbor scene which he called *Sun Rising: an Impression*, were preoccupied with the visual beauty of the world and of the images to be made of it, and in many of their paintings the meaning attached to the sensory pattern was of little importance. The Abstract Impressionists of the third quarter of our century are also preoccupied with sensory experience, but it is quite as proprioceptive as visual. So-called action paintings like Pollock's *Autumn Rhythm* (Fig. 4–15) are visible records of the artist's gestures and movements, predominantly sensory in quality with little or no explicit meaning.

POLLOCK. *Autumn Rhythm.*

(1912–1956; American.)
Oil on canvas, 105″ × 207″.
The Metropolitan Museum of Art,
   New York.
George A. Hearn Fund, 1957.

Fig. 4–15.

There used to be a rather general assumption that where an artist sets out to "represent" reality, or some part of it, the resulting work should be as nearly as possible an exact copy of nature and that the degree of exactness will depend on the artist's skill. This is far from the case. Even where the purpose is to celebrate the very specific character and sensory quality of reality, as in Chardin's *Still Life,* the artist does not "hold up a mirror to nature." In the process of copying, the total experience of perception with its attendant meanings and attached feeling would be dismembered. The life would go out of the image leaving a dead imitation instead of a living re-creation.

It will be useful to compare four paintings of cathedrals: Constable's *Salisbury* (Fig. 4–16), Corot's *Chartres* (Fig. 4–17), Monet's *Rouen* (Fig. 4–18), and Matisse's *Notre Dame* (Fig. 4–19). They all represent recognizable cathedrals, but with what a personal vision did each man see his building! In the first two one cannot escape the sense of importance that the artist attaches to things as things, identifiable as towers, portals, traceried windows; and the stone masonry of which they are constructed, solid and permanent as befits a six-hundred-year-old structure. The symbolic meaning of each part of the image is important.

Not so with Monet and Matisse. These painters cared less for the informing character of their images and perhaps more for their sensory quality. Monet seems primarily to celebrate the shimmer of hot sunlight on yellow and gray stone and the shifting patterns of lavender and blue and green that fall in the shadows where we suppose the western portal to be, although it is not defined as such. Matisse withdraws even further from the cathedral as a stone structure, solid and tangible. He seems to use its well-known and well-beloved form rising above the Seine simply as an occasion to celebrate the act of the celebration itself, the act of painting. One feels his joy in the resistance of pigment and canvas to his brush and in the textural as well as in the visible quality of the paint. And yet out of this very personal "celebration" there emerges a great form, a massive shape with a timeless, brooding personality not unlike that of the pyramids of Egypt. Monet's *Rouen* and Matisse's *Notre Dame* are both a long way from what the visitor to these great buildings remembers, while Constable's *Salisbury* and Corot's *Chartres* are closer both to photographs and to the "beauty" which we "recollect in tranquility." It is clearly a matter of varying intention on the part of the painter: each is communicating to us something which has meaning for him, but he selects from the richness of experience and celebrates what matters most to him personally.

CONSTABLE. *Salisbury Cathedral.*

(1776–1837; English.)
Oil on canvas, 34¼″ × 43⅝″.
*Copyright The Frick Collection,
    New York.*

Fig. 4–16.

A further comparison might be made between the seventeenth-century *View of Delft* (Pl. IIa) by Jan Vermeer, and Monet's *View of Amsterdam* of two hundred years later (Pl. IIb). In Vermeer's painting the rose-red roof tiles of the houses to the left of the picture, the pale pink of the distant buildings in the center, and the blue roofs and turrets to the right count both as tiles, bricks, and slates, and as sheer color. Moreover, the modulation of the color

ART AS EXPERIENCE

COROT. *Chartres.*

(1796–1875; French.)
Oil on canvas, 24½″ × 19½″.
The Louvre, Paris.

Fig. 4–17.

from light to dark indicates the slopes of the roofs, the rounded forms of the turrets and towers, the contrasts between shadowed and strongly sunlit surfaces, so that we know what we are looking at in solid substance and in space as well as in surface patterns.

In Monet's *View of Amsterdam,* one cannot be sure whether the houses flanking the canal are of brick or of stone; nor are we told much of their forms other than that their high, shouldered facades are crowned by characteristically Dutch gables. But we are not

THE ARTIST'S IMAGES

MONET. *Rouen Cathedral, West Facade, Sunlight.*

(1840–1926; French.)
Oil on canvas, 39½″ × 26″.
National Gallery of Art, Washington. Chester Dale Collection.

Fig. 4–18.

MATISSE. *A Glimpse of Notre Dame in Late Afternoon.*

(1869–1954; French.)
Oil on canvas, 28½″ × 21½″.
Albright-Knox Art Gallery, Buffalo, New York.

Fig. 4–19.

concerned: what catches and delights the eye is the shimmer of sunlight and the beautiful, dappled surface of the canal and of the buildings. Gerard Manley Hopkins echoes Monet's theme in his poem "Pied Beauty": "Glory be to God for dappled things."

Compare the canals in the two paintings. The water at Delft is much closer to our memory image; it is "watery," with unsteady reflections of houses, trees, ships. The canal at Amsterdam is flecked with countless touches of light, and reveals the texture not of water but of paint. Monet has given us what is probably a very accurate picture of the way the water of the canal looked on a particular afternoon, ruffled by a breeze, brilliant with colors borrowed from the green and rose and gold of the surrounding city as well as from the blue of the Dutch sky. It is a most particular view, personal to the artist and peculiar to his mood. Vermeer's painting is also very personal in feeling, but it has that general quality which makes one say "that is the way I have seen it too."

Both painters were fascinated by visible reality, but Vermeer was more interested than Monet in the idea associated with his visual impressions—with what they added up to when given their usual meaning; Monet was more concerned with the sensuous qualities of light, shadow, and color, with the look of the city as a whole, than with its individual parts.

Descriptive Images of Reality

For most people the real world consists of the things that can be touched and handled as well as seen or only thought about. A book on a table is "solid" because it resists muscular action when we press on it or grasp it in our hands. The idea of "solidity" is, in fact, not derived from vision at all, though certain visual characteristics tend to be associated with it. Something can "look" solid, but if there is any doubt, we have to make contact with it to be sure.

The most important of the visual characteristics of solidity are apparent continuity of surface, apparent volume, and an apparently unchanging shape. "Apparent" is used advisedly, because appearances can be deceptive. A cumulus cloud, for instance, or a bank of mist in a valley, tends to look solid while its shape remains visually unaltered. The sense of its solidity is diminished if it changes visibly in contour or surface, and disappears entirely as the cloud or mist envelops one in an airplane or on the ground. The lack of any resistance of the cloud on contact entirely dispels our sense of its solidity.

ART AS EXPERIENCE

Ideas of solidity and weight tend to be associated with one another, because both are derived from our sensations of muscular tension in pushing against or handling physical objects, or lifting them with some degree of effort. The appearance of solidity and weight, or their absence, can be a very important factor in our responses to works of art. In this connection compare the figures of the soldiers in Manet's and Rouault's paintings of the mocking of Christ (Figs. 4–1 and 4–2).

Solidity and weight tend also to be associated with ideas of volume, since objects must occupy some space to be solid and, in general, larger objects tend to be heavier than smaller ones, though there are, of course, very great differences in that relation. The sense of volume is greatly enhanced by vision, particularly under appropriate conditions of lighting. If a round object is lit from the front it will appear relatively or absolutely flat; if it is lit from the side as in the Velasquez still life (Fig. 4–10), the gradations of light and shadow on its surface enormously enhance the effects of volume and solidity. Bruegel (Pl. I) and Holbein (Fig. 4–9) depended much more on eloquent, descriptive contours than on light and shadows, contours that serve to recall for us both the mental act of limiting an object within a boundary, and the tactual-muscular act of pressing along the edges of an object to test its solidity. At the same time it should be noticed that in the work of an artist such as El Greco and in any art of which the purpose is not "material realism," strong effects of volume and solidity have been neglected or avoided (Figs. 2–9 and 4–23).

By the volume of an object is meant the amount of space it occupies, actually or in imagination. But the space itself is something other than the volume of objects we can touch and handle. The room in which one sits has a volume, most of which is obviously not occupied by solid objects. Nor does one think immediately of the air the room encloses if the idea of its volume of enclosed space occurs. We can neither see, touch, nor handle space, though we may speak loosely of "seeing space" when we gaze at a far horizon or the sky, and a designer may even speak metaphorically of "handling space" when he designs the related volumes of a building or a piece of sculpture. But what we actually see and handle is the matter *in* space. To the artist, then, the problem of the aesthetic use of space cannot be separated from the use of solids.

The concept of space is illusive yet it is one of the most important that we possess, not only in its practical relevance but also in its imaginative implications. No practical purpose can be achieved without the movement of objects in space, whether the purpose is as simple as the cooking of an egg or as complex as international trade. Moreover, man from time immemorial has looked up at the stars with wonder and awe, has watched the flight of birds, and has wondered what lay beyond his terrestrial horizon. As we have seen, some of our aesthetic response to a great bridge (Fig. 2–5) is bound up with our ideas of the immensity and illusiveness of space, a portion of which the bridge seems to have brought under control. Though we may today talk hopefully (or fearfully) of interplanetary travel, and describe cosmic space with abstract words, its size is literally unimaginable. With the exception of the still relatively few astronauts, people in general have no "images" to deal with it, only abstractions. The artist cannot represent the vastness that astronomers measure in light-years, but is forced into using visual abstractions, or metaphors, of his own. Van Gogh, in *Starry Night* (Fig. 4–20), unites his recall of bodily movement through space to visual memories of astronomical photographs of spiral nebulae. The resulting visual metaphor is a vivid and moving image of the vastness of the heavens, and of man's position between it and the earth beneath his feet.

If we can neither see, touch, nor handle space, how do we come by our understanding of it, and out of what experiences does the artist fashion his images? The English word *space* comes from the Latin *spatiari*, meaning "to wander," and this suggests that from early times space was looked on as something vast in which one got lost. Indefinite vastness remains one of the chief characteristics of space as we think of it, though the self-confidence of our scientists today leads us to put the emphasis on exploration rather than on getting lost.

The dictionary distinguishes between absolute space, which is indefinite extension in all directions, and relative space, a portion of extension, the intervals between objects or points in space.

It is the second kind of space with which we deal every day in our practical lives. This also forms the basis of many of the artifact-images of space in our Western Renaissance tradition. We are aware that physical objects occupy space, and, though we realize their existence by touch and their size and weight by handling them, we also *see* that they are of different sizes, that they occupy different positions in space, and that the same object looks different when seen at different distances from us.

When, in about 1400, the attention of Italian artists began to focus on their visible and tangible environment, interest centered

ART AS EXPERIENCE

VAN GOGH. *Starry Night.*

(1853–1890; Dutch.)
Oil on canvas, 29″ × 36¼″.
*Collection, The Museum of Modern Art,
    New York.*
*Acquired through the Lillie P. Bliss
    Bequest.*

Fig. 4–20.

first on the representation of physical objects in all their bulk and
solidity, and then proceeded to ways of understanding and recording the relations existing between them in space. The Renaissance
artist was content to add up distances of relative space and to disregard or only hint at the existence of absolute space. In Masaccio's

MASACCIO. *The Tribute Money.*

(1401–1428; Italian.)
Fresco, Brancacci Chapel, Santa Maria
  del Carmine, Florence.
Photo: Alinari-Art Reference Bureau.

Fig. 4–21.

The Tribute Money (Fig. 4–21), the space in which the group of disciples stands about the central figure of Christ exists for us chiefly because of the individual bulk of each figure and of the clarity of emptiness between them defined by the contours of their bodies. The building, solid and measurable, must occupy space and so this too is assumed and added to the area in which the disciples stand. The figure of Peter removing the coin from the mouth of a fish at the water's edge is smaller than his figure as he stands by Christ receiving directions from Him, and we automatically read the cause of this diminished size as the distance from the group to the lakeside. We are giving to the image of the smaller figure "meaning based on previous experience." Thus the artist builds up a credible image of the scene with a number of instances of limited space. By the soft tonality of the successive banks of hills, and the diminishing clarity of the contrasts, Masaccio attempts for the first time in Western art since the Romans to suggest the body of dust-laden atmosphere that fills the space between us and the horizon, even to suggest that extension is continuous beyond the horizon itself.

                                              ART AS EXPERIENCE

To find artistic equivalents to this element of our world which is at once so intangible and so inescapable, to perfect a system by which the illusion of three-dimensional space could be projected on a two-dimensional plane and the relative sizes and positions of objects in space could be logically plotted, the Renaissance mind invented linear perspective. This is the name given to the system by which the artist makes all lines and surfaces that are supposed to run straight into the distance disappear into a single vanishing point. The vanishing point may be high as in Leonardo's *Last Supper* (Fig. 2–10), or low, as in the Perugino illustrated (Fig. 4–22), or to the left or right of the center of the picture, but its position will always be on the eye level of the viewer, the horizon of the picture. Parallel lines, like the rails of a railroad track, converge as they recede from the viewer, and objects get smaller as they recede. The distance at which the viewer is supposed to be in front of the picture will control the speed with which objects diminish in size. So-called "one-

PERUGINO. *The Handing of the Keys to Peter.*

(1445–1523; Italian.)
Fresco, Sistine Chapel, The Vatican, Rome.
Photo: Alinari-Art Reference Bureau.

Fig. 4–22.

point perspective" assumes that the viewer remains in one position in relation to the picture, or the artist in relation to the scene represented. This may be seen in Masaccio's *The Trinity* (Fig. 7–2). But it is possible to compose a picture with a number of vanishing points, in which the artist and the viewer take up a number of different positions in relation to the picture, as in El Greco's *View of Toledo* (Fig. 4–23). The result will "read" spatially and expressively, but lacks the consistency of such a painting as Perugino's *The Handing of the Keys to Peter* (Fig. 4–22).

Linear perspective, because of its emphasis on line which is so readily translatable into terms both of movement and of tactility, invites us to move imaginatively into the space represented, following the "railroad tracks," touching the sides and edges of buildings as we move along beside them, sensing with our whole bodies their solidity as they block the way in one or another direction. In Leonardo's *Last Supper* (Fig. 2–10), as we have seen, linear perspective is used both as a coordinative, clarifying device and as an expressive means. On the horizon behind Christ's shoulders there are three vanishing points: just above Christ's right shoulder the parallel lines of the top of the left wall and of the tapestries on it converge; those of the coffered ceiling converge behind the head of Christ; and those of the right wall, at a point above His left shoulder.

While the effect of these perspective lines is to clarify and measure the space, they also lead the attention to the central figure, the physical and spiritual focus of the picture. Linear perspective here is vital both to coherence and to expressive content. The three vanishing points may, like the three windows, have symbolized to Leonardo and to his patrons the doctrine of the Trinity.

Both linear and atmospheric perspective play important expressive roles in Bruegel's painting of *The Unfaithful Shepherd* (Fig. 4–24) who abandoned his flock to the wolves. Bruegel places the shepherd almost on the picture plane as though he were about to hurl himself out of the picture entirely in his haste to save his own skin. His bulk and strength are such that he could easily have dealt with the wolves had he not cared more for his own safety than for that of his charges. In the near middle distance, the flock are frantically scattering before the attack without any chance of reaching the safety of the home-farm on the distant horizon. The irregular ruts of a wagon road, and the straggling row of trees to the left suggest with their distantly converging lines how far the sheep would have to run to safety. The tonality of the landscape pales very gradually from the relatively strong intensities of the red and green of

ART AS EXPERIENCE

EL GRECO. *View of Toledo.*

(1541–1614; Spanish.)
Oil on canvas, 47¾″ × 42¾″.

The Metropolitan Museum of Art,
*   New York.*
Bequest of Mrs. H. O. Havermeyer, 1929.
The H. O. Havemeyer Collection.

Fig. 4–23.

BREUGEL. *The Unfaithful Shepherd.*

(c. 1525–1569; Flemish.)
Panel, 22″ × 33½″.
Johnson Collection, Philadelphia.

Fig. 4–24.

the shepherd's clothing and of the grass and shrubs in the foreground to the almost neutral tones of the farmhouse and its surrounding trees as they merge with very little contrast into the sky at the horizon. The desolate emptiness of the space between the fleeing shepherd and the distant farmhouse is conveyed both by atmospheric and by linear perspective devices, but the perspective counts for little expressively, while the emptiness of space in which the deserted sheep have no place to hide is all-important to the expressive content of the picture.

ART AS EXPERIENCE

Space can also present itself to the consciousness as a vast field of light-dark and color of which the whole absorbs our interest rather than any of its parts. This experience is exclusively visual. Space is then regarded not as a sum of distances between physical things, but as a mysterious whole in which material things are secondary. Goya's print called *The Giant* (Fig. 4–25) is one of the most convincing and moving statements of this kind of space-image in all the history of art. Goya's meaning is no more explicit than is his statement of space. Though the title and our interest center in the tremendous figure, it is not its massive power that is memorable, but the ultimate loneliness and impotence of even a giant in the immensity of unmeasured space.

While the Renaissance mind concerned itself with the measurable, limited space between objects, even if those objects might be situated as far off as the eye could reach, there was already in the work of Leonardo and of some of the German painters of landscape early in the sixteenth century a suggestion of that other kind of space, of "unlimited extension in all directions." We have seen in El Greco's *Adoration of the Shepherds* (Fig. 2–9) that by the end of the sixteenth century, space had begun to be presented as beyond human measure, absolute not so much in the sense of being unknown as unknowable. This is so largely subjective that it is hard to visualize, but we experience it under certain very familiar circumstances. Think of a moonless, overcast night sky which seems to hover over the unknown; or of a thunderstorm, by night or by day, with the dazzling flashes of lightning illuminating great volumes of cloud-filled space, and silhouetting briefly dark against light or light against dark. Eerie shapes without solidity at indeterminate distances we recognize as "houses," "trees," "hills," only because we are familiar with such shapes at other times.

El Greco has suggested a similar experience in his *View of Toledo* (Fig. 4–23). The great square fortress of the Alcazar, the groping tower of the cathedral, and the blue-gray city walls all have the weightless evanescence of buildings that seem about to be lost either in darkness or in some great cataclysm. The men who struggle up the hill toward shelter are reduced to tiny specks, while the wraith-like figure on the pale horse seems about to be swallowed up by the stream he is fording. Here are no measured intervals: distances are impossible to judge either within the picture or between us and the city. Nothing is definite, nothing sure except the undefinable dread that seems to hang over the city like a dream of foreboding.

Goya. *The Giant.*

(1746–1828; Spanish.)
Etching and aquatint, 11¼″ × 8″.
The Metropolitan Museum of Art,
  New York.
Dick Fund, 1935.

Fig. 4–25.

The Varying Sensory Quality of the Artist's Images

Let us examine now a number of works of art to discover what kind of sensory recall, visual and tactile (largely exteroceptive), or bodily (interoceptive and proprioceptive), the artist has relied on most heavily; and what kind of sensory response the images awaken in you. Admittedly there is a danger here: one may look at a painting or a piece of sculpture with only this question of sensory quality in mind and, coming to a quick conclusion, mentally label it as "primarily visual," "mainly proprioceptive," or "very tactile," and then turn to the next. The dangers are first that one does not stay with the image long enough to respond to any but its most obvious qualities, and second, that one has no chance to inquire into the relation of its sensory quality to the artist's purpose, or to the total expressive content of the painting or sculpture. So be forewarned and do not indulge in the practice of "labeling."

Our first two illustrations were used earlier (Figs. 3–2 and 3–3). Look at Beckmann's *Man in the Dark* (Fig. 3–2), and try to recall an occasion in which you had to "feel" your way through a totally dark room to the light switch. In order to intensify your recall, imagine that you have been waked in the middle of the night by the telephone, ringing with the urgency we tend to ascribe to untimely telephone calls. You probably found your way partly by remembering spatial relationships between, let us say, your bed and the table, the table and the door. You may have had these memories corrected by bumping into a chair or encountering the table top with your groping hands before you had expected to. The sensory image that you have recalled, or that you are imagining, probably has nothing visual in it at all. It is made up of a pattern of proprioceptive sensations, punctuated or accented by the tactile encounters between your shins and the chair leg, your hands with the table top, then with the door jamb and knob, and finally, with the electric light switch.

It is the total, bodily alertness that possesses one in such a state of temporary blindness that Beckmann expresses in his small figure, *Man in the Dark*. The necessarily acute awareness is concentrated in the large, groping hands, and in the cautious feet whose size the artist has expressively exaggerated. He has also emphasized the vacancy of the face; its passivity conveys with utmost clarity the temporary subordination of sight and vision to touch, and to bodily balance and movement.

Is it accurate to describe Beckmann's image as proprioceptive to the exclusion of all visual and tactile quality? As you look away briefly from the reproduction, can you recall vividly the shape and look of the figure? As you look at it closely, do you feel any impulse to touch it or to handle it firmly; does its texture or solid volume make any appeal to you? For this writer the response to it is only a very little visual, and not at all tactile: Beckmann awakes a profound sense of empathy, a physical feeling-into the figure of the *Man in the Dark* that brings back strong recollections of past experience. At the same time there is suggested a significance that goes beyond mere recall. Perhaps it is the *look* of the man's face, the visible contrast between the facial passivity and the alert hands and feet that suggest a theme which goes beyond the simple representation of the subject.

What would the sculpture convey to you without its title? Students have been asked this question in the presence of the original sculpture but with its label covered. The answers were illuminating. There was never any doubt that the figure represented a blind man or one temporarily blind, but there was the further suggestion that the artist was not so much describing a particular person as he was symbolizing fumbling, groping humanity.

In contrast to Beckman's *Man in the Dark*, Rubens' drawing of a *Blind Man* probably seems initially more beautiful (Fig. 3–3). But is there the strong recall of bodily sensations; do you feel yourself groping in the darkness with this man? Probably not. Rubens has produced a very beautiful image of a blind man. We sympathize with him, but we do not empathize; our own proprioceptive experiences are not called into play. It seems to be an image in which the major appeal, the major quality, is visual; in which there is some tactile quality, though little, while proprioceptive quality is almost completely lacking.

The Rubens drawing is patently beautiful while the Beckmann sculpture is almost ugly. They both have power to move us but in quite different ways and degrees. It has been said that "beauty is in the eye of the beholder," and while we should not twist the meaning out of its original context, it does seem probable that the word *beauty* is most applicable to visual images; that it is definitely a quality attached to exteroceptive experience, to visible, tactile, and audible sensations but rarely, if at all, to proprioceptive except by empathetic transfer. One does not feel beautiful though one may be conscious that one appears so to others. And so, when a work of art almost flaunts its ugliness, as for instance, the individual images within Picasso's *Guernica* (Fig. 3–7), and yet moves us profoundly, the chances are that we are responding not to visual qualities but to strong proprioceptive elements in the artifact-image.

Antonio Pollaiuolo's little sculpture of *Hercules Crushing Antaeus* (Fig. 4–26) owes its particular quality to the fact that the sculptor had not only watched people in violent action, but that he had also known how it feels to tense and strain one's muscles, to suffer pain, to gasp and shriek. The emphasis he has given to the contraction of muscles in both figures, including their faces (and it is noteworthy that none of the muscles is very large though most of them are highly contracted) is more true to bodily experience than it is to visual observation.

But what of our sensory experience as we look at the sculpture? We can properly speak of our sensory "images" for while they are intense they are literally "imaginary." We must imagine ourselves handling the figures: we feel the hollow in Hercules' back, close our fingers around his bulging calves, or restrain the kicking feet of Antaeus as he struggles to touch the ground. By a very slight effort of the imagination, we bring into play both our proprioceptive and our tactile sensory receptors. We feel intensely the reality of this mortal combat, enjoying the tingle of armchair excitement in the presence of danger which is not really a danger because it is not our own, and a vicarious surge of physical power as we feel ourselves into the body of the hero. One hardly needs to know the story of the giant Antaeus whom Hercules was required to kill, so graphically and emphatically is the story rendered. Antaeus was the son of the earth-goddess and drew his prodigious strength from contact with his mother. In order to vanquish him, the hero had to keep the giant from touching the ground, for each contact brought the son of Earth a new surge of power.

Antonio Pollaiuolo was a painter and engraver as well as a sculptor and a goldsmith. In his engraving of the *Battle of the Naked Men* (Fig. 4–27) each figure is as densely solid as are the bodies of Hercules and Antaeus. The strong, continuous contours never appear to be the edges of two-dimensional shapes—like paper dolls—but are like the ever disappearing edge of an egg. One is never in the slightest doubt about the three-dimensional reality of these fighting men. Nor is the artist concerned merely to portray visually beautiful and tangibly real human bodies. These men are caught up in homicidal fury, engaged in a life-and-death struggle which we can enter into because of the strong appeal the artist makes to our proprioceptive imagination. Though Pollaiuolo repre-

POLLAIUOLO. *Hercules Crushing
Antaeus.*

(c. 1432–1498; Italian.)
Bronze, H. 14″.
National Museum, Florence.

Fig. 4–26.

POLLAIUOLO. *Battle of the Naked
Men.*

(c. 1432–1498; Italian.)
Engraving, 15¾″ × 23″.
*The Metropolitan Museum of Art,
New York.*
Joseph Pulitzer Bequest, 1917.

Fig. 4–27.

sents each figure as though it were a contour map, and the whole
group as though they were modeled in relief, the contour lines are
made to carry the directional movement, the stresses and strains,
thrusts and counter thrusts.

Look at the figure in the right corner leaning over his fallen
enemy: follow the line of his arm up from his hand on the dagger's
hilt, back of the head, down again along the thigh and bulging calf
to the raised foot. In another moment with one upward pull of the
dagger, the victor will straighten his back, ready for the next comer
—except that behind him an unseen enemy is bringing his battle

THE ARTIST'S IMAGES   125 axe down with a finality implicit in the tremendous calf and thigh muscles, the taut abdomen, and the crossed arms that hold the axe.

In the combat taking place at the left of the print the outcome is more questionable. For every thrust there is a counter thrust to balance it. The push of the leg of the man whose foot is planted in the groin of his opponent is balanced by the forward lunge of the upper figure; each dagger point is kept from reaching its mark by the force of an opposing movement.

These brief references do not begin to exhaust the relationships that make up the complex design and drama of the print, but they will serve to draw attention to the strongly proprioceptive as well as the tactile character of Pollaiuolo's imagery. The artist surely felt the action in his own body even more vividly than he saw the lunging forms of the men.

There is, however, visual quality here as well. The somewhat stylized plant forms of the background are like incised ornaments on a metal surface, and the light forms of the nudes moving against the dark are beautiful as sheer visual pattern entirely aside from their expressive character. The power of the print, however, lies primarily in its tactile and proprioceptive—more particularly, kinaesthetic—imagery.

FRA ANGELICO. *Last Judgment.*
(1387–1455; Italian.)
Panel, 41½″ × 83″.
San Marco Museum, Florence.
Photo: Alinari-Art Reference Bureau.

Fig. 4-28.

A very different temperament was that of Pollaiuolo's fellow Florentine, the Dominican monk known to history as Fra Angelico, whose imagination worked most fully and happily in terms of visual imagery. The *Last Judgment* (Figs. 4–28 and 4–29) may have been painted by an immediate follower, but the imagery is characteristic of Fra Angelico. Paradise is represented where the blessed souls join hands with angels in a dance of joyful but restrained thanksgiving. We see them moving in stately measure through the flowery meadows of Paradise, and we recognize it as a dance because their gestures and attitudes and the slight movement of their clothing correspond to our memory images of dances we have watched. We feel no impulse to join them but are content to remain as spectators.

FRA ANGELICO. *Paradise.*

Detail from *Last Judgment.*
Photo: Alinari-Art Reference Bureau.

Fig. 4–29.

MATISSE. *The Dance.*

(1869–1954; French.)
Oil on canvas, 8′ 6⅝″ × 12′ 9⅝″.
*Collection, The Museum of Modern Art,
    New York.*
*Gift of Governor Nelson A. Rockefeller,
    in honor of Alfred H. Barr, Jr.*

Fig. 4–30.

Compare this with a dance by Henri Matisse (Fig. 4–30). Without describing the look and hard feel of taut muscles as Pollaiuolo did, the painter indicates their pull and stretch with lines that are themselves instinct with life. We feel pulled into this dance ourselves. Matisse's lines correspond with the tensions we have known in our own bodies if we have ever followed the caller's command, "All join hands and circle left," and have had our arms almost pulled out of their sockets by our boisterous neighbors. The images in Matisse's painting are not visually descriptive. No amount of stretch

ART AS EXPERIENCE

and strain would make a group of nude people *look* this way, but the painter has made us feel them proprioceptively in a way that no visual description, however vivid, could give us. The painting is in fact a rather realistic rendering of a proprioceptive image.

Our own daily experience of solid mass and of texture is less extensive; our direct, tactile images are far less numerous than are those of visibility, because, of course, unlike visual images which have the indefinite and variable range of the human eye, tactile images are limited by the reach of the human arm and by the relatively few contacts the human body allows itself. There is more agreement among people where solidity and texture are concerned than where color and shape are in question; while there is much less agreement in matters of proprioceptive feeling than in either. We shall discuss here only one example, Rubens' *Wolf and Fox Hunt* (Fig. 4–31), in which the appeal is made about equally to our eyes and to our tactile sense.

The *Wolf and Fox Hunt* was commissioned by the Marquis of Spinola, who later commanded the Spanish troops in the Netherlands, and it can be assumed that the *Hunt* was intended as decoration for a great house or palace. The feast of color can only be appreciated in the presence of the original painting; strong reds and greens confront each other in the costumes and in the saddle blankets; the fox's coat is a beautiful cinnamon; that of the greyhound, almost milky white; the wolf's rough coat is a blue-gray. The intense colors are given a foil in the pale blue of the sky and the misty distances of the flat plain.

But Rubens is not content with a visual statement of his theme of throbbing vitality. The lady and gentleman on horseback are made very much of flesh and blood, healthy and strong, while the two huntsmen share this quality but have also an earthiness that sets them apart from the mounted gentry. It is, however, the animals that hold our attention most. In them, Rubens (or his assistant Snyders whom Rubens described as "particularly skillful" in painting animals) has combined with beautiful visual images of lithe shapes and expressive movement, superlative qualities of tactility. One should take time to run one's hand over the sleek body of the greyhound, and then for contrast with his well-groomed coat, over the rough texture of the wolf's fur. Then feel the fur of the little fox, standing up all along his back, as he snarls defiance at his overpowering enemies. And finally, stroke the well-combed manes of the horses, and slap the gray's rump to hear the resounding thwack.

RUBENS. *Wolf and Fox Hunt.*

(1577–1640; Flemish.)
Oil on canvas, 96″ × 148½″.
*The Metropolitan Museum of Art,
    New York.*
Kennedy Fund, 1910.

Fig. 4–31.

Exteroceptive and Proprioceptive Creative Types

"Every man is a special kind of artist" with dominant preferences
for visual, tactile, or bodily imagery, but it is impossible to find
among artists of stature instances where one kind of sensory experience has been drawn on to the exclusion of the others. However,
as has already been noted, Prof. Viktor Löwenfeld has established
the fact that two major creative types exist which he has called the
"visual and the haptic" but which we shall call the "exteroceptive
and proprioceptive," aware that neither classification is wholly satisfactory. In calling the second type "haptic" (from the Greek word

ART AS EXPERIENCE

meaning "to grasp") Prof. Löwenfeld emphasizes the importance of the role of the tactile receptors in establishing the individual's relation with the solid substances of his environment. Let us, instead, call this type "proprioceptive" since its major characteristic is the ultimate reference of every question and of every experience to what is crucial and central, the sense of self. This is, as we have seen, primarily based on internal, bodily sensations complemented by tactile impressions and, to a very slight degree, by visual. We shall, then, translate Prof. Löwenfeld's terms "haptic" and "visual" into "proprioceptive" and "exteroceptive." [2]

Each type has its own way of establishing orientation in the world of reality, of coming to feel at home in its immediate circumstances. The exteroceptive relies on vision. For him, seeing is not only believing; it leads at once to a sense of assurance, of faith in the environment. The other type, the proprioceptive, must experience a new situation more slowly, moving about in it, handling its various parts (and here the experience becomes in some degree exteroceptive); above all, feeling himself into new relationships with the space and with its contents. As Prof. Löwenfeld has shown, an aviator of the exteroceptive type, when the proprioceptors responsible for his bodily orientation have been rendered useless by the gyrations of the plane, will trust the evidence of his eyes and rely on the reading of his instruments. A pronounced proprioceptive type will not be able to learn to fly because he cannot ignore his bodily sense; his test of reality remains proprioceptive and he cannot risk ignoring its findings by acting on the evidence of his eyes alone.

Artistically, the exteroceptive type remains essentially an observer, the proprioceptive, a participant. We have already seen in our discussion of dreams in the previous chapter that there is evidence of the existence of the two creative types among non-artists. It was certainly an exteroceptive type who dreamed of her playmate hanging from the limb of an apple tree. On the other hand the author of the dream of playing tennis with eggs is quite likely to be a proprioceptive type.

It would be a mistake to assume that every dream or every work of art embodying proprioceptive feeling is the work of the proprioceptive creative type. As we have already noted, nightmares and dreams of strong emotional content tend to make use of bodily imagery, and the same is true of works of art. It is characteristic of

[2] See Viktor Löwenfeld, *The Nature of Creative Activity*, 2nd ed. (London: Routledge and Kegan Paul, Ltd., 1952), Chapter 5.

some of the greatest that they embody every kind of sensory quality. Grünewald's figures in the *Crucifixion* (Fig. 4–4) offer convincing proof. Furthermore, some artists of very great gifts will spend their youth working in a mode of imagery that happens to be in favor at the time and only in later years develop their full powers in a different mode. This is admirably demonstrated in the work of Francisco Goya.

If we had only the work of Goya's first twenty-five years, we should count him a brilliant portrait painter and decorator of the exteroceptive type (Fig. 7–5). But the works of his late middle and old age, the bull fights (Fig. 10–24), the disasters of war (Fig. 10–9), and the "dark paintings" (Fig. 7–6), while losing little of their visual quality, though color matters less than light and dark, are primarily important for their extraordinary proprioceptive power. Goya was essentially a proprioceptive creative type trained to satisfy the prevailing taste for strongly decorative, which is to say largely visual art, who only realized the full extent of his powers after his deafness cut him off from the exteroceptive world of sound and forced him back into the inner world of self.

Mental Images and Schema

As we have seen, in some works of art the artist's imagination is more concerned with the symbolic process that accompanies perception than with perception itself; meaning then becomes at least as important as sensation and emotion. The term *mental image* is frequently used to signify a picture existing in the mind without the presence of an external object to which it corresponds. This description applies also, of course, to a memory image. But the term *mental image* can be used legitimately in a more limited sense to describe a specific kind of memory image differing from its fellows in a degree of simplification, of generalization or abstraction.

If you were asked to describe your mental image of a sailboat, unless you are a sailor and have a rich and varied active knowledge to draw on, the chances are that you will describe something like a slice of melon seen from one side with a vertical at one end and a right-angle triangle whose hypotenuse runs from the top of the vertical back toward the opposite end of the melon slice. While this bears little resemblance to a sailboat, the very simple shape is readily acceptable as standing for a sailboat, and most people would recognize it. It is a very general image, stripped of every accidental or individual effect. It is a kind of mental construct made by thinking first of the boat, then of the mast, then of the sail, and by putting these separate parts together as intelligibly as possible. There was no thought of the enjoyment one might have in looking at the final result. It is not an aesthetic image, either in purpose or function.

The "stick" figures which stand for men on a population chart bear no resemblance to the direct image of a man; they depend on memory of direct perception only insofar as they have the normal human equipment of a head and trunk, two arms and two legs, distributed more or less as is usual in human beings. There is no description of sensory qualities, of shape, solidity, color. The mind has imagined and the hand fashioned these figures simply for factual communication. Even the "fact" is a very general one: the figure may be man, woman, or child. The important thing is that it stands for a human being, not a horse or a tractor.

The sailboat and the stick figure are ideograms or schema; to be very precise, they are artifact-images of mental images, shorthand signs rather than the record of sensory experience, and they serve no aesthetic purpose whatever. They are "seen" in a void, separated from nothingness by a clear outline. Their silhouetted shapes are informative and all-important. Ideograms and schema begin to claim our attention when they are employed for an aesthetic purpose, when as in the art of children and in much of primitive, ancient, early medieval, and modern art they are the vehicles of feeling as well as of intelligible meaning. Note the schema in Picasso's *Guernica* (Fig. 3–7), especially the light bulb in the almond shaped "eye." Picasso makes constant use of schema, as does Paul Klee, sometimes for expressive purposes, to convey meaning or feeling; often for decorative purposes.

In children's drawings the schema begins to appear when the child has for some time been giving apparently arbitrary names to aimless scribbles. The schema seems to result partly from an accidental likeness between a scribble and some object important to the child, and partly from his urgent desire to make a picture of this important thing. The "important thing" may be anything, a house, a person, the sun, or the moon. The little English boy aged almost three who produced the sheet of cars shown in Fig. 4–32 distinguished carefully between "ordinary cars and American cars." The only other object that he had drawn with intention at this time was a moon. Here he was clearly noting an accidental likeness between a scribble and the moon, and one that was easy to repeat.

Cars.

Child, age 2½ years.
Pencil.

Fig. 4–32.

The Ice Age horses of Lascaux (Fig. 4–33) are perceptual images in which the salient characteristics, the shapes and the three-dimensional solidity, are recalled with great accuracy and recorded with infinite skill and subtlety. In the hunt (Fig. 4–34) from a later Neolithic cave in eastern Spain the boar is the representation of a direct, visual image, though not re-created with anything like the verve or artistry of the earlier painting. The Neolithic huntsman, on the other hand, is a "stick figure" come to life. As a hunter himself, the painter has had all his visual attention on the quarry, and felt no urge to study the *appearance* of his fellow huntsmen. But the speed of the chase he has felt in his own body, and recalling the proprioceptive experience, he has vitalized his schema. His image records what is important to the artist: the visual appearance and tactile substance of his quarry, the speed and skill of the hunter.

In the Egyptian fishing and fowling scene (Fig. 4–35) the artist has used a much more elaborate schema. Where the Neolithic artist's intention was to express with schematic brevity the speed of the hunt, the Egyptian's purpose was to reproduce in detail the varied life of a landowner along the Nile. Menna is engaged in a favorite sport; his Neolithic ancestor, in a triumphant struggle for survival.

ART AS EXPERIENCE

Frieze of Ponies and a Bull.

Prehistoric cave painting.
Lascaux, Montignac, France.
*Photo: Caisse Nationale des Monuments
   Historiques.*

Fig. 4–33.

No style ever had so long and continuous a life as that of ancient
Egypt, and no art has so consistently depended upon the use of a
schema. The figure of Menna, a nobleman of the fifteenth century
B. C., is cast in the same schematic form (a *mental construct*, as it is
frequently called), that had evolved in Egypt before 3000 B. C. and
continued in use with very minor changes until the opening of our
own era. The Egyptian schema for a human figure is not the happy
accidental creation of a child or of a child-like people, but a highly
sophisticated construction resulting from an analytical approach to
the problem. And yet the process is not unlike that of the child

Neolithic Boar Hunt.

After Maringer and Bondi, Art of the
  Neolithic Age, *Fig. 150, p. 119.*
New York: Frederick A. Praeger, Inc.,
  1944.

Fig. 4–34.

who, when asked how he went about his drawing, said, "First I
think and then I draw my think." The Egyptian ignores the unity
of the body as he sees it, but studies its parts, each of which he
draws as he "thinks" it. The head is drawn in profile which is the
most easily recognized view and the most intelligible. An oval
might be mistaken for a fruit, a circle for the sun. The eye has a
special significance as the window of the personality; it will not do
to reduce its size or tamper with its known shape by foreshortening.
The artist therefore draws it as he knows an eye to be, almond-
shaped with two concentric interior circles. Shoulders, at least on a
man, should be broad, and to seem broad and strong, must be
viewed from the front. Legs are for walking, and the clearest way
to show walking legs is from the side, one in front of the other.
Seen thus, the foot also displays its most foot-like aspect.

And so the Egyptian schema develops: a profile head in which
is placed a full-front eye; full-front torso and shoulders; hips, legs,
and feet seen from the side. Within this schema considerable action
is possible, as witness Menna. And within the range of social and
religious importance, the schema varies from strict adherence to the
formula in the representation of important people—gods, pharaohs,

ART AS EXPERIENCE

noblemen, and priests—to freedom and some description of natural-istic detail in the figures of children, servants, and other less important people. With the latter the artist relies more on direct perception and less on the traditional mental construct.

The matter of size in Egyptian imagery does not depend on visually apprehended relationships. As in children's art, it is arbitrary but not accidental. Bigness reflects social importance, and accordingly Menna, the lord and master and father, towers over his children and servants, dominating the group with his heroic size and dual appearance.

The arbitrary system of proportion, together with the Egyptian artist's complete disregard of third-dimensional space, characterize other arts where the "word" also takes precedence over the visual image, where the main interest and intention lie in communication rather than in celebration. Proportion is essentially a system of visual relationships, and, as we have noted, one sees deep space in terms of the proportionate sizes and the varying tonality of things

Egyptian Fishing and Fowling Scene.

Copy in tempera of an Eighteenth
  Dynasty tomb painting.
(Fifteenth century B.C.)
*The Metropolitan Museum of Art,
  New York.*

Fig. 4-35.

Akhenaten   Worshipping   the   Aton.

Relief.
Empire Period.
National Museum, Cairo.
Hirmer Verlag, Munich.

Fig. 4–36.

existing in that space. It requires an intellectual effort to "think" space, and when one does, it is apt to be in either wholly abstract, two-dimensional terms as in the sixth-century mosaic (Fig. 1–4), or in remembered visual and kinetic images, such as those of Bruegel's *Unfaithful Shepherd* (Fig. 4–24).

When the child-artist imagined his cars (Fig. 4–32) he did not see them in a spatial context; he "thought" them as entities existing in their own right without reference to each other or to space. This is also true of the Paleolithic artist whose animals are highly visualized in themselves but bear no proportionate relations to each other and are, as it were, suspended, with no solid ground beneath their feet. The prehistoric artist developed a marvelously visual image under the urgent drive of what he probably conceived to be necessity, while he remained content to disregard space as the child does in the schematic stage of his development.

The Egyptian schema or mental construct evolved as a means of making the artifact-image of a human being first intelligible and then decorative. Compared with the bodily feeling expressed in the Neolithic huntsman, the Egyptian figure is sedate and restrained. One searches almost in vain through the annals of Egyptian art to find any expression of emotion. The exception is found in painting and sculpture of the Tel el Amarna period when, in the fourteenth century B. C., a heretic king for a time upset the whole elaborate hierarchy of the priesthood and the pantheon of gods. Declaring that there was only one God, the creator of heaven and earth, the Pharaoh Akhenaten set the example of worshipping this creative power in the form of the sun's disc, the Aton (Fig. 4–36). A relief shows Akhenaten with his wife and one of his little girls in the act of worship, while the Aton reaches down protective, generous hands toward them. In the figures of the king's family, the old schema is modified and, since the purpose was to express feeling, the modification was toward the representation of proprioceptive rather than visual quality. Compare these figures with the sculpture *Youth Imploring* (Fig. 3–1).

But the king who initiated the revolution in religion and in art died, and his daughter's husband, young Tut-ank-amon, was not strong enough to resist the gathered forces of reaction. After Tut-ank-amon's death, the old hierarchic regime was re-established and Egyptian art returned to its traditional use of mental imagery strictly devoid of human feeling but carried to new heights of decorative brilliance and hieratic formality.

Suggestions for Further Reading

ARNHEIM, R. *Art and Visual Perception: a Psychology of the Creative Eye.* Berkeley: University of California Press, 1954.

This is of great value particularly in the author's analyses of works of art. Its weakness lies in the degree to which the author ignores the role of the non-visual senses both in the creation of art and in its enjoyment.

BAUDELAIRE, C. *The Mirror of Art.* J. Mayne, Trans. and Ed. Garden City, N. Y.: Doubleday and Co., 1956. (A Doubleday Anchor Book, A 84.)

One of the first critics to give due importance to the irrational element in art; especially interesting in relation to the art of the twentieth century.

CASSIRER, E. *An Essay on Man.* Garden City, N. Y.: Doubleday and Co., 1953. (A Doubleday Anchor Book, A 3.)

Chapter 4 is interesting in connection with the artist's images of space.

CLARK, SIR KENNETH. *The Nude: A Study in Ideal Form.* New York: Pantheon Books, 1953. (Bollingen Series XXV.) (Also a Doubleday Anchor Book, A 168; Garden City, N. Y.: Doubleday and Co., 1959.)

Valuable in connection with our chapter on the artist's images.

CLARK, SIR KENNETH. *Landscape into Art.* Boston: Beacon Press, 1961. (A Beacon Paperback, BP 117.)

In this book and the preceding one on the nude, the author throws light on the creation of two of the artist's favorite themes throughout art history. As the importance of religious art declines, these two become central to the artist's purposes. While Sir Kenneth's approach is not historical, a great deal of history is implicit.

GOMBRICH, E. H. *Art and Illusion: A Study in the Psychology of Pictorial Representation.* New York: Pantheon Books, 1960. (Bollingen Series XXXV.)

A fascinating study. Like Arnheim, Gombrich gives the non-visual senses less than their due.

LAMING, A. *Lascaux.* London: Penguin Books, Ltd., 1959. (Also available as a Pelican Book, A 419.)

A clear account of one of the most interesting of the prehistoric caves with illustrations of both the paintings and the engravings, and a discussion of the theories concerning the purposes and meaning of this earliest art.

LEONARDO DA VINCI. *The Notebooks: A New Selection.* Selected by P. Taylor. New York: Mentor Books. (A Mentor Classic, MT 312.)

SMITH, E. B. *The Dome.* Princeton, N. J.: Princeton University Press, 1950.

Interesting in connection with the concept of space.

5. Imagery and Style and the Purposes of Art

The Concept of Style

THE concept of style provides us with the means of comparing the work of one artist with that of another. By style we mean, in this connection, the total character of a work of art. Style has been described by Charles Rufus Morey as the "imprint on artistic expression of a point of view, be it the point of view of an individual, an epoch, or a race." [1]

An artist's style will result in large measure from his choice and use of imagery, in short, his imagination, but the formal and expressive character of the individual work will answer to the artist's immediate intention and to the particular function this work is to perform. A painting intended as an aid to devotion (Fig. 1–4) will have a very different character from a narrative scene (Fig. 4–21, 5–11, or 10–18). The one will tend to be static and self-contained; the other, active and open. Style is also affected, and in large measure controlled, by the tradition in which the artist is bred, and by the materials and technical procedures that lend themselves to his purpose or recommend themselves to his taste or to that of his patron. More will be said of this in Part II.

[1] C. R. Morey, *Christian Art* (New York: W. W. Norton and Co., Inc., 1958), p. 45.

Style and Imagery in Greek and Roman Sculpture

While the relationship between imagery and style is implicit throughout this book, it may be useful to take the discussion of images a little further in this connection before turning to the artist's purposes.

In the central stream of European art the schema makes its appearance generally at the beginning of a new tradition. The earliest type of "artifact-image of a mental image" in Greek art (Fig. 5–1) has little decorative quality and only a very simple, forthright, expressive power. The artist hardly attempts to differentiate among the various sensory data that have gone to make up the mental image. The basic shape is sufficient to convey the idea of a human form. If, however, one compares the Cycladic idol with the figures on a population chart, the aesthetic function of the idol at once is marked in contrast to the practical, mental function of the ideograms.

Woman.

(2500–2000 B.C.; Cycladic.)
Marble statuette, H. 2′ 6¼″.
Photograph by courtesy of the Ashmolean Museum, Oxford.

Fig. 5–1.

As the use of the schema develops, with constant technical repetitions and with a growing knowledge of and reference to nature, details are added and the various parts are related in a coherent pattern that has great decorative appeal to the eye (Fig. 5–2). The sixth-century (B. C.) Greek statue of a youth is constructed part by part as intellectually as was the Egyptian painted figure of a nobleman fishing. There is a similar emphasis on what the artist knows rather than on what he sees. But there is this difference: the Greek artist is not bound by his tradition. The style of the Kouros lasted hardly a century, while Egyptian style, as we have seen, maintained itself for three thousand years.

Where the simple shape of the Cycladic idol is sufficient to stand for a worshipful being, the statue of a youth is the result of careful study of a human body, and the resulting image is both tactual and visual in origin. The eyeball, for instance, is thought of in three-dimensional terms as something one could feel tactually, not simply see as a plane with an inscribed circle. The visual effect of curly hair is conceived again tactually but represented as a series of three-dimensional knots arranged in a repetitive visual pattern. The complete symmetry of the body, the balance of right and left, forms a total pattern of great beauty, but the final figure lacks any sense of organic growth. It is rather a tidy accumulation of decorative parts which add up to the representation of a young man.

This highly decorative use of mental imagery, or, to put it another way, this decorative elaboration of the simple mental image, is a characteristic of what is known as archaic style. One finds it cropping up all over the world at various times, but generally where the value set on the idea is still very strong and the technical skill of the artist is highly developed.

At the beginning of the fifth century B. C., Athens in league with her fellow Greek city-states defeated the aggressive imperialism of Persia and there resulted a tremendous upsurge of confidence both in themselves as Greeks and in their gods. This new impetus led artists and patrons to look critically at the old, archaic images; beautiful, no doubt, but inadequate to express the new prideful humanity of the Greeks. The sculptor recognized that he could go no farther toward patterned ornament in the embellishment of his image, so he apparently re-thought the image of a human being or of a god in human form. The *Apollo* from the temple of Zeus at Olympia (Fig. 5–3) is an idealized figure of a man, still strongly tactual in its sensory origins, but conforming to the new canon of ideal proportions (the

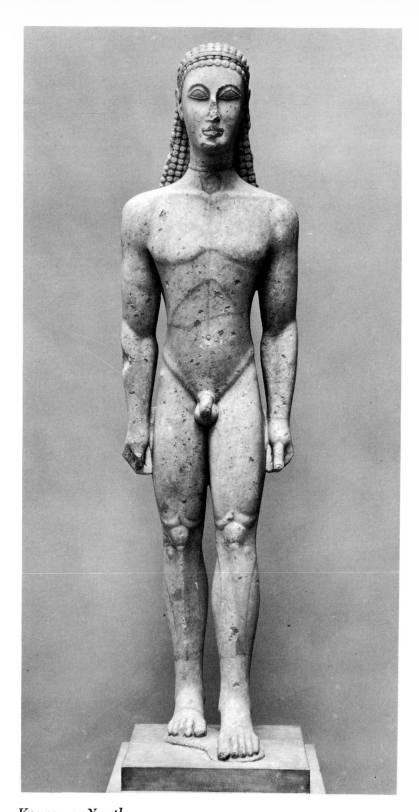

Kouros, or Youth.

(c. 600 B. C.; Greek.)
Marble, H. 6′ 1½″.
The Metropolitan Museum of Art,
  New York.
Fletcher Fund, 1932.

Fig. 5–2.

Apollo.

West pediment of the Temple of Zeus at
    Olympia.
(c. 460 B. C.)
Marble, over life size.

Museum, Olympia.
Hirmer Verlag, Munich.

Fig. 5–3.

body was to be five times the height of its head). No longer does the figure appear to be an accumulation of parts, but it now has the look of organic growth and unity.

A hundred years later the artist again shifted his emphasis. The change is not so abrupt between the Olympian *Apollo* and the *Hermes* of Praxiteles (Fig. 5–4); the artist has not re-thought his image, but instead of aiming to embody an ideal of majesty and dignity in the figure of a god made after an image of man, the sculptor has bent all his effort toward creating an image which will *look* as much as possible like a beautiful human being. Visual imagery almost wholly takes the place of tactual; the eyes are no longer firmly constructed as eyeballs in sockets, but the effect of a half-closed eye is achieved. The neatly "set" hair of the Olympian Apollo has given place to an effect of real hair rumpled to look natural.

These four sculptured figures (Figs. 5–1 through 5–4) trace the change from an artifact-image of the idea of a human or divine figure (Fig. 5–1) through a highly developed, schematic rendering of this mental image (Fig. 5–2), to an idealized representation of a direct, exteroceptive image (Fig. 5–3), and finally to one in which the sensuous, perceptual qualities of form and texture, light and shadow have become more important than the idea expressed (Fig. 5–4).

The same subtle change from a highly conceptual type of imagery to one that is strongly perceptual or phenomenal may be seen in a comparison of the relief of the *Mourning Athena* (Fig. 5–5), found on the Acropolis and dating from about 455 B.C., with one of the wingless Victories from the Nike balustrade which originally surrounded the little temple of Athena Nike at the entrance to the Acropolis (Fig. 5–6). This figure dates about 410 B.C.

In the earlier relief, there is a slight reminiscence of the Egyptian construct. The shoulders are seen almost in full front, while the bent head is turned in profile. The feet also are in profile though the folds of the skirt again suggest a full front view. Actually the transitions between these "views" are so subtly modulated and expressively motivated as the goddess mourns before a gravestone, that it is only on close scrutiny that we realize the conceptual construction behind the image. The evidence suggests, however, that the sculptor has first *thought,* and then carved into the stone his beautiful, conceptual image.

The arms are bare and their round firmness is very marked—strong tactile images—but beneath the heavy folds of drapery there is no indication of the body. Where the material of the dress or chiton is pulled smooth across the breasts we see their gently swelling

PRAXITELES. *Hermes with the Infant Dionysos.*

(c. 330–320 B. C.; or copy, late first century B. C.)
Marble, H. 7′ 1″.
Museum, Olympia.
Hirmer Verlag, Munich.

Fig. 5–4.

curves. But the artist is in no way concerned to celebrate the beauty of the female body. The body of the goddess is sufficiently reminiscent of direct sensory experience to be intelligible and expressive of the idea of mourning. The over-all shape of the image plays the chief expressive role, while the visual quality of the image is largely concerned with pattern as in the earlier archaic *Kouros* (Fig. 5–2). Tactile quality is more important. We have already noted the firm solidity of the arms. There is also in the rounded form of Athena's helmet a strong appeal to the tactual sense: one wants to

Mourning Athena.

(470–450 B.C.)
Marble.
National Museum, Athens.
Hirmer Verlag, Munich.

Fig. 5–5.

Nike Adjusting Her Sandal.

Balustrade of the Temple of Athena Nike.
(c. 427–424 B. C.)
Marble, 42″ × 20″.

Acropolis Museum, Athens.
Hirmer Verlag, Munich.

Fig. 5–6.

cup one's hands around it, and to feel in contrast to the containing-ness of the helmet, the flat elegance of the curved edge of the crest. Even the folds of the drapery have a heavy, tangible quality. In making his image of the goddess believable, the sculptor relies more on tactility than on visual quality.

This is less true in the case of the Nike bending to adjust her sandal. (She has often been described as tying her sandal, but it takes two hands to tie anything, and her left hand was never in a position to assist.)

When one examines closely the position of the body one finds a very formalized set of relationships behind the seeming naturalism; a large element of ordering has gone into the formal structure of the relief. Note the way in which the several axes of the shoulders, the breasts, the groove in the abdomen just below the rib cage, and the hips fan out from a common center placed roughly where the outer edge of the right arm passes behind the thigh. One's eye picks up the triangular area beneath the right breast and the larger one between the thighs, but these spaces and the forms that define them are softened by the ripple of drapery.

The whole figure is contained within a great oval, a frame marked now by the contour of the left arm, now by the lines of drapery down to the left ankle and up to the right knee where the movement is picked up by the contour of the right arm and returned to its starting point.

It is worth noting that what we have referred to as the contour of the left arm is not realized as a tactile image which we feel under our hands, a clearly defined edge of a rounded volume as in the right shoulder of the Nike and in both arms of the *Mourning Athena*. The contour of the Nike's left arm is only suggested visually by the folds of material that crease away from and around it. We apprehend this left arm of the Nike visually, not through our sense of touch. The draperies of the Nike flow in a seemingly casual manner, but actually they are formalized to produce a beautiful pattern of cascading curves which serve secondarily to reveal the shape of the lovely body beneath the thin material.

The sculptor of the Nike has exploited almost equally the beauties of vision and of touch—though the balance inclines toward vision—while the conceptual content of the image which has lost its earlier function of intelligibility, is concentrated in a single theme, the celebration of beauty for its own sake.

Greek and Roman art continued for more than seven hundred years (roughly 500 B.C. to 300 A.D.) to be preoccupied with the beauty and power of the human body, and, in the latter part of this period, with the celebration of the beauty and worth of the whole world of sensory experience. Antique art of the Classical period is strongly exteroceptive in imagery, a characteristic of self-confident ages in human history.

In the later days of the Roman Empire as political, economic, and social distress increased and human confidence weakened, the thoughts and hopes of many, pagan and Christian alike, were more and more centered in a future life and in a good which should transcend the life of the senses. Then the art of antiquity showed a tendency to turn to "the mysterious centers of thought and feeling" of which Gauguin was to speak almost two thousand years later. As the artist ceased to celebrate the world of the senses, his images became crude; they lost their classical justness of proportion and their vitality. Classical art had become decadent when Christianity, with a new and overpowering concern to propagate an idea, seized upon these debased forms as a means of communication. Once more the idea, "the word," mattered supremely.

It will be of interest to examine an instance of late pagan art, *Apotheosis of an Emperor* (Fig. 5–7), in which many of the characteristics which were later to be developed in medieval times are already apparent.

On a fourth-century ivory plaque an unidentified Roman emperor is shown making his triumphal way to heaven. Although the Empire had become officially Christian at the beginning of the fourth century, there are in this plaque no specifically Christian connotations, though analogies at once come to mind. There are, rather, statements and suggestions of the imperial pomp and pagan religion of ancient Rome. In the lower part of the plaque, the emperor, sceptre in one hand, leafy olive branch in the other, is enthroned beneath a gabled canopy on a chariot drawn by four elephants, each with its rider. In the upper part, still seated but no longer on a visible throne, the emperor is borne aloft by two winged figures. His destination is identified as the sky by the signs of the zodiac behind which, in the right corner, is the haloed figure of the sun god. In the center of the plaque, a nude figure with flying cloak drives the four horses of a chariot as it too takes off for the upper regions from a three-tiered, draped altar, while to the left of the horses' hooves two great eagles also climb steeply. The detailed meaning of the plaque is not clear to us, but its relation to other, more readily identifiable scenes justifies our reading it as the apotheosis of triumphal ascent of an emperor into heaven.

Apotheosis of an Emperor.

(Late fourth century A. D.)
Ivory plaque.
*Courtesy of the Trustees, The British
Museum, London.*

Fig. 5–7.

If one compares this scene of triumph with that on the Triumphal
Arch of Titus of three hundred years earlier (Fig. 5–8), one is immediately inclined to see here the decadence of an older, more accom-
plished art; and technical decadence there certainly is in some degree. In the Arch of Titus, figures are foreshortened as seen from
the side; the horses, while treated in the same way as in the ivory,

ART AS EXPERIENCE

Chariot Relief.

Arch of Titus, Rome.
(Late first century A. D.)
Photo: Alinari-Art Reference Bureau.

Fig. 5–8.

the far horses being actually ahead of the near for legibility's sake, are allowed to disappear one behind the other, and space is more subtly suggested than in the ivory and is more convincing. The earlier triumph throbs with movement and vitality entirely lacking in the later. But if one looks for the cause of this change not to the general decline of Roman institutions in the fourth century, but to the individual artist's purpose, one comes on an important clue. The first-century sculptor presents the triumph of Titus returning with the spoils of Jerusalem as nearly as possible as it happened in the streets of Rome. It is a creative image based on direct sensory experience though he modifies it to meet the requirements of relief sculpture, and in order to express a theme while recording an event. The fourth-century sculptor, on the other hand, was not concerned to celebrate the visible splendor of the triumph but rather to expound the idea that earthly pomp and the world of the senses pass away, and that the final triumph is in the translation of the soul to heaven. This is not to be seen with the physical eye but only apprehended by the eye of the mind. And it was with the eye of the mind that the artist constructed the scene, "thinking" each part of his story separately, each image and its separate parts, and finally spreading them out for us to read within the stringent limits of his available space and frame.

The little gable resting on two slender columns is seen full front, but since without the sloping roof it would fail to convey the idea of a protection over the Emperor's head, the artist has included the roof at the only angle possible in the available space. The Emperor's shoulders and torso are in front view, but his legs, almost in profile. The platform juts out in a corner under the left foot entirely inconsistently with the line of the gable and of the plinth that supports the nearer column. Some third dimension is indicated in the receding heads of the elephants, but it is cancelled out by their feet planted firmly on a line with the wheels, the line being parallel with that of the gable and of the plinth and at an angle to the elephants' heads and to the platform.

We are not here dealing with the complete disregard for the third dimension which we found in Egyptian painting. Here the handling of space is complicated by a tradition of visual naturalism, the monuments of which were certainly familiar to the artist. (The Arch of Titus was standing in Rome in the fourth century as it had in the first and still does in the twentieth.) On the other hand, the artist had no desire to study the ancient monuments and to copy them consistently, and so he fell into the practice of using certain outward tricks—like the slanting line of the horses' and elephants' heads—almost as an inherited schema, useful to him in making intelligible the ideas he had to communicate.

One could multiply the examples of mental imagery among the details of the ivory: for instance, the two small wheels behind the nearest elephant bear no more structural relation to the chariot than do the wheels of the child's cars (Fig. 4–32) but they transform what would otherwise appear to be a very solid piece of masonry into a vehicle. The sky is indicated by the signs of the zodiac and by

ART AS EXPERIENCE

the presence of the sun god, mental images standing for the starlit and for the sunny heavens. One sees the zodiacal signs representing the months, September through January: Libra with her scales; Scorpio; the centaur archer, Sagittarius; the goat, Capricorn; and the water-carrier, Aquarius. These are signs rather than symbols. Apollo's halo is, on the other hand, a symbol of his divinity, while the rays of light about his head merely identify him as the god of the sun.

Purposes and Style

The style of the ivory plaque with its rich use of schema rather than of direct images of perceptual experience answers the artist's purpose which was primarily to convey an idea, the apotheosis of an emperor. But we have seen ideas expressed in perceptual images— Giotto's figure of *Justice* (Fig. 4–5), for instance, or Mantegna's *Mother and Child* (Fig. 1–6), the theme of which is maternity. Clearly there are other factors involved with a change of purpose in the creation of this new style. Among them may be counted the lack of technical experience of the artist who, no longer caring deeply about reproducing the visible and tactile world, had never perfected himself in the imitative skill exercised by the sculptor of the Arch of Titus (Fig. 5–8). But the chief factor is the relative value attached to the *idea* as against the *direct sensory image*.

It has already been pointed out that an art which celebrates the visible and tangible world is characteristic of periods of human confidence. When the ivory plaque was carved, Europe was entering on a period in which man's confidence in his ability to control his physical circumstances, even to cope with the world in which he found himself, was badly shaken by the collapse of Roman imperial power and the loss of that peace which Roman law and the Roman legions had given Europe for several centuries. At the beginning of the Middle Ages, art was asked to provide images of a spiritual order that should make good the loss, and to represent the power and glory of heaven in convincing but appropriately other-worldly splendors. This the mosaics of the sixth century supplied. Glorious in color and glittering with gold, they were themselves fit offerings to the unseen powers of a spiritual order.

Such another period of human confidence as had characterized the world of Greek and Roman antiquity was not to reappear until the Renaissance, though there were signs of the rebirth long before the fifteenth century.

Purpose and Function as
Means to Aesthetic Evaluation[2]

We have had frequent occasion to refer in passing to the purpose or intention of the artist, but the matter is sufficiently central to require more than passing comment. On the face of it, it would seem logical that the character or style of a work of art should be wholly molded by the artist's intention since the making of art is certainly an intentional activity. It is, however, far less simple than one might expect. Accidents and irrational, unintentional acts play an important part in the formation of any work of art, and the artist himself frequently denies having a purpose that can be explicitly stated. The creative process is its own excuse. The role of purpose, whether conscious or unconscious, also varies from age to age as the patron or consumer plays a significant or an insignificant part. The degree to which the patron who "pays the piper" also "calls the tune" is a study in itself.

For the purposes of such an introductory study as ours, there is another reason for considering the artist's probable intentions. How can we judge of the artist's success unless we have some idea of what he is trying to do? The purpose and function of a practical artifact can generally be assumed from its form, and one can judge of its quality largely on the basis of how well it works. It has been suggested earlier that the same test can be made of an artifact whose general purpose is not practical but aesthetic. It is, however, much less easy to discover the particular purpose behind an aesthetic artifact, and its function will probably differ slightly with each person responding to it. Suppose we assume that one very basic purpose behind a work of art is to convey thought and feeling; then it may be said to "work" in the degree to which it is successful in communication. But this brings us at once onto very shaky ground, since there arises the question of the sensitivity and understanding of those who are expected to receive the communication. Obviously the value of the painting or sculpture, its success or failure, cannot rest on the reception accorded it by a person totally unprepared to understand its significance.

For this reason, it is temptation to fall back on the word "expression" and let judgment rest first on the degree to which the artist believes he has expressed what he felt, and second on the

---

[2] In somewhat different form this material dealing with the artist's intentions appeared in the summer of 1960 in the *Journal of Aesthetics and Art Criticism* under the title "Francisco Goya and the Intentions of the Artist."

quality of his feeling and thought. Here again one has difficulties, because the artifact will then be incapable of objective valuation, and will have to be accepted or rejected entirely on the prejudiced opinion of its maker. Obviously, this is no solution to the problem of the final judgment of the quality of an aesthetic artifact.

We can only suggest a rule-of-thumb answer to this question, but it is a rule which if followed long enough is sure to take the inquirer onto firm ground even in the midst of a welter of subjective variables. Try to apply to the aesthetic artifact the same test you employ for its practical brothers: the test of use. How does the painting or sculpture work aesthetically, how does it affect you? If we honestly adopt an open mind and an open-eyed awareness and curiosity, the work of art will itself suggest its function. And from an understanding of its function, we can work back to the artist's purpose and to the complex of thought and feeling to which he gives meaningful form.

Among aesthetic artifacts there is a great variety of communication. At one extreme the work of art may, by awakening our sense of injustice or our pity, move us to action we would not otherwise have undertaken. Art of this kind is a form of propaganda, and like other aesthetic artifacts it may be good, bad, or indifferent. The best examples of this type of art outlive the specific evil at which they were originally aimed; or, to put it another way, the evil, losing its immediate occasion, becomes generalized. However, it is the artist's ability to present his subject in general terms, with a broad human significance, that makes it important.

In this connection it is interesting to note that Goya's great series of prints in which he presented incidents of the Napoleonic war in Spain as human "disasters," as well as many of his anti-clerical and political prints made during the period of the restoration of the Spanish monarchy, were not published until long after the artist's death. By the time they appeared, their message had been generalized by the passage of years, and the prints were, as they are today, anti-war rather than anti-Napoleon, against human venery and abuse of power rather than against the power of a specific body.

At the other extreme from the art of social consciousness in this matter of communication, lies the very personal, very private art in which the artist seems only to wish to share his feelings and ideas with others of a sympathetic mind. Among the artists whose work has this private character, the same great names appear, among them Goya, Daumier, Picasso, all of whom have used their art in the interests of humanity but as frequently, or more frequently, for their own delectation and satisfaction.

A useful distinction can be made between private and public purposes of art. The purpose behind the building of a great cathedral, Salisbury for instance (Fig. 4–16), is largely public, though the architect or master mason, and probably the masons and sculptors as well, involve themselves in the public purpose to such an extent that it becomes their own even while they may remain anonymous. Constable's purpose, on the other hand, when he painted his various images of the cathedral, must surely have been to communicate his private delight in the majesty of the great building as it rises above the wet meadows of Wiltshire and the houses and gardens of Salisbury.

While the purpose of the building is public in origin, it functions both publicly and privately; and though the purpose of the painting is private, its function may be said to be public as well as private since it allows us to share the artist's delight and to participate to some degree in the meaning the cathedral has for him.

The value of the work of art does not, however, depend finally on its public function. Some works of art have little or no public function because of their relative unintelligibility, but may still be exceedingly valuable—beautiful and meaningful—to their makers and to the few understanding persons for whom they have meaning, to whom they speak.

To return briefly to Henri Matisse's analysis of the dual impulse behind the creation of art—the desire to make an icon or holy thing, and the desire to share experience—it would seem that the impulse to make a holy thing might be more broadly stated as the basic urge to create, to bring into being and to give life to something that had no previous existence; to create living, meaningful forms analogous to but in no sense identical with the forms of nature. Matisse's second purpose, the urge to share the quality of experience, may well be considered a matter of communication. Interpreted broadly, all artifacts that have an aesthetic rather than a practical purpose are in some degree communicative whether or not the "meaning" is publicly understood. Thus, instead of giving the two purposes the equality of siblings, as Matisse does, they can be seen as existing *seriatim* in the creative process, the one generating the other.

The Artist's Intentions

At the risk of oversimplification one can make a useful classification of four major types of aesthetic purpose, all manifestations of the central creative impulse to which we have already referred:

they are the impulse to decorate, to celebrate, to expound ideas or express feeling, and finally to exorcise devils. Clearly, they overlap and in practice are rarely wholly separable. Of the four, the first can be identified as a mainly hedonistic impulse to adorn oneself or one's environment and the things that go to make it up. The decorative function of both aesthetic and practical artifacts is so obvious as to be frequently overlooked today. The decorative purpose may be private as in the interior design of one's home, or in the making of one's own flower garden; or it may be public as in the murals decorating public buildings, or in the design of a park.

In the case of the garden or the park, to make the environment more sensuously pleasant, the materials that nature provides are organized in accordance with a plan, formal or informal as suits the taste of the owner or the fashion of the time. Whether the artifact be a garden, a piece of pottery, a decorative painting, or a work of sculpture, the decoratively pleasing quality will lie in the ordered variety of its elements. This suggests patterned ornament, but representational images may in themselves be primarily decorative, and they are frequently used to give order and interest to practical objects. As we have seen, the Greek wine cup (Fig. 2–7) is made far more agreeable and entertaining to use by the addition of the picture of the ancient voyager.

The statue of *Apollo* (Fig. 5–3) from the Temple of Zeus at Olympia was originally the central figure in the decoration of the pediment or triangular gable of the temple. It was part of a highly organized complex of architectural decoration, but the group also served to celebrate Greek unity and devotion to the gods. The purpose of the sculpture might be termed both decorative and expressive.

On the other hand, the decorative panel of the Arts (Fig. 5–9) that Boucher painted for Mme. de Pompadour in 1755 has no other purpose than to provide an unobtrusively charming background for gay supper parties and amusing conversation. This is decoration with no other aim than to please.

We have used the word *celebration* in connection with art more than once, and in the interests of clarity it may be well to define the term. According to Webster, *celebrate* means

1. To perform publicly and with appropriate rites; solemnize
2. To honor with solemn rites
3. To proclaim; publish abroad
4. To extol, sound the praises of.

Boucher. *Painting and Sculpture.*

(1703–1770; French.)
Oil on canvas, 85½″ × 30½″.
(One of eight panels.)
Copyright The Frick Collection,
  New York.

Fig. 5–9.

The emphasis on *public* rites and on *publishing abroad* links celebration with communication. The words *honor, extol,* and *praise* almost complete the meaning as the word is used in art criticism. However, in some degree our use of *celebrate* borrows from its synonym *commemorate* since the function of an aesthetic artifact of this kind is to commemorate the quality of an experience already past.

The work of art celebrates or commemorates not so much an object or an event, as the artist's experience of it, his perception or the feeling attached to the act of perception. Our feelings are often quite as profoundly touched by experiences that move us to horror, or disgust, or intense sympathy, as by those producing responses of love and joy. Goya's *The Third of May, 1808* (Pl. IVa) records, shares, and commemorates; it does not, of course, "celebrate the event with praise and honor."

In this great painting Goya commemorates and does honor to the Madrilenos who had risen against Napoleon's soldiers in violent street fighting only to be captured and put to death. But Goya's painting does more than record the execution. He tells with excruciating sympathy of the way each man went to his death, stumbling or striding up the hill into the patch of lantern light, there to meet the firing squad. Some tremble and bury their faces in their hands; one falls on his knees in prayer. The man who is next to die flings his arms up and glares defiance, while the man beside him, with hands clenched looks up to heaven. The dead pile up and those still to come press on from the gate of the city seen dimly in the background. In contrast to the detailed study of facial and bodily expression among the condemned men, the firing squad are blocked in like so many trigger-pulling automata, without any kind of human expression. Goya commemorates the courage of the patriots, but he also celebrates the infinite variety and richness of human nature which was to him a theme of endless fascination and interest.

A third specific purpose may be described as the intent to inform and persuade, to express in aesthetic terms, ideas and feelings that seem important to the artist and/or to his patron. In the great ages of communal faith this purpose generally originated with church or priesthood. Christian art of medieval Europe owed its character largely to the desire of the Church to present its teachings in understandable and persuasive form to a largely illiterate people. The artist, for the most part an anonymous craftsman following the explicit directions of his patron, was expected to instruct his audience in the doctrines and the lore of the Church, to lend force and conviction to its values, and to make its saints venerable and lovable.

Since the Reformation, church patronage of the visual arts has dwindled fast, and the aesthetic purpose has tended to originate not with the Church but with the individual artist. His intention has been more to express personal feeling than to instruct or persuade. Yet Rembrandt would hardly have printed a large edition of *Christ Crucified* (Fig. 10–19) had he not been fairly sure of an audience.

The Egyptian wall painting (Fig. 4–35), while very decorative, clearly belongs under this heading of persuading and informing. The owner of the tomb on one of whose walls the hunting and fishing scene is represented looked forward to a renewal, in the land of the dead, of all the pleasures of a happy life on his Nile valley estate. To insure this prospect, it was the custom to cover the walls of a tomb chapel with magical pictures which could be expected to come to life when the dead man entered the next world. On one wall would appear a hunting and fishing scene such as this; on another the nobleman might be seen protected by a canopy from the sun, watching the ploughing or the grape harvest on his estate; on still another, he and his wife would be shown feasting with their friends while musicians and dancers provided entertainment. There was originally an actual offering table in the chapel to which the mortuary priests brought suitable provisions, but to be doubly sure of an adequate diet throughout eternity, there was also represented on the wall a banqueting table, and piled high beside it the special delicacies of fruit, vegetables, meat, and drink to which the dead man had been accustomed in this life.

The magical efficacy of the tomb painting depended on its informative, legible character, but any nobleman of taste and any self-respecting painter would wish the tomb to be as beautiful as possible. The orderly, balanced pattern of the composition, the device of repeating the major figure in symmetrical juxtaposition to its counterpart, and the beautiful line of the young girl's body as she bends to pull a water lily—these are only a few of the evidences of the strong decorative sense that the Egyptian possessed. The painting is both informative and decorative; we can only hope that its magic also proved persuasive.

Persuasion is not peculiar to religious art, however. In a more self-conscious age Jacques Louis David, leader and spokesman of the artists of the French Revolution, on more than one occasion set forth his passionate conviction that the artist has a responsibility to society. "Each of us is accountable to the nation for the talents which he has received from nature: if the form is different, the end ought to be the same. The true patriot ought to seize eagerly every way of enlightening his fellow citizens and of presenting to their eyes increasingly the sublime traits of heroism and virtue." [3] To David one of the functions of art was to enlighten men. Again in his Project for the Committee of Public Safety for the Fine Arts, Article 2: "Republican Artists, while our heroes assure the triumph of liberty and prepare for peace by victory, it is your task to make it loved, it is for you to embellish it." [4] This is clearly a demand for persuasive art. David's own painting of *The Death of Marat* (Fig. 4-3), the revolutionary journalist and member of the Chamber of Deputies, is a most persuasive record of an event, a deeply moving memorial to a patriot who was the victim of political assassination.

Jean Paul Marat (1743–1793) was one of the most colorful personalities of the French Revolution; a scientist and physician who in 1786 had given up his scientific career to embrace one of political journalism. As editor of "L'Ami du Peuple" he had become identified with the title of his journal, "Friend of the People," and waged constant war against those whom he regarded as seeking personal power within the framework of the Revolution. He was often forced to hide in the sewers of Paris to escape his enemies, and, as a result, contracted a painful skin disease from which he was slowly dying. To ease the pain he sat long hours in a warm bath where, with a board across the sides of the tub, he was at work when Charlotte Corday was admitted. Her plea was that she had information concerning the whereabouts of some escaped Girondins, and Marat wrote their names on a slip of paper before she stabbed him to death.

Marat had been David's friend, and the painting is simply inscribed on the upturned packing box which holds his ink pot and pen, "To Marat, David." One is inclined to think that it was the artist's own deep feeling, not his sense of political responsibility, that prompted the utter simplicity of the portrayal: the stillness that pervades the picture, the geometric order of verticals and horizontals that suggests a final equilibrium; color shading from blue-gray to black in the background, and paling to white where the light falls on the dead man's cheek and forehead, on the white cloth around his head, and on his bare left arm and the slip of paper in his hand.

---

[3] Quoted by Milton Brown in *The Painting of the French Revolution* (New York: The Critics Group, 1938), p. 51.

[4] *Ibid.*, p. 52.

We have already spoken of the expression of feeling and emotion as it belongs to the more or less public arts of persuasion, but we have yet to note the artist's private impulse to give vent to feeling for its own sake, to externalize it in visual forms. This is closely related both to his desire to celebrate the quality of experience, of which something has already been said, and his need to exorcise private devils, of which more will be said later, but it may be useful to look at each impulse separately and to consider each kind of resulting expression.

In the twentieth century the desire to express feeling itself instead of feeling about something, to focus directly on the emotion instead of on the object or the circumstances that arouse it, has almost taken over the field (Fig. 4–15). This is due to a very complex set of circumstances which, since we are a part of them and ourselves influenced by them, we probably cannot hope fully to understand. As society asks less and less of the artist, depending almost not at all on his interpretations of reality and on his judgments of value, he of necessity draws more and more into himself. Lacking the evidence of value to society which his artistic forbears generally had in some degree, the modern artist is forced to find in the fact of his own existence as a living, sentient being, and in the quality and variety of his own feelings, the material of his art. In some measure this accounts for the variety of forms taken by the visual arts in our own century. Since the purpose (when it can be identified) originates in the subjective feeling of each individual artist, the forms are legion and the images tend to be proprioceptive.

It would certainly be a mistake to convey the impression that before the twentieth century there was no "expressionist" art. There have been periods, notably the Byzantine and medieval Christian, which have been primarily characterized by the expression of feeling. There have also been instances of great expressionist artists working as El Greco did, in a period chiefly devoted to the celebration of the world of sensory perception. In this connection compare Titian's *Adoration of the Kings* (Fig. 5–10) with El Greco's *Adoration of the Shepherds* (Fig. 2–9). Titian celebrates the tangible, visible qualities of the Mother and divine Child, the sumptuous retinue of the kings, the sleek, well-groomed horse, and the imperturbable little dog. He uses all these elements and more to tell his story. El Greco on the other hand tells his story entirely in terms of its emotional meaning for him. The distortions of El Greco's figures seemed to his contemporaries, and to generations after, the result of faulty eyesight. It was not until a generation of artists at the end

ART AS EXPERIENCE

TITIAN. *Adoration of the Kings.*

(c. 1477–1576; Italian.)
Oil on canvas, 56″ × 89⅞″.
The Cleveland Museum of Art.
Mr. and Mrs. William H. Marlatt Fund.

Fig. 5–10.

of the nineteenth century began themselves to turn their eyes inward
that people could see in the emaciated, tensely drawn out figures of
El Greco's shepherds the expression of their wonder and yearning
toward the miraculous Child, and in the bodies which are rendered
almost immaterial by the tricks light and shadow play on solid
things, a suggestion of Greco's own feeling that the nativity of Jesus
was one of the great mysteries of all time.

Finally, a fourth aesthetic purpose can be identified. There are
many aesthetic artifacts that come into being from the artist's need
to exorcise private devils; as Blake said, to "give a form to the devil
in order that it may be cast out." The artist actualizes the phantoms
that beset him and thus subdues their power.

It is recorded [5] that during the Battle of Britain, bombed out children first suffered a period of shock, and then began to play at bombing. By this means they apparently subdued the terrifying phantoms of their nightmares and found their way back to psychic health. The artist's "play" also deals on occasion with painful reality under the comforting cloak of make-believe. Some actual experiences are too painful to keep in our conscious minds, and some emotions are so unacceptable that we must repress them. Both have a way of forcing themselves back on our attention in dreams and nightmares, to quote Hadfield, "objectified and personalized into living creatures such as vampires or crabs, or monsters or witches, insisting by persevering recurrence and with threat of mental illness on being faced and dealt with." [6] The term *nightmare* originally referred to the monstrous creatures themselves, literally night-mares; it later came to include the whole dream in which they appeared.

It seems probable that most of the monsters and grotesque creatures of art owe their ultimate origin, and certainly their vitality, to the same mysterious source from which our nightmares come, bred in that still relatively little known world of the human unconscious and subconscious mind. It further seems very likely that they owe their concrete, artifact existence to a healthy human impulse, akin to that of the bombed-out children, to objectify the dread creatures; to have them out where we can take a good look at them in broad daylight.

For the tough minded, artists and laymen alike, this may be of only academic interest, but even the healthiest among us have our nightmares and are occasionally ready to echo the old prayer:

From ghoulies and ghaisties,
And long-legged baisties,
And things that go "bump" in the night
Good Lord deliver us!

Monsters are found the world over; frequently, as in St. George's dragon, they embody the principle of evil against whom the champion of good persistently triumphs. They generally bear some relation to actuality though in a distorted and often completely metamorphosed way. The actuality, however dimly remembered, which serves as the material parent of the monster was probably originally something seen or touched or handled in the world outside the

[5] J. A. Hadfield, *Dreams and Nightmares* (London: Penguin Books, Ltd., 1954), pp. 96–102. (Also available as a Pelican Book, A 294.)
[6] *Ibid.*, pp. 176–78.

GRÜNEWALD. *Temptation of St. Anthony.*

(c. 1470–1528; German.)
Panel from Isenheim Altarpiece.
Oil on panel.
Unterlinden Museum, Colmar.

Fig. 5–11.

artist. Its metamorphosis, the selection and joining of incongruous parts, and above all, the feeling that breathes through it derives from sensations felt inside the artist's own body, and from the emotions of which he is probably only partly conscious as his monster takes objective and personalized form.

Consider the creatures that torment St. Anthony in Grünewald's painting at Colmar (Figs. 5–11 and 5–12). It seems possible that the creative process may have been something like this. In trying to put himself in the place of the anguished, guilt-ridden Anthony, the painter ascribed to the saint some of his own worst nightmares. While he had precedent in earlier renderings of the same subject, he imagined the monstrous creatures besetting the saint in the personalized, objective forms taken by his own repressed emotions. These personifications of evil took the elements of their fantastic, hybrid forms from the painter's experience of real creatures, of shiny black gastropods, of snakes, of clawing vultures. These, and many besides, the painter called up out of memory, each still clothed in the dread of an actual encounter, and perhaps of subsequent dream

GRÜNEWALD. Detail from *Temptation of St. Anthony.*

Unterlinden Museum, Colmar.

Fig. 5–12.

Romanesque Capital.

The Cuxa Cloister.
Marble.

The Metropolitan Museum of Art,
*   New York.*
The Cloisters Collection, Purchase, 1925.

Fig. 5–13.

visitations. But as they took form in the painting they were meta-morphosed into new species, new living monsters as credible as they are fantastic and terrifying.

There are two different types of artifact-monsters, identical in ultimate origin but one more evolved than the other: one has, in effect, been longer in captivity. The more evolved are those that have taken a recognized place in the illustrated pages of human consciousness, like the familiar devil with horns and a forked tail,

IMAGERY, STYLE, PURPOSES

DuBuffet. *Businessmen's Lunch.*

(1901–   ; French.)
Oil on canvas, 35″ × 45¼″.
Collection of Prof. and Mrs. Henry R. Hope,
   Bloomington, Indiana.

Fig. 5–14.

or St. George's dragon. These have become accepted symbols of
evil, and when one meets them, instead of the quality of very personal dread that surrounds a nightmare, there is the almost pleasurable recognition one accords the villain in a familiar drama.

The other type of monster is less evolved; it has not yet achieved
the general acceptance and significance of the dragon or the devil.
The second type is as various as the individuals whom they first
tormented in dream or fantasy. Such are the innumerable creatures

ART AS EXPERIENCE

of ill assorted parts who adorn the capitals of medieval cloisters (Fig. 5–13), of whom St. Bernard complained bitterly that they diverted the brothers from their meditations with their "shapely mishapenesses," for while it seems probable that they originally took form in the unconscious of the stone-cutter who carved them, they certainly lent themselves admirably to purposes of decoration.

Sometimes these unevolved monsters take on a human form, as in Jean DuBuffet's *Businessmen's Lunch* (Fig. 5–14), or in Bosch's *Christ Before Pilate* (Fig. 5–15), where the tormentors of Jesus are the embodiment of human stupidity and cruelty. "Giving a form to the devil in order that he may be cast out"; creating images in which the quality of experience is celebrated, images which by their own

BOSCH. *Christ Before Pilate.*
(c. 1450–1516; Netherlandish.)
Oil on canvas, 31½″ × 41″.
The Art Museum, Princeton University.

Fig. 5–15.

authority serve to organize and set to rights our ideas and our feelings, explaining ourselves to ourselves and to others; providing a bridge between the artist and his audience; and finally, and most simply, adding visual delight to our sometimes humdrum lives—these are some of the purposes and functions of art; these are the business of the artist.

Suggestions for Further Reading

ACKERMAN, J. "A Theory of Style," *Journal of Aesthetics and Art Criticism,* Vol. XX, No. 3; March, 1963.
> Strongly recommended. This article raises basic questions without giving dogmatic answers. It can be studied with profit at various levels of understanding.

ALFORD, J. "Art and Reality 1850–1950," *The College Art Journal,* Vol. XVII, No. 3; 1958.
> This article elucidates with great clarity the relation between style and patterns of thought and feeling. Very valuable for the serious student.

CARPENTER, R. *The Esthetic Basis of Greek Art of the Fifth and Fourth Centuries.* Bloomington, Ind.: Indiana University Press, 1959. (A Meridian Book, MB 19.)
> Essential to an understanding of Greek art.

LÖWENFELD, V. *The Nature of Creative Activity,* 2nd ed. London: Routledge and Kegan Paul, Ltd., 1952.
> One of the key books for the approach to art made in this textbook.

MOREY, C. R. *Christian Art.* New York: W. W. Norton Co., Inc., 1958.
> In very small compass this book illustrates the relation between art and cultural pattern.

SCHAPIRO, MEYER. "Style," in *Anthropology To-day: An Encyclopedia Inventory.* A. L. Kroeber, Ed. Chicago: University of Chicago Press, 1953.

WÖLFFLIN, H. *Principle of Art History: The Problem of the Development of Style in Later Art.* M. D. Hottinger, Trans., from the 7th German edition. New York: Dover Publications, Inc. (Paperback no. T 276.)

II. THE ARTIST

LOOKS AT ART

6. Gilles

The Initial Response to the Painting

In this chapter we shall examine a single painting as the *Land of Cockaigne* was considered in Chapter 1. Our point of view will have shifted in two respects: first, the painting is very different from the Bruegel and has different things to show us; second, the author of this part of the book is a practicing painter whose training and attitudes affect the approach. But in spite of these differences, the approach demands the same willingness to take the time *really to look*, to look without prejudice and to bring to the looking every bit of your own relevant experience.

It is intended here to direct your attention to things you might not have noticed, and show you ways to use your experience that may not have occurred to you; the assumption will be that nothing essential is truly hidden, and the problem is for you to organize and understand what you see in ways which are meaningful because of what you already know. Of course, there are some pertinent facts which will enter the discussion, but these become meaningful in this context only when you have truly looked at the work of art. The facts only serve to extend an experience already begun.

The Detailed Inventory

Now, let us turn to the painting which will concern us for the rest of this chapter. Antoine Watteau has represented an actor of the *Commedia dell'Arte* named Gilles (Pl. III). What do you see in the picture? Your attention probably goes first to the main figure of Gilles, but what attracts your attention after that? Perhaps it is some detail in the central figure's dress, posture, or look; or the other figures behind him; or the foliage and sky. As in our study of the *Land of Cockaigne* we shall begin with an inventory of what is in the painting. (The assumption will be that you already have an impression of the painting as a whole and feel a certain attitude toward it.)

The trip through this painting is clearly of a different order from the one we made through the *Land of Cockaigne*. The earlier picture read like a moral tale, while *Gilles* is closer to a character sketch or a biography. In the Bruegel the detail is related to the painting as a whole in a direct, literary way; in the Watteau, although it has literary significance, the detail serves more to create an atmosphere, a setting for the chief character.

Full-length in roughly the center of the painting is a man in a white silk costume; he wears tan shoes with rose-red silk ties, and on the back of his head is a tan hat which appears to be held on by a pink band which the hat partially covers. He faces us almost directly; his arms hang limp at his sides and seem swallowed up, as does the rest of his body, in the fullness of the costume; his hands, feet, and head look as though they are hooked on like those of a doll or marionette. He stands on a small hill or ridge above the ground level of the rest of the painting and there is some ground cover and part of a bush near his feet; the color is a mixture of tan and green.

Immediately behind him in the picture space are three men, a woman, a statue, and a donkey. To Gilles' left is a man with his back to us and with his face turned so that we see his profile; his costume appears to be of the same rose-red silk that ties Gilles' shoes and the gesture of his body and the jaunty angle of his hat seem to indicate a degree of worldliness in contrast to Gilles' look of simplicity and awkwardness. Behind the man in red are the woman and another man. The woman, except for a certain beauty, is not distinctive; the man is clearly a special type—note the fantastic brim on his hat and the amazed expression on his face. Near these three figures is a sculptured bust with vines overgrowing its pedestal. On Gilles' right is a grinning man in a black cap and costume with a white ruff around his neck riding into the painting on a donkey. In the background there is foliage of a variety of kinds and to the left there are clouds behind the trees; the upper part of Gilles' figure appears against a pale blue sky.

THE ARTIST LOOKS AT ART

The Formal Structure

We shall now read or describe the painting in another way. What kind of shapes and colors does it have and how are they placed within the rectangle of the painting? How do they relate to the recognizable objects already identified?

The dominant shape is that of the figure of Gilles. The buttons on his coat seem both to touch the front of the picture plane and bisect the rectangle (the last is not really true—the midline falls close to the inside of his left arm); the smaller shapes—hands, feet, arms, legs, pockets, head, and ruffled collar—reinforce this effect by being almost bilaterally symmetrical. The highly repetitious character of the central figure is very important: contrast this figure with all of the rest of the painting. If you block out the figure of Gilles (placing a couple of fingers over him will do) you will see a suggestion of a pattern which is directly opposed to the pattern of form in the major figure. There is a kind of zig-zag starting with the tree branch in the upper left and moving down to the other side of the painting to a point above the head of the man in the black cap; then the line returns across the painting following the four heads in the middle-ground, and is paralleled by a line which passes behind Gilles' feet. But there is another pattern and shape discernible, although a little less distinctly, in the middle- and background. Start with the hand of the man in red silk and follow the line up to his head, up the chest of the statue and the trunk of the tree, out the lower limb and in an arc behind Gilles to the trees on the other side; from there to the black-capped man, to the head of his donkey, to the lower edge of the white pants, and finally to the starting place.

This gives us three shapes: the oval of Gilles' body, a zig-zag, and a circle. These are not just flat geometric figures on the surface, because they also function in the illusionistic space of the painting. The zig-zag starts well back in the picture and in the line of the ridge brings us almost to the front of the picture space. The circle starts in the front of the middle-ground (the space occupied by the figures) and goes to the deepest part well into the background and then returns to the middle-ground. Finally, the subtlest of the shapes is that of Gilles. In a general way it is an oval, but if we look at it a little more closely, there is the oval of his torso which rests on two rectangles formed by his pants legs whose rectangles are echoed in the forearms. This composite is topped by a circle made of the head and hat, while the whole group of shapes is set in an illusionistic space by the values used for each. By value is meant lightness or darkness of the color regardless of its hue (red, blue, etc.) or of its intensity (brightness or dullness). The lightest value in this figure is the oval of the torso; the darkest is that of the rectangles of the legs, and in between is the value of the head and hat. Because dark values seem to recede and light ones to come forward, Gilles seems to have his back arched and his hips thrown forward; the whole combination of shapes is bent like a bow.

This brings us to the color and to the patterns we find in it. Gilles' costume, the sky, and the clouds are closely related in color, with cool blue, blue-gray, and white dominating the foreground and background; sandwiched in between are the greens, tans, reds, and black of the predominantly warm middle-ground. The separation of the cool blues and grays from the warm tans and red is certainly not absolute, especially between the foreground and the middle-ground; the tan of the hat and shoes, the rose-red of the ribbons, and the pink flesh tones relate closely to the colors in the middle-ground. The color is used both to clarify the space and to put things in their proper places, while simultaneously the colors tie these parts together.

The Painter's Means

Let us examine now the way the painting was made: what materials and techniques were used, and how these affect the "look" of the painting.

The painting was done in oil on canvas. The colors were ground with oil (probably either nut or linseed) into a paste and applied with a brush to canvas. The canvas was first covered with white, probably non-oily, ground. The paint was applied generally in two ways: as an opaque substance covering any color underneath; and thinly and transparently as a glaze allowing the color beneath to strike through. The opaque painting or *impasto* is most clearly seen in the pure whites on Gilles' coat and in the flat blue sky. The glazing or use of transparent paint is common to most of the painting; in the reproduction it is most evident in the red coat and hat of the man to the left, and in the foliage.

These two ways of applying paint tend to have a characteristic look about them which contributes to the over-all effect of the painting. (The use of these techniques is not common to all oil painting.) The opaque painting has about it a certain flatness—one might also say a certain straightforwardness and simplicity—because of the direct character of its application. The glazing, because it is transparent and is often built up of successive layers of different colors, has a much less stable look: the glazed areas appear to shimmer and dance; their movement in space gives a vitality and liveliness to the surface of the painting.

Watteau's technical handling of the paint is closely related to his feeling for light and for the way light exposes form and color. Along with the relative thickness and opacity of the paint, the shape and size of Watteau's characteristic brush strokes are tied to his interest in a particular kind of light.

For Watteau light reveals form and color, but these are phenomenal rather than conceptual. They are things to be seen, and he represents them as such; in this his painting is like the Monet (Pl. IIb) rather than the Bruegel (Pl. I). In the Bruegel color and form are more closely related to what we "know," to our ideas of color and form. In Watteau's painting, light not only reveals these qualities; it also seems to dissolve them. The edges between one form and the next and one color and the next are not precise as in the Bruegel. The fickle character of natural light is a strong element in Watteau's art. Light and the qualities it reveals are constantly changing from one moment to the next, and certain kinds of surfaces emphasize this; consider in this painting, for instance, the silk and the leaves—the visual appearance of each varies distinctly with any change in light.

Glazing, we have noted, when it is used with a certain kind of brush stroke, can very readily show these qualities while it also gives solidity to the forms. Glazing can be used, of course, in different ways for very different results; e.g., compare Van Eyck (Fig. 7–9) and Bruegel (Pl. I). And the same or a similar brush stroke can be used without transparent paint, as Monet does in his *View of Amsterdam* (Pl. IIb); but to obtain a sense of both the changing surface of visible things and their volume the technique of glazing is ideal. The thicker, opaque paint used in this painting over relatively large areas is not common in Watteau's work. Its use here is particularly suited to the problem of presenting a figure who is both *in* a landscape and *on* a stage set. This is one of the underlying themes of the painting which will be developed later. For the moment we can leave the technical aspects of the painting, only noting that the most highly glazed areas are sandwiched in the picture space between areas of heavier, flatter paint.

A Subjective Approach

Now that we have examined the painting in several generally objective ways, concerning ourselves first with the recognizable things in it, then with the shapes and colors which dominate it, and finally with the way it was put together, we are in a position to look at it from a subjective point of view. Most of what has been said above is not very meaningful in this context unless we now consider: "How does the painting affect me?" Do you see anything that you can relate to other kinds of experience and how in turn are these related to what has been observed in the painting? In this process we may notice things which have not been seen before or which have not seemed significant. These can enrich and redirect the earlier responses to the painting.

First, look at Gilles and his posture. He stands facing us directly with his feet close together, his arms forward, in front of his body; his back looks arched and his costume is very full, especially his jacket. As mentioned earlier, his head, hands, and feet look like those of a doll or a marionette; they seem to be tacked onto the costume. This results from our inability to see clearly the body beneath the costume, and because his knees, hips, wrists, and elbows are hidden we can only guess how and where his body is articulated. His elbows are not only hidden, but in the area where they should appear there is a large amount of surplus material which seems to restrict movement. Similarly hidden is the point where his neck meets his shoulders; Gilles' ruffled collar, not his spine, appears to hold his head in place, and his shoulders are pushed forward in order to hold his arms in position. This causes his upper chest to drop and meet his lower chest which is pushed up by the arching of the small of his back; a complicated gesture which is necessary in order to fit his body into the bulky costume he wears.

Assume this position; you will probably have the feeling of not knowing what to do with your body, the sense that your body is not put together right and does not belong to you. If you have performed in amateur theatricals, the position may seem quite familiar. Watteau has captured here the feeling and look of the awkward performer.

Gilles' face is paradoxical. Whereas the body is ill at ease and awkward, the face is self-assured, confident, and relaxed. His facial expression makes the gesture of his body a pose: he is a professional performer and this is his part, and his face betrays him because this is a portrait and not a scene from a play.

WATTEAU. *Gilles.*

(1684–1721; French.)
Oil on canvas, 72½″ × 58⅝″.
The Louvre, Paris.

Pl. III.

Watteau. Detail of *Gilles.*
The Louvre, Paris.
Fig. 6–1.

The figures behind him do seem to be performing some dramatic incident; they appear indifferent to everything except what they are involved in among themselves. To observe them is for us like watching a performance, but in the case of Gilles we are being presented to a performer who is half his role and half himself.

This is amplified by the fact that Gilles is not only in front of the other actors, but also above them, and by our identification of him with the figures behind, he is also above us. He is, in physical fact, above the viewer, for the actual picture is about six feet high and is hung a couple of feet off the floor. In this position he dominates us but is at the same time somewhat unstable; his lack of stability is reinforced by his clumsy gesture and awkward posture. The effect is that neither he nor we have control of the situation and both are a little ill at ease. We are meeting a character from a play rather than watching him, and his position above us is unnatural.

If we block out the bottom half of the painting this unnatural feeling is strengthened by the figure of Gilles "pasted" on the flat blue sky. Seen this way, the painting becomes a poster rather than an ordinary portrait.

The Theme

Now, if we turn back to our earlier observations perhaps we can tie them together and fill in the relationships between the different approaches we have made to the painting.

Each time we have considered the painting there has been one strongly recurrent characteristic, its clear division into three areas: the foreground containing the central figure, the middle-ground with the other figures and foliage, and the background of sky and clouds. The foreground and background are similar in the relative flatness of the paint and form, and in color; between is the much more complicated middle-ground with its varied contents of sculpture, human figures, bushes and trees, and an animal. The formal movement is more involved in the central portion, which occupies more pictorial space, and the brush strokes are smaller and the paint transparent. The distribution of forms is asymmetrical, with a far greater concentration of objects and background on Gilles' left. The action is also distinctive in the middle-ground where the figures seem to be acting parts in a play. Gilles looks as though he should be a character in this play but has stepped out of it to be presented to us. He is separated from his fellow actors by several devices: he is not in the same part of the picture space; his face no longer contains the expression of his part, although his body does—the gesture of his body is that of his character, Pierrot, but in repose rather than in action like the other characters. His body is posed in the most recognizable aspect of the type of character he plays, and he is placed above the other actors and above the viewer. He is on dis-

Watteau. Detail of *Gilles.*

The Louvre, Paris.

Fig. 6–2.

play before us and he is aware of it. His inaction, symmetry, and the way in which he is silhouetted against the blue background give him the appearance of a poster portrait; the characters behind tell what the play will be in which he is a performer. Perhaps he is given the central position in the painting because he is the star, or perhaps, as Germain Bazin has suggested, the painting is a parodied *Ecce Homo.* This forces us to look at *Gilles* in relation to the artist and to his time, and allows us to infer something of what the artist's purpose may have been.

Relative Aspects of Watteau's Life

Antoine Watteau's life is as fascinating as his art, and this often makes it tempting to turn a discussion of his painting into a study in romantic biography, for as an individual he appears as typical of his age as is his work. He was born in Valenciennes in 1684 shortly after that city became a part of France; his youth and early training were during the last years of the reign of Louis XIV, the golden age of France. Watteau came to Paris as a young man in his 'teens and worked as a drudge for a dealer in cheap pictures; at twenty-one he entered the studio of Claude Gillot for a short period and then the studio of Claude Audran in the Luxembourg. While he was working under Audran, the young painter was deeply influenced by Rubens' work; he made many drawings after Rubens' paintings and assimilated the painting techniques used by Rubens in his later life. Having failed to win the *Prix de Rome,* Watteau returned to his home in Valenciennes, and there continued to work and to develop. After a short time, he returned to Paris where he became an Associate of the Academy. He only needed to paint a diploma piece in order to become a full member, but this was not done for five years and then only after pressure was applied; the painting Watteau executed for this purpose was the *Embarkation for Cythera.* In 1719 he made a trip to England to consult a certain Doctor Mead, but returned to France in increasingly bad health. Two years later Watteau died, apparently of tuberculosis, in Nogent-sur-Marne.

As a person he is reported to have been very touchy and sensitive, always dissatisfied with his own work and the work of others. He is said to have felt much more at ease drawing than painting and he was constantly drawing, wherever he was. Subject to depression and aware that he was a sick man, Watteau worked a great deal and was impatient with any interruption. The mixture of lightness and ennui which is so characteristic of his age and his art was also a part of his personality; the delicate beauty of figure and dress floating over a current of the vanity and tragedy of life—so common in Watteau's paintings—summarizes both the age and the artist. It is this quality which makes Watteau seem so much like Mozart, who closed the age that Watteau began.

The year 1717 was an important one for the painting we are considering since in that year the *Commedia dell'Arte*, the Italian improvisational comedy players, were again allowed to perform in France. They had been banned some years earlier by Louis XIV, and after his death the return to Paris of the Italian *Commedia* signalized the end of the puritanical measures which had marked the last years of his reign.

The world of the actor and the musician was fascinating to Watteau; one or the other recurs in a majority of his paintings. One senses that these types and their relation to society struck a very sympathetic chord in the artist; Watteau may have felt that he too was a kind of histrion or entertainer who put on his act and then was sent away. These traveling actors and musicians, in any case and for whatever reasons, are the subject of the painting *Gilles* and as such require an explanation.

The *Commedia dell'Arte* was a form of popular theater which started in Italy and was transplanted to France with very few changes except that the stock characters had French rather than Italian names. The plays were not written out; there was just an outline of a plot and in this framework the players improvised their parts. The actors specialized in one character which they usually played, the characters being a limited group of types: the rake, the beautiful woman, the cuckold, the inept servant. The character Gilles played was that of a simple valet named Pierrot who constantly got things mixed up, whether they were messages to his master's lover, or his master's clothing. The bumbling servant, often with underlying common sense, is a familiar figure in literature. One needs only to think of Cervantes' Sancho Panza or Hacek's Good Soldier Schweik to find the same characteristics.

An Artist's Dialogue With the Painting

Up to this point, with the exception of the discussion of technique, we have followed closely the approach employed in the discussion of the Bruegel painting in Chapter 1. The reasons for this are simple: to look at a picture thoroughly is a necessary preface to any further consideration of it and to look at it from various points of view enriches and varies the study, which otherwise might become just staring, not seeing. Let us turn now to some more personal kinds of relationships which artists often have with paintings, and to some less general observations about *Gilles*.

Painters frequently have with the work of other artists what might be called a "dialogue"; that is, they see their own work and the work of another artist as making comments about the same thing. The painter will often "take a phrase" in the form of a figure or layout from another artist and base a painting on it. The artist may also re-do the work of another in his own style. This kind of conversation usually happens between the painter and another artist with whom the painter feels a rapport or sense of familiarity. In this it is also analogous with a dialogue in the common use of the term. Of course, this is not a "real" conversation since one of the artists is usually long dead and much of the relationship is simply a construct on the part of the living artist, but it is no less real for the living artist in terms of his work and how he develops it.

This represents a way to have a relationship with the past—with the history of art—which is not objective and impersonal. It gives the study of works of art warmth and humanity which can be lost if the painting is only seen as a monument of eighteenth-century art, for example, embodying certain formal and iconographic qualities. It should be added that these qualities are significant and very important, but there is something more. The artist looking at art of an earlier time may see that another artist has tried to do the same thing, or things very similar to what he has tried to do. Watteau had a relationship like this with the seventeenth-century Flemish master Rubens. The French artist was fascinated by Rubens' technique. He also borrowed some facial types from the earlier master; the face of the woman in *Gilles*, for example, is very close to a Rubens type.

To this writer it is the positioning and the posture of the central figure that are most interesting. A comparison with a sculptural figure may make the point clear. Look for a moment at the Chinese terra cotta in Fig. 9–1. Do you recognize the similarity even in these two widely dissimilar works? They are both almost bi-laterally symmetrical, that is, balanced on either side of a median line. But our recognition of this is visual; it is a response to a visual pattern. There is a hidden quality to which we are likely to respond more strongly. We are intensely aware of the spine of each of the figures. This writer's response, and it is by our definition an aesthetic and proprioceptive one, is in the small of his back. In neither of the illustrations can we see the back of the figure, yet the whole posture of each seems to depend on how the spine is set, on the position of the shoulders and the placement of the feet.

Look now at the area of Gilles' knees: they appear to be locked. This seems to fit what has already been observed about the theatrical character represented, but if we did not know any of that, would we respond to this feeling of locked knees? Gilles clearly could not move quickly and could be easily pushed over; how right is his position high in the picture space then, and how well this matches the theme of the painting!

The dialogue between the artist and another artist's work is, of course, not limited to posture and positioning of the figures. Another response is also to the central figure, but in this case it has nothing to do with its being a figure. Notice the transition of color in the costume; how it so subtly moves from gray at the top of the neck through the broken gray and white, to a lighter gray, then to white and down the figure to gray again. Throughout the whole modulation, the sudden value shifts vitalize the whole form, while relative warmness or coolness of the grays and whites cause slight but fascinating spatial relationships to occur in the form as a whole. To see these requires practice, but is worth a little effort.

From this point of view, *Gilles* could just as well be a bottle, a table cloth, or a non-descriptive shape. The fact that the painting is of a human being is no longer as significant as it was when the thing which concerned us was the spine or the knees. What is important to notice in this type of examination is that neither concern is exclusively "right." "Rightness" and "wrongness" are not meaningful terms when the interest is a personal one, when the work of art concerns us subjectively rather than objectively. The initial objective description is essential, but it is only the beginning of the "dialogue" between you and a work of art. It is important to remember this because so many arguments over works of art rest on a confusion between "what is there" and "what interests me."

The relationship of an artist to any work of art is often two-fold. The work of art concerns him both professionally ("How is it put together?") and personally ("He feels the same way about that as I do"), and these two kinds of interests affect how an artist looks at a painting: he often sees it as both a school and a confidant. You may ask: What does this mean to me since I am not a painter? The best answer is that, although you may not be a professional artist, you are in many ways similar to the professional artist and you can have similar personal relationships with works of art. The relations between the viewer and the work of art are numerous, and one of the most important tools you can develop is the ability to see from a variety of points of view.

THE ARTIST LOOKS AT ART

7. The Painter's Means

The Genesis of a Work of Art

Between the conception of a painting and its completion there is a process of development and growth from an intangible idea to a concrete artifact. In the beginning the painting may be no more than an attempt to capture a certain gesture, a relationship of colors, a kind of light, a particular quality of paint or the feeling of a mood; in some cases the artist may just start painting with no notion of what he is interested in developing with the paint and will find his theme as he works. This process of the artist working and looking at what he has done, making studies, putting the paint on and taking it off, noticing some characteristic of the painting which indicates further possibilities within the painting at hand or for future pictures: this is a part of every artist's work.

As paintings are studied, with respect and awe, they often become so hallowed and are given such significance that it is difficult to remember that they are objects with technical and physical properties, the product of a man who has manipulated material into the form it has. In the act of working with the materials the artist forms his purpose, his intention; he gives the seed of his idea a place in which to grow, a context of material and technique in which it can be realized and made manifest. The kind of paint, the type of support, and the tradition of the painter constitute a geography in which the purposes of the artist can find their way; they make up the limits and the conditions within which and through which an intention becomes a painting.

As this analogy of the seed and the soil suggests, a large part of the final form of the painting is the product of the process of development rather than of the conception with which the artist started, and the materials of the painter are a central part of this realization.

Technical Considerations

A painter works with colors on a support. His central technical problems are in finding ways to make the colors adhere to the surface and in discovering the proper tools with which to apply the paint. In order to keep the paint on the support some kind of binder is either added to the pigment or applied to the support so that the color will be held in a chemical bond to the surface of the wall, canvas, paper, or wooden panel. The procedure of the common forms of painting consists in applying to the surface of the support the pigment suspended in some liquid, the medium; in time (the time varies), the medium dries leaving the pigment bound to the surface of the support.

Different kinds of painting solve this problem in different ways, and the artist develops procedures that suit the technique or techniques he chooses. The painter's method of painting constitutes an aspect of his style and of his way of developing a painting.

Other, very tangible problems involve the artist: the size of the painting and the place where he works. These are an important part of the physical act of painting and can be profitably taken into account by the viewer. The place where the artist worked is especially pertinent to mural paintings since they were often executed where they are viewed. To see some of these factors in operation let us turn first to a series of murals in the Brancacci Chapel of the church of the Carmine in Florence. They were executed in the technique known as fresco by one of the masters of the early Renaissance, Masaccio.

Some Paintings Executed in Fresco

Consider first *The Expulsion of Adam and Eve* (Fig. 7–1) and note the general characteristics of Masaccio's style—the simple palpable form and the direct naturalism of his figures and their gestures. The color is muted, but this is largely due to the accumulation of dirt through the years and to a fire that destroyed much of the church in the eighteenth century. (One small section of one of the paintings was covered for many years and there the color is much

MASACCIO. *The Expulsion of Adam and Eve.*

(1401–1428; Italian.)
Fresco, 6′ 9″ × 2′ 10¾″.
Santa Maria del Carmine, Florence.
Photo: Alinari-Art Reference Bureau.

Fig. 7–1.

closer to its original state and much less dark and gray than are the rest of the paintings.) In spite of its muted nature, it is possible to see in the originals that Masaccio's color falls into two general schemes: one based on red, blue, a cool gray, and flesh; and the other emphasizing green, yellow, tan, a warm gray, and flesh. *The Expulsion* is an example of the first with the main emphasis on color (in the sky and on the archangel) in the top half of the painting. The leaves, incidentally, are a much later addition and are interesting only in that they allow us to compare two grossly different kinds of painting. The foliage points up the fact that it would be very hard to call Masaccio a facile, clever painter. His greatness rests on grounds other than skill: on his seriousness (who could call him trivial?), his inventiveness, and his honesty. What is meant by honesty is simply this: he never tries to fool us into thinking he can do what he cannot. Look for instance at the poorly articulated hands of Adam. If you question their clumsiness compare them with Adam's upper abdomen and the naturalistic skill with which it is executed. Masaccio could have hidden the hands but he did not, nor did he use anyone else's device to solve the problem. His inventiveness may be rooted in this honesty and the willingness to follow his insights without cheating on the details.

It is possible to develop this point by comparing these figures with the drawing and the painting of *The Libyan Sybil* (Figs. 10–1, 10–2) by Michelangelo. Michelangelo appears to have worked with much more ease and certainty than does Masaccio. There is none of the clumsy articulation of detail or posture, and the posture is much more complex in the painting by the later master. Masaccio's work always looks as though the artist were feeling his way along, searching for the forms he needed.

When one examines Masaccio's work more closely, one's sense of its searching and serious character is reinforced. The handling of the paint is broad, and the space confronts us like space seen through a window or a doorway; it is straightforward and direct. His forms are simple and are often shaped like a pyramid. His attention went to the large, over-all shapes rather than to the detail. Throughout Masaccio's paintings the gestures of his figures are dramatic, but not histrionic.

In order to see the qualities of Masaccio's technique more closely, let us turn to *The Trinity* (Fig. 7–2), a fresco in another church in Florence. The broad handling is easily noticed in the detail of the head of God (Fig. 7–3), in the beard and hair: these are treated as masses, not as an accumulation of detail. The detail, even if it were easy to execute, would be lost because of the scale (the figures are close to life size). The scratched line around the head of God which was used in laying out the painting cannot be seen from the floor. We are given some indication of the artist's awareness of the painting's permanent place: he shows the source of light to be falling directly on the painting. Since the painting is on the north wall of the nave, the light that falls on the painting comes from the windows in the south wall—from above, much as Masaccio has painted the light in his painting. What would the source of light be, then, for *The Expulsion* in the Brancacci Chapel if Masaccio was consistent in this? It would be above you and to your right as you look at the painting and that is precisely where it is. A device of this kind which the artist can depend on is meaningful to him and to you because it extends the painting outside its edges to the larger context of the building which includes both its viewers and the painting. Due to this larger relationship he can obtain effects that are impossible without it. Look at *The Trinity* again. Where does the artist assume the viewer's head will be? From the way the perspective is articulated, the person looking at the painting is facing the step up to the floor where Mary and St. John are standing, and on which the cross is stationed. We are then at John's and Mary's feet, and Christ, God the Father, and the Holy Ghost rise above us toward the ceiling. A step below kneel the donors who gave the money for the painting. They too are above us, but we share the same space. At least, there is the sense of their coming out from the wall into the nave rather than receding into the wall as the other figures do. We are joining them in devotion (or they are joining us) in the larger context of the church. The religious figures rise above them and us, both in the way the figures are presented to us by perspective, and in physical fact. The way in which the donors enter the space where we are standing includes us in the painter's constructed hierarchy.

Since in fresco painting the pigment is applied in water-color to wet, freshly laid plaster, particles of lime in the plaster surround the particles of pigment; thus, as a fresco dries the color becomes less intense, or whiter, than in the original pigment. With its colors of low intensity, fresco is well suited to an artist who, like Masaccio, is concerned with deep space and the weight and tactility of objects in space. Especially in *The Trinity* and in *The Tribute Money* (Fig. 4–21) the tactility of objects and the space they occupy are given almost equal importance. The space in each painting is different. In *The Trinity*, an architectural space embraces the figures; it arches over them forming an architectural mandorla or "glory" about them.

Masaccio. *The Trinity.*

(1401–1428; Italian.)
Fresco, 22′ 3½″ × 15′ 6″.
Santa Maria Novella, Florence.
Photo: Alinari-Art Reference Bureau.

Fig. 7–2.

MASACCIO. Detail of God the
Father from *The Trinity*.

Photo: Alinari-Art Reference Bureau.

Fig. 7–3.

The kind of space represented in *The Tribute Money* is not closed or architectural but is open and filled with atmosphere. One measures the space, step by step in a marked recession: the side wall of the building, its porch, the trees, and the mountains. There are instances of diminishing scale, which are signs of what is forward and what is back. The space is not, however, measured with the clarity of the coffered ceiling in *The Trinity*.

Fresco Painting: Technical Considerations

Fresco is one of the major mural painting techniques; as such frescoes are usually large in scale and an integral part of a building. A fresco painting occupies a permanent place, fused to the walls and not made to be moved. Fresco painting is done in roughly the following way: the wall to be painted is prepared by covering it with a number of coats of plaster; then the painting is laid out by scratching the outlines into the final layer of plaster while it is still damp. The final painting follows and the pigment is mixed with water or water and lime so that it will bind to the damp plaster. The artist needs to have a very clear idea of what he is going to do, since he must work rapidly before the plaster dries, and the technique allows for very little over-painting. Artists frequently use cartoons or full-scale drawings which they transfer onto the wall in order to have the plan carefully worked out before beginning the actual application of paint. Delacroix is said to have remarked that the necessity for having everything ready at once in fresco gives a feeling of excitement directly opposed to the indolence which oil painting gives. Some painters in oil might question the "indolence" inspired by their medium, but it is certainly true that there is not the same race against time in oil that there is in fresco.

Fresco technique also lends itself best to a relatively broad and flat handling, and subtle gradations of light are not easily executed in fresco. This is one of the reasons frequently given for Leonardo da Vinci's avoidance of this technique. The *Last Supper* (Fig. 2–10) was done in oil. It certainly would be very difficult, if not impossible, to obtain in fresco the shimmering turn of form which is so characteristic of Leonardo's work and which we have also seen in Watteau's. There is also a strong bond between a mural painting and its location. Since a mural is not movable and is painted where it is to be seen, there are a number of constant conditions which artists in other media cannot expect. For instance, the relationships to the building space, the kinds of light, the position in relation to the viewer and to other paintings close at hand are much more constant than they would be for an easel painting.

In size a mural is usually large so that it rises above the spectator and can be awe-inspiring and even overbearing. It is possible for a fresco to envelop the person looking at it. The qualities which are most common in fresco are, then, broadness of handling, a constant environment, and a relatively large size.

Easel Paintings

How different is the task of a painter of easel pictures; how little can he depend on the environment of his work. But, on the other hand, he is also free of the restrictions of a given space and a certain building. He is free to paint without the dictates of a particular context. This freedom is appreciated by many artists, and they are very willing to suffer the disadvantages of being responsible only to the edges of the painting. This is the most striking difference between fresco and oil painting: the movability of an easel picture. (Reference here is to oil painting as it is usually done on canvas or wood panel; it is possible to use oil for wall painting, but it is not common.) The artist rarely paints an oil painting where it will be hung and often does not see his work after it is situated. Even if he does he has very little control over how and where it is shown, what kind of lighting the painting has, and what it is placed next to.

Let us consider the Spanish painter Francisco Goya as an example of an artist who painted easel pictures in oil paint. Goya lived the greatest part of his life in Spain (although he did go to Italy as a young man and he died in France). He is often described as a Spanish artist *par excellence;* however, his national character and the great intensity of his work will not be of special concern in this discussion. Emphasis, instead, will be on describing his work as typical of a certain kind of artist working in a certain kind of material. Goya's technique of painting has not usually concerned his commentators. The reasons for this are several. First, his technique is largely *a la prima* application of paint, that is, direct painting with little under-painting and glazing. It offers little opportunity for the exposition of the stages or steps in the making of the painting. Second, Goya was not an experimenter in oil technique and only simplified the means that were common in his time. Third, and most significant, is the fact that his work lends itself to so many other kinds of criticism, social and political, psychological, and ideological; *how* Goya paints seems unimportant beside *what* he paints, and the sources of his art. But if, as an artist, you want to study oil painting in its simplest and most direct form there is no better "school" than a late Goya.

Consider, for example, the portrait from the Frick Collection of *Doña Maria Martínez de Puga* (Fig. 7–4). One's initial reaction to this painting is likely to be that its verbal equivalent is "frank." This may not say very much, but it does give some indication of the lady's direct gaze and solid stance and the simple, confident way the portrait is painted. The figure is cut off at the hips by the bottom of the painting; it is cut again by the two colors of the background between the shoulders and elbows. These divisions of the figure certainly do not add to the charm and beauty of the lady; they are only ways to show her to us. The lighter value of the upper background silhouettes the set of her shoulders and her dark, curly hair, and draws attention to her face. The darker value of the lower background minimizes her dark dress, and these two darks set off her hand, fan, and scarf. This is not a clever painting; we can tell what the different stuffs—gold, silk, lace—are, but Goya does not amaze the viewer with his skill in rendering different materials. Neither does he display his sitter in theatrical light as Rembrandt might have done nor in a shimmer of paint as in a Renoir portrait. Perhaps the only way to approach the technique of a painting like this one is to suggest what Goya has done by indicating what he has not. Goya's portraits are an excellent "school" for a painter because he does not seduce with his technique. With his boldness and simplicity he can teach us many of the possibilities of *a la prima* painting. Perhaps the most profound lesson in this painting is how much strong, sure drawing with the paint can mean to an artist and how, if the artist chooses, this drawing can produce a great painting without technical display. Goya is, perhaps, the first artist after 1500 to teach this lesson which has meant so much to twentieth-century painting.

It is sometimes argued that the technical means must change with the subject, and if this is taken to mean that all aspects of technique should change, it is clearly not true. But there is some truth in the argument, as two paintings can show us.

The best place to start is with the kind of light the artist uses to expose his subjects. In the portrait of Doña Maria there is no clearly defined source of light. The lady appears to be standing in the diffused daylight of her home or the artist's studio, and we are not given indications of either time or place. This is, of course, very fitting if the painting is to present a person's appearance apart from

GOYA. *The Third of May, 1808.*

(1746–1828; Spanish.)
Oil on canvas, 8′ 9″ × 11′ 4″.
The Prado, Madrid.

Pl. IVa.

KLEE. *Around the Fish.*

(1879–1940; Swiss.)
Oil on canvas, 18⅜″ × 25⅛″.
Collection, The Museum of Modern Art,
New York.
Mrs. John D. Rockefeller, Jr.

Pl. IVb.

GOYA. *Doña Maria Martínez de Puga.*

(1746–1828; Spanish.)
Oil on canvas, 31½″ × 23″.
Copyright The Frick Collection,
  New York.

Fig. 7–4.

the environment. The idea that an individual lives in a certain way and comes out of particular circumstances is not significant to Goya in this painting. This is not, however, always true of Goya's portraits. Consider, for example, the portrait of *Don Manuel Osorio* (Fig. 7–5) in which the things which represent his world become an important part of the theme of the painting.

The second painting, *The Third of May, 1808* (Pl. IVa) is a very precisely described event. It is dated "3 May, 1808," and the sky is dark. The patriots are flooded with light from a lamp and are making their last gestures and cries before they are executed. The "timeless" element is the firing squad. Their backs emphasize the repetitiousness of uniform and stance. They are the ubiquitous, anonymous executioners acting on orders. Each of the patriots is a clearly differentiated individual or at least a type. Each is described as a person by the way he behaves in an extreme situation much as an actor presents the character he is playing. In this painting we see one of the most dramatic events conceivable. But compare this with Masaccio's *Expulsion*. Masaccio can rely on the weight of religious tradition in his painting of the Adam and Eve story. Any person who is at all familiar with the biblical tradition will know what came before and what follows the incident painted. The painting is not independent of its place in a large tradition; if it were, certain things in it, the angel for instance, would appear nonsensical.

Goya cannot depend on a tradition to fill his painting with meaning. Unless we have studied the history of his time we know nothing of who the soldiers are or whom they are executing. The force of the painting must come from general feelings about killing and from the nature of the presentation. Many easel paintings are divorced from a constant situation not only by their portability but also by their subject. Goya's answer to this problem was to address his art in many cases to situations which are highly charged with emotion of extreme and general kinds—like war, death, senility, insanity, worship, and vanity. However, Goya's portraits are not for the most part representative of any of these or other emotions; yet they have a related power. Much of the strength of Goya's paintings rests on his technique, and we cannot afford to content ourselves with a study of his subject matter alone.

This point can be made very specifically with one of the so-called "dark paintings." These were painted by Goya for his own house outside Madrid and represent some of his most personal and interesting work. Look at *Two Old People Eating Soup* (Fig. 7–6). The subject is strange and the presentation of it is almost ghoulish. It is

THE ARTIST LOOKS AT ART

GOYA. *Don Manuel Osorio de Zuniga.*

(1746–1828; Spanish.)
Oil on canvas, 43⅜″ × 23″.
The Metropolitan Museum of Art, New York.
The Jules S. Bache Collection, 1949.

Fig. 7–5.

GOYA. *Two Old People Eating Soup.*

(1746–1828; Spanish.)
Oil mural transferred to canvas,
  20⅞″ × 33½″.
The Prado, Madrid.

Fig. 7–6.

kept from being a horror picture similar to many we can find in the nineteenth century by the simple fact that it is well done—the drawing and paint handling are masterful.

How the work is done is as important as what it is about. The two are so closely tied to each other that in many ways it is senseless to try to separate them. This is especially true if the subject of a painting is looked upon as a much larger thing than the title usually indicates. If what the painting is about is seen as including characteristics like the quality of paint and drawing, the kinds and relationships of color, the size and format of the painting, and the tradition and style of the painter, then it is clearly very difficult to separate the "how" from the "what."

THE ARTIST LOOKS AT ART

As has been indicated in Part I, "What the painting is about" is the theme of a painting, not merely the subject, and the techniques and forms are a part of that theme. If we allow ourselves to talk about the sharp angles or the heavy shapes we are not just thinking of an angle that is less than ninety degrees or a shape that is large in the painting. We imagine something of the heaviness of the shape if we were to lift it and the sharpness of the angle if we were to run into it. These experiences seem to be very much a part of what a painting is about.

Painting in Oil: Technical Considerations

Oil paint offers the greatest range of handling of any techniques. This is one of the reasons why it has very nearly dominated painting since the middle of the sixteenth century. Oil can be used for almost any kind of painting, but it has been used most in painting pictures which are portable and usually hung on walls. This is commonly referred to as easel painting. The scale of an easel painting is not clearly set, but generally it will be big enough to be seen from four or five feet and not too big to go through a door. These observations may sound trivial unless you realize that one of the most important characteristics of a painting is its scale in relation to human scale, and the size of the space which surrounds it. Museums frequently swallow up small paintings in the large space of a public building. This has led many artists to paint what they call museum paintings, that is, paintings which are too big for homes but which will fit the space of a museum. Goya's *The Third of May, 1808* (Pl. IVa) and Picasso's *Guernica* (Fig. 3–7) are both cases in point; they are not for private, domestic use. The artist who paints easel paintings in oils generally works in the following way: he applies his paint on a support of either canvas or wood, the surface of which has been prepared in such a way as to isolate the support from contact with the oil paint. The reason for this is that the oil in the paint would in time rot the wood or canvas. The isolating is finished with a ground which gives the artist a luminous surface to work on.

The colors are ground into a paste with the addition of oil—usually linseed oil—and can be applied directly in this form. The painter will often thin the paint with oil, varnish, turpentine, or a combination of these. The artist can use oil paint in many ways, and in his technique alone, we can find clues to the attitudes underlying his work and the factors which are constant in the "world" he constructs.

He can make the paint very thin and transparent and supply it as a wash which veils the ground with color while the ground gives luminosity to this color; he can use the thin, transparent paint as a glaze to alter the color slightly and to develop a sense of solid form. The artist can also keep the oil color opaque and apply it flatly and directly; or by not thinning it at all, he can build rich, thick, heavy textures. Most artists do not do just one of these things in a painting —they use the paint in widely different ways in making a single picture. The ways they choose and the sequence of their methods tell us something of the artist's attitude toward his work. It should, however, be emphasized that no single aspect of the work of art tells everything and that learning to understand a painting is a process of bringing to bear all the available information. The reader needs to remember that the work of art as a whole is much more than technique.

Consider again the *Two Old People Eating Soup,* especially the thickness of the paint and the way it is drawn into by the brush. The pull of the sticky paint as it was pushed around the socket of an eye, down a nose, around the bowl of the spoon or across the top of the blanket is a part of the meaning of the painting. The statement and how it is made are wrapped in, around, and through each other. In Goya's work, as in Masaccio's in a somewhat different way, the form and technique do more than indicate something of the meaning. They are a part of the meaning. Much of the excitement of looking at paintings is in the discovery of how each artist uses his materials, his feelings, and his ideas.

The variety of the painter's methods is revealed vividly if we turn now from Goya's paintings to those of Paul Klee, the Swiss artist. Much of Klee's work is in water-color, both transparent and opaque, and most of it is small in size. Both the technique and the size contribute to the differences in ways of going about painting.

The *Comedie* (Fig. 7–7) can show something of what we mean. This painting is only related to *Two Old People Eating Soup* insofar as both are concerned with aspects of what it means to be a human being. But what different sides of that condition! For Goya, in his painting, feelings about human life are shown as a part of senility, sickness, and hunger; for Klee in *Comedie* this state is summarized in the puppet-like movements of figures on a stage indicating how both in the theater and in social life we only play roles which are transparent and farcical. It would seem that both artists are telling us of things that must be faced, but they are very different things and must be faced for different reasons.

KLEE. *Comedie.*

(1879–1940; Swiss.)
Monotype and water-color on paper,
  12″ × 17⅞″.
*Reproduced by courtesy of the Trustees
  of the Tate Gallery, London.*

Fig. 7–7.

There is in Goya's painting a kind of fleshiness about the paint, a hint of the soft but resilient and sometimes sticky feel of a body. In Klee's painting there is none of this. His paintings rarely appeal to the sense of touch. The appeal lies more in the pictures we form in our minds of simple ideas. It is one of Klee's greatest concerns to show in the least terms and the simplest images, the things, people, and emotions about which we feel very strongly.

THE PAINTER'S MEANS   203

First, the technique is the simplest: just stains and lines on the surface, which is not to say that this is not very difficult to do well, but it is not complicated and does not *display* virtuosity. Second, the over-all shapes of the figures are simple and made up of variations on geometric shapes presented in a direct, uncomplicated way with little illusion of space. The shapes that make up the frieze of figures are broken up and decorated with straight lines, dots, dashes, and curliques and laid against a regularly modulated background of color and value.

The painting can be seen as a joke. It makes an ironic comment on the way of life it represents, and at the same time enjoys that human folly. The painting also points to the kinds of similarities which may occur to us. For instance, how some people when dressed up actually look like they are turning into a plant, a lamp, or a tower as the four figures on the right-hand side of the painting do. The segmented drawing contributes to this and leads to further notions of, as we have mentioned, puppets and dolls, and leads us to additional understanding, through pictorial metaphors, of how we look and how we live. It is wise to remark here, that although Klee's work seems, so often, to be about things that are within the range of language, it is hard to find words to reveal some of the meanings in it.

As we have noted above, the danger of talk *about* the painting is that we tend to lose its directness, its simplicity and richness of meaning.

Another painting by Klee carries this matter further. *Around the Fish* (Pl. IVb) is a still life in oil on canvas. It looks fairly easy; it is such a delightful picture. Klee is able to paint some of the beauty and some of the unpleasantness of seeing a fish on a table. He equates it with a flower put in water and with a cut cucumber. Much of what he sees he reduces to repeated geometric shapes, curves, circles, and straight lines. The simplicity of his conception again is striking. The colors like the shapes are simple and separated from each other. Everything is clearly defined, a characteristic, as has been pointed out earlier, of mental imagery.

The remark is often made that Klee's paintings are child-like, and this comment is almost as frequently denied. Consider this painting for a moment in the light of these comments. The simplicity, clear definition, and picturing of a thought is like the work of a child. This particular painting is also almost jewel-like; its clear bright colors glow on a dark ground. The fairly shallow space is also reminiscent of children's paintings, and the painting's freshness gives a feeling that both the viewer and the artist are seeing these things for the first time, a feeling akin to the naivete of a child.

It is, however, a mistake to assume that Klee's work is childish; that it is untutored, primitive, and unreflective. Klee's is an extremely reflective kind of painting. He is constantly forcing himself and the viewer to reconsider his thoughts and perceptions. In *Around the Fish* we are confronted with a group of still-life objects among which is a man's face with an arrow pointing at it, an exclamation mark, a sun and moon, and a cross. Two of the flowers in the foreground seem to be growing out of what should, in the everyday world, be a table. The relationships among the objects in this and in many of his paintings are humorous, and like many jokes, the humor can lead us to reflection on how we see the world. Through these qualities of simplicity and humor, Klee opens us to thought just as does the work of many children.

Turn now to another of Klee's paintings, *The Twittering Machine* (Fig. 7-8). The media are water-color and ink. The water-color is used as a stain to tone certain areas with slightly different colors; the ink is used for the line drawing of the four "twitters," their crank and stand, and the mottled dark spots around the machine. The drawing was probably done first by a technique, which Klee often used, of applying ink to a surface and then placing the paper on the inked surface. By drawing on the back of the paper he picked up the ink in those places he wanted it. The mottled areas are caused by the paper's contact with the inky surface. After this the water-color was applied to the dampened paper, or the water was put on the paper after the paint. In either case we can see how the paint was made to run and blend on the surface.

The small size of the painting, although not the *cause* of this play of technique, makes this way of working possible without a great deal of preparation. The painting can be easily handled, while its small size gives both the artist and the viewer a sense of ease and intimacy with it.

The Technique of Water-Color

The term *water-color* covers a number of different materials that share the quality of being soluble in water. The most common difference among the various water-color paints lies in the material that binds the pigment to the painting surface. In some, animal glues are used; in others, vegetable substances, while in some newer materials the binder is a plastic. With the exception of the latter,

KLEE. *The Twittering Machine.*

(1879–1940; Swiss.)
Water-color and ink, 16¼″ × 12″.
Collection, The Museum of Modern Art,
  New York.
Purchase Fund.

Fig. 7–8.

it is difficult to build a thick, textured paint surface in water-color, so most artists rely on thin paint and the washes and staining to which watery paint lends itself.

Until recently water-colors were small in scale and were used most often for the illustration of books or as an extension of drawing. In the second case the water-color is simply used to tint and accent the drawing. When painting is used for illustration it of necessity becomes subservient to the text, and this role irritates modern sensibility, but the literary nature of many water-color paintings is hard to ignore. Klee's work, as we have seen, has a very strong literary quality though it does not specifically illustrate a text.

Water-colors are usually close to the size of a book page. As such they should be held and looked at, rather than hung on the wall to be seen from a distance. One of the disadvantages of museums is that there we can rarely hold the painting to achieve the kind of relationship with a small painting which seems so natural for it. (This is possible, however, in the print and drawing rooms in many museums.) The small painting, like prints and drawings, and unlike fresco and large easel paintings, clearly has this characteristic: it lends itself to a very comfortable and intimate appreciation. Instead of being a part of a building or a painting on an impersonal wall, it is a thing to be taken out and looked at like a book and put out of sight until it is used again.

Considerations of Technique as Related to Aesthetic Character

We will turn now to a series of individual works in order to see in a variety of uses of a single medium or of mixed media some of the range of possibilities in easel painting.

Picasso's *Weeping Woman* (Fig. 3–6) impresses the viewer most by the directness and the heaviness of the painting. The drawing is bold, dark, and muscular. The color is flat and bright. There is almost no modulation of the color within an area and it is usually painted within the limits of strong black outlines. The whole seems to be a denial of the gentleness and grace of the painting of half a century earlier, of Impressionism. Compare it for instance with Monet's *View of Amsterdam* (Pl. IIb). How Picasso's technique matches the subject of his painting! How well it shows the bold, harsh distortion of grief, the brutalizing effect of tears.

Compare it to the portrait of Giovanni Arnolfini and his wife by Jan Van Eyck (Fig. 7–9). What differences come first to your mind? The immediacy, speed, and violence of Picasso contrast sharply with the distance and patience of Van Eyck. The Arnolfini double portrait is painted on a panel in oil and tempera. The figures are placed in an illusion of space which is shown by the illusion of light. The term *illusion* is not used here to suggest that Van Eyck is trying to fool us, but to draw attention to the fact that Picasso uses neither light nor space to create an illusion. Picasso's painting, as has been pointed out, has less to do with our visual and tactile perception of the world outside ourselves than it has to do with our physical awareness of our own bodies.

Van Eyck is very much concerned with his sense of touch and vision. Each thing represented, even though it has a meaning other than a formal or phenomenal one, is represented with the greatest care for how it looks and feels. The painter uses his brush and paint to differentiate the kinds of qualities of the materials and objects in the space and the light in the room.

If we contrast the Van Eyck and the Picasso with Rembrandt's *Portrait of Himself* (Fig. 7–10) another group of differences and similarities comes forward. The quality of the paint in the Rembrandt is thick, often thicker than that in the Picasso, but it is handled in a different way. The paint is built up over a period of time; the brush moved much more slowly in Rembrandt's hand than it did in Picasso's. Rembrandt, like Van Eyck, is interested in how forms look in light, but he is much less interested in the sense of touch, and his kind of light, the light that he describes in painting, is not the kind that Van Eyck paints. The way in which Rembrandt paints the clothes he dressed himself in indicates less how they would feel to the touch than how they look when light catches clothing made of different fabrics and cut and sewn in different ways. Consider the full sleeves and folds around his wrist, the puckered cloth around his chest, and the twisted rope of fabric around his waist. In each we can see the thickness and the body of the paint, in each it is handled in a way that suits the look of the kind and condition of the cloth. Around the wrist, the paint was pulled in easy curves; across the chest there is a flick of paint above the pucker and pulling straight down below; but the pull in neither of these places is as great as in the sash. In each case the gesture or stroke of the brush imitates the movement of the cloth.

Van Eyck shows us the way materials move, but not through the way his brush moves. While Van Eyck describes how material looks, Rembrandt duplicates its gestures with his own.

Van Eyck. *The Arnolfini Double
   Portrait.*

(fl. 1422–1441; Flemish.)
Oil and tempera on oak, 31⅞″ × 23¼″.
*Reproduced by courtesy of the Trustees,
   The National Gallery, London.*

Fig. 7–9.

REMBRANDT. *Portrait of Himself.*

(1606–1669; Dutch.)
Oil on canvas, 51⅛″ × 40¼″.

Copyright The Frick Collection,
  New York.

Fig. 7–10.

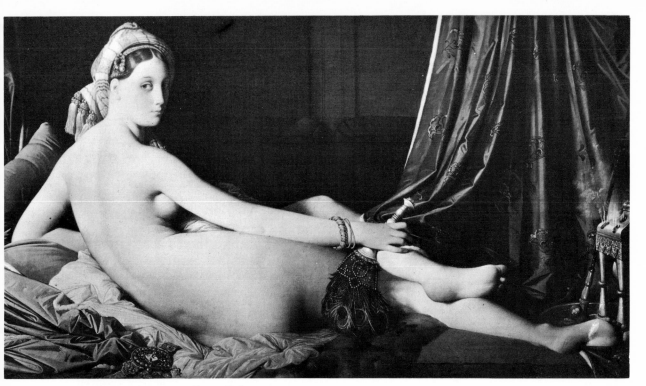

INGRES. *La Grande Odalisque.*

(1780–1867; French.)
Oil on canvas.
The Louvre, Paris.

Fig. 7–11.

More closely related to Van Eyck than Rembrandt's *Portrait* or Picasso's *Weeping Woman* is *La Grande Odalisque* by Ingres (Fig. 7–11). The *Odalisque* is like the double portrait in two particularly apparent ways: first is the smooth, enamel-like surface of both. The artist in each case seems to have eliminated as far as he could any brush marks or indication of what happened before the painting was finished. Neither artist allows us to glimpse the work and time that went into the painting. We can only see the product of his work and not its progress. Second is the emphasis on line in the paintings. The forms within the painting are clearly distinguished from each other by the precise, fine line. It is almost always possible to know where the edge of each part is and where the next part begins. Another look at the Rembrandt makes this clear. Try, in his *Portrait of Himself,* to trace around the hat at *exactly* where it ends and the background begins. Then try to do this with the Ingres, the Van Eyck, and the Picasso. In the last, doesn't the question of the inside or the outside of the line come up? Why didn't that question arise with Van Eyck or Ingres? Is it only that the line is too thin?

It is interesting that there are two versions of this *Odalisque* by Ingres. One is in the Metropolitan Museum in New York and another, the painting reproduced here, in The Louvre in Paris. They are very much alike except that the one in New York is in *grisaille*, that is, it is painted in different values of a blue-gray, while the one in Paris is painted in a range of colors. This indicates something of Ingres' concern with line and form as they can be seen apart from differences in hue of the things he paints. To Ingres, draughtsmanship was the essence of painting. He is quoted as saying, "To draw is not simply to reproduce outlines; drawing does not consist merely of making strokes; drawing is as well the expression, the inner structure, the ground work, the form. . . . If I had to put a sign above my door, I would write *School of Drawing* and I am sure I would turn out painters."

An artist who, like Rembrandt but very unlike Ingres, *is* concerned with the sticky quality of paint is the American painter Willem de Kooning. In his *Woman, I* (Fig. 7–12) we can find many of the concerns we have been considering. Perhaps the only interest he has eliminated is the representation of things as they are seen and touched. There certainly are in this painting the passion and distortion we saw in Picasso, and the gesture of the hand as it lays on the paint, which we saw in Rembrandt; but here it does not refer to the movement of fabric or flesh. Finally, there is a strong use of drawing which, however, never quite encloses the form as it did in the Picasso, the Ingres, and the Van Eyck.

The aspect of de Kooning's painting that needs particular emphasis is the gesture of the hand applying the paint. This is by no means his only concern, nor is he the first artist to show the viewer something of the act and tools of painting. It is possible to find this in the work of many painters, but in de Kooning's work one is especially aware of it. You can almost feel the twist in your wrist as you look at the large hooked strokes around the breasts; and you feel it in your shoulder when you see the broad brush stroke down the side of the painting. The brushes used are big ones; we are aware of the different sizes used. Note, for instance, the drawing around the eye and the stroke across the lap. The paint in all cases is a thick, sticky stuff made of bright pigments ground in oil. The act of painting is full of movement and involves materials to paint with and on. De Kooning makes us very much aware of this.

THE ARTIST LOOKS AT ART

DE KOONING. *Woman, I.*

(1904–   ; Dutch-born American.)
Oil on canvas, 75″ × 58″.

Collection, The Museum of Modern Art,
  New York.

Fig. 7–12.

Throughout this chapter the intention has been to make the reader aware of a number of different kinds of experiences of which the working artist is aware. Much of his awareness is of the medium he is using and the way or ways he finds to use it. We should not take a narrow view of technique and think of it only as the particular material the painter paints with: oil, fresco, water-color, or some other medium. There are other physical considerations like size and situation; there are the choices of how much the artist will show of the process of making the painting, what qualities he will emphasize in both the material from which he draws and the material with which he works. The artist will often not know what he is doing until he has finished. He will feel his way through his experiences, both in the painting and outside it, searching for whatever he may find. A person looking at a painting must often work in the same way, feeling his way along, referring now to the painting and now to memory, and now to a hope or "hunch." Learning rules about how a painter works will not lead to understanding; allowing yourself to learn from a painting will.

Suggestions for Further Reading

CONSTABLE, W. G. *The Painter's Workshop.* New York: Oxford University Press, 1954.
　　An interesting picture of methods and procedures at various times in the history of art.

DOERNER, MAX. *The Materials of the Artist and Their Use in Painting.* New York: Harcourt, Brace & World, Inc., 1949.
　　Useful in a study of the materials used by various artists.

GOLDWATER, R., and TREVES, MARIO, Ed. and Trans. *Artists on Art, from the XIV to the XX Century.* New York: Pantheon Books, Inc., 1945.
　　A valuable anthology of statements by artists about art.

HOLT, ELIZABETH GILMORE, Ed. *A Documentary History of Art,* 2 vols. Garden City, N. Y.: Doubleday and Co., 1957. (A Doubleday Anchor Book.)
　　A selected anthology of the literature of art history.

MAYER, R. *Handbook of Materials and Techniques.* New York: Viking Press, 1957.
　　Useful in connection with the individual palettes of various painters.

POPE, A. *Introduction to the Language of Drawing and Painting.* Cambridge, Mass.: Harvard University Press, 1929.
　　One of the best and clearest statements of a theory of color. It has been described as "Art explained to a scientific age."

THOMPSON, D. V. *The Materials and Techniques of Medieval Painting.* New York: Dover Press, 1956.
　　Of particular interest for the author's discussion of the sources of the medieval painter's colors, and for the character of his technical procedures.

8. Moore's Two-Piece Reclining Figure

A Recurrent Theme in the Work of Henry Moore

Many artists in a lifetime of work return again and again to a theme or to a cluster of themes related to a certain subject. It has been suggested that this is a part of the nature of artistic activity: that individual artists and even whole civilizations have only a few notions and these notions simply occur over and over in different forms. An artist like Vermeer, who devoted most of his known work to the subject of an interior of a room and the theme of the beauty of ordered security; or a civilization like the Hellenic, which so often used the subject of the nude male to embody an idea of human excellence—these are but two examples of this thematic recurrence. Whether this is the case for all art is questionable, but for certain individuals this pattern of recurrence is clearly evident; Henry Moore is one of these artists.

Moore's work can be seen as turning around several subjects— reclining figures, abstract forms, seated figures, and heads. He has made a large number of pieces of sculpture in which there are often recognizable representations of parts of the human body. It is one of these reclining figures (Fig. 8–1), a later example of this subject in Moore's work, that will be central to the discussion in this chapter.

MOORE. *Two-Piece Reclining*
Figure No. II.

(1898–   ; English.)
Bronze, H. 50″, L. 99⅛″.

Collection, The Museum of Modern Art,
New York.
Given in memory of G. David Thompson, Jr.,
by his father.

Fig. 8–1.

The posture of Moore's figures has two constant characteristics: the head is set erect on the shoulders, while the upper torso rests on one or both elbows. Sometimes the figures rest on the small of the back with knees up and feet close to the buttocks; at other times they lie on one hip with bent knees. (See Fig. 8–2.)

The representation of a human being lying down with the upper torso supported on one or both elbows has appeared fairly often in art. Examples which can be seen in this book are the *Dionysos* from the Parthenon (Fig. 8–3), Michelangelo's *Adam* (Fig. 8–4) and his *Night* (Fig. 9–7), and Ingres' painting of the *Odalisque* (Fig. 7–11). As these examples indicate, the purposes for which this posture has been employed are varied. The position has been used, among other things, to embody a feeling of repose and sensuality, a sense of weight and oppression, an idea of solid stability; or to represent a

MOORE. *Recumbent Figure.*

(1898–   ; English.)
Hornton stone, H. 35″, L. 50″.
*Reproduced by courtesy of the Trustees
  of the Tate Gallery, London.*

Fig. 8–2.

fall due to a wound or death. Through all of these themes there is the common thread of the pull of gravity on the weight of a body which is off its feet. In different contexts the posture denotes the various attitudes we can have toward ourselves and others in a horizontal position. Michelangelo's sculpture seems to represent the weight and oppressiveness which can be associated with a reclining figure, and Ingres' painting, the sensuality and indolence.

Moore has stated that for his early work he found little in the Greek tradition which could stimulate him. He has, in fact, said that his interest in the reclining figure was awakened by a Mayan lime-

Dionysos.
East pediment of the Parthenon.
Marble, L. 5' 8".
Courtesy of the Trustees, The British Museum, London.
Hirmer Verlag, Munich.

Fig. 8–3.

MICHELANGELO. *Creation of Adam.*

(1475–1564; Italian.)
Fresco, ceiling of Sistine Chapel,
   The Vatican, Rome.
Photo: Alinari-Art Reference Bureau.

Fig. 8–4.

stone sculpture of a rain god (Fig. 8–5). In this piece he found more than just the posture; he also found a use of materials which appealed deeply to him. The closeness of the Mayan figure to the shape of the block from which it was carved and the stone-like look of the forms seemed to Moore to show a kind of honesty, a "truth to materials," that was lacking in much Western art. (He did believe that some European art, like Romanesque and early Gothic, had these qualities of honesty and truth to materials. It is doubtful that it is the truthfulness of the way the artist worked that produced this sense of honesty; it seems more likely that it was the common association with probity of simple shapes, directness of gaze, and relative symmetry.) Moore was able to find in this piece a point of departure and the rationale he needed to work. Given this direction the

Chac-Mool, the Rain Spirit.

Mayan.
Limestone, L. 58½".
Museo Nacional de Antropologia, Mexico.

Fig. 8–5.

artist and his sculpture were able to go ahead gradually, to develop and to discard in the course of development many of the initial justifications for working in a particular way.

The Sculptor's Craft

A sculptor like Moore is deeply concerned with the craft of sculpture—the physical construction of the sculptured object and the various skills that go into making sculpture. Artists of all kinds are involved with the techniques and principles that lie behind and insure a durable work of art, but there are some who are only interested in putting down what they think or feel, and see technique only as a vehicle for this expression. Although an artist like Moore puts the expressive content at the center of his work, the sculptor's craft has more than a subservient role to play in his work. The technique and how it is manifested in the finished work is a part of what is expressed. The artist shows the viewer something of the process by which the final result was obtained. This working-through of a piece is an essential part of the finished object.

The different surfaces which can be noted on the two reclining figures (Figs. 8–1, 8–2) and the expressive associations which these different textures have are part of this complex of meaning and craft. The smooth finish on the stone of the earlier piece required different tools and different gestures to produce than the scraping and rasping which gave the rough skin to the later bronze.

Moore has always worked as both a carver in stone and wood and a modeler in plaster and clay. He is equally at home in building up his pieces and in carving them out of a block of material. In this range of technical resource he is unlike many contemporary artists, who although they may know different techniques, are only at ease with certain materials. Because of this ability to make his sculpture in a number of different ways, Moore has been able to expand the motifs he is attracted to in both form and material.

The Relation of Theme to the Sculptor's Experience

Before an artist finds any motif which appeals to him he will often have had experiences which are related to the motif in a number of ways. The experience of the position and posture of the body is one of the most obvious forms of an occurrence which is not necessarily artistic but which all of us share, and which has been a steady source of motifs in art. Many other ways of being related to a motif are possible, and a number of these have been suggested in Part I of this book. As far as the posture of the reclining figure is concerned, we have all lain or seen others lying on beds and in bathtubs, on beaches and on lawns. We have braced ourselves up on our elbows and felt the push against our shoulders and necks. These may not be clearly remembered, and it is important to realize that they need not be; these experiences are a part of our lives. Moore, in this piece (Fig. 8–1), characterizes the sense of the undramatic recurrence of the posture. It is more like rising from sleep than fall-

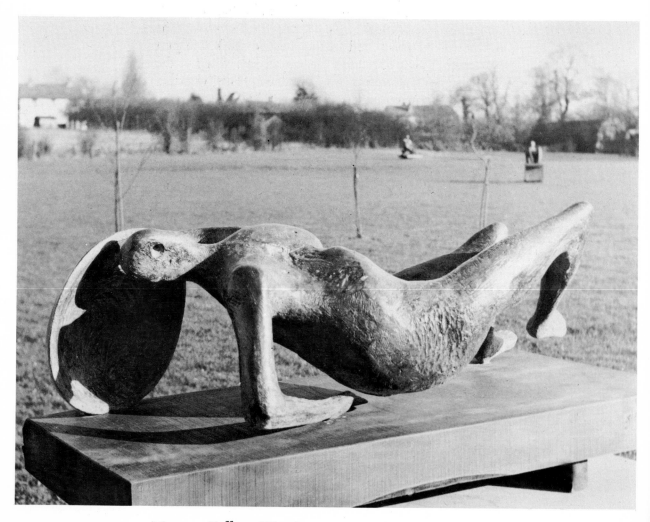

Moore. *Falling Warrior.*

(1898–   ; English.)
Bronze, L. 58″.
Walker Art Gallery, Liverpool.

Fig. 8–6.

ing from a wound. He has in other sculpture, like his falling warriors, depicted the more active, theatrical side of the reclining human body.

If we contrast one of these falling warriors (Fig. 8–6) with the reclining figures, the themes of both may be put into higher relief. The fallen figure is off balance; he is hitting the ground, not lying on it. There is no sense of repose and inaction. There is a dramatic action and that is of failure and injury. The center of the thematic difference is, then, the difference between lying down and falling down. Moore seems also to indicate that this is a difference between men and women. The reclining figures, when they have a recognizable sex, are all women; the fallen figures are men. Woman, for Moore, is passive, secure, and reliable; man is active, violent, and liable to be hurt. It can be noted that Moore's fallen figures do not occur until the 1950's when the artist expanded or developed new aspects of much of his work, and was able to find in the forms of classical Greek sculpture a meaningful point of departure (Fig. 8–7).

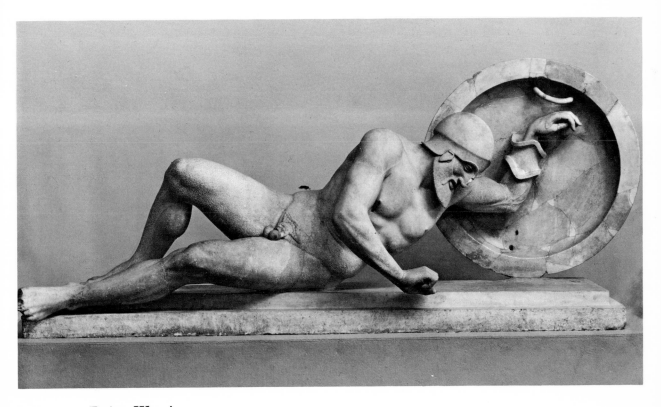

Dying Warrior.
East pediment of the Temple at Aegina.
(c. 490 B. C.)
Marble, L. 72⅞″.
Glyptothek, Munich.

Fig. 8–7.

We also have many experiences of shapes disposed in space. People and things are always in a spatial relationship to each other, and exploring these relationships is an early activity of human life. The knowledge of the space around us and of the things which break it up—or break into it—is needed for life just as the knowledge of our posture is necessary. We experience space and shapes largely through sight and touch, and posture largely from our proprioceptive sensations. This is all part of our basic human store of knowledge, important to all of us, though, in most, relegated to the area of automatic response. We need not *think* in order to turn aside from a large object directly before us in space. But the artist in his related forms activates the relationships; he brings into conscious, aesthetic awareness relationships that are basic and vital to human life.

The shapes in Moore's sculpture frequently bear a strong similarity to some natural formations. This is not surprising since he has spoken so often of his interest in material and in the ways that the forces of nature give forms to things. Weathered rocks and driftwood immediately come to mind, and larger formations like mountains and river beds also seem relevant. He is highly selective; there are not, for instance, any crystalline forms in his work, and his selection leans toward the smoother, more flowing, closed shapes. The lighter, more open forms in nature and space, like clusters of leaves and twigs or feathery clouds, are also absent from Moore's work. He relies almost completely on the natural formations which lie close to the earth or those, like the trunk and lower branches of a tree, which rise from the ground thickly, with a muscular look about them. A sense of solidity and stability is common to such natural formations; it is this quality that Moore relies on together with the feeling of timelessness which is common to these natural forms and to his work.

What concerns us here is not that this sculptor's work is not encyclopedic; every artist selects from his sources whatever they may be —nature, social life, his own personality, and so on. Our concern is, rather, to discover what is chosen and what is discarded of the possible forms and the feelings and associations common to those he uses. There will never be absolute concurrence among individuals in these affective attitudes, but it is possible to agree roughly on what kind of experience the work appeals to, and it is even more possible to agree on the kinds of experience which are *not* called up by the work of art. There comes to mind no instance in Moore's work which could be called wild and frenetic or light and gay; in most instances it is serious, monumental, heavy, and stable. By ascribing these latter qualities and not the former, the associations with timelessness and security are derived.

The *Two-Piece Reclining Figure No. II*

The bronze *Two-Piece Reclining Figure No. II* (Fig. 8–1) is an example of Moore's later work (1960) in which human posture and rock-like forms are given an almost equal place in the sculpture. The work is in two sections: the head, arms, and upper torso form one part; and the legs and hips, the other. The anatomy of the figure is only suggested, roughed in, but the implication of its hidden structure is unmistakable. The head is a short column rising from the top of the left-hand block, and the lower legs are represented by a break in the bottom of the block to the right and an indication of knees at the top of this block.

The two pieces of this figure look like large chunks of weathered and carved stone, but the stones have been carefully placed in relation to each other like those in a Japanese garden, or, as the artist has said, in natural formations like the cliff at Étretat, shown here in a painting by Monet (Fig. 8–8). The use of separate but combined shapes also suggests the bringing together of two human beings in a spatial and psychological connection. Moore seems to suggest that any body, whether it be organic or inorganic, is related to others as parts of the human body are related to each other. We are not made to feel a sense of dismemberment, that a human being has been pulled apart. Rather, because of the solidity and the evocation of security this piece has and gives, there is instead a sense of the strong ties between separated entities. These characteristics of the piece exemplify the artist's interest in nature's ways of shaping materials, and in suggesting what is necessary to life. He uses the human body and its parts as a model.

The *Two-Piece Reclining Figure No. II* is a bronze cast. It was probably worked out initially in plaster. The metallic look of the bronze is not emphasized; the piece is not polished to be bright and smooth. Moore has gone beyond his earlier need to be "true" to materials. He seems to have felt that it is more significant to be true to the shapes and textures that he responds to as he works than to follow any notion of how the material "should" look. This has been very much his practice throughout his work even when he has believed otherwise.

MONET. *The Cliff at Étretat.*

(1840–1926; French.)
Oil on canvas, 25¾″ × 32″.

*The Metropolitan Museum of Art,
   New York.*
*Bequest of William Church Osborn,
   1951.*

Fig. 8–8.

The *Recumbent Figure*

The *Recumbent Figure* (Fig. 8–2) dating from 1938 was carved in stone in smooth forms. It is a single piece, but the formal relationship between the head and shoulders and the legs is similar to that of the two-piece figure. The stone is smoothed and shows its grain like the figures in wood which are contemporary with it. It is striking that the various sculptures of a given time in Moore's life are quite similar even though there is a difference in material. It would appear that it is much more his own reactions and needs that affect the form and finish of the sculpture than it is the demands of the material with which he is working. The subjective demands of the sculptor's personality usually overrule any objective demands of material, and he has always had a confident command of a variety of materials through which to work out ideas.

Moore's Use of Texture

During the war Moore did a series of drawings in the air raid shelters of London. These drawings seem to have been the starting point for an interest in more naturalistic representation and more roughly textured forms which appeared in some of his sculpture after the war. In these drawings he uses an interesting technique involving chalk, pen and ink, and water-color wash. They are sketched in with pen and ink, and chalk; then the whole drawing is washed over with water-color which does not adhere to the chalky areas except in small spots. In the *Pink and Green Sleepers* (Fig. 8–9) the light chalk gives the drawing a strong relief; it highlights and wraps around the shapes of the bodies and blankets. It is the appearance in Moore's work of rough texture and the realization of this texture in draped material which concerns us here. These characteristics are also present in the *Two-Piece Reclining Figure,* but in a different relationship to representation. In the drawing the turn and texture of the form are shown through the representation of light as it is reflected from various kinds of surfaces. Light cannot be the subject of sculpture to the same degree as in painting since sculpture does not deal with the same kind of illusion, that is, the depiction of three-dimensional objects on a two-dimensional plane. A piece of sculpture can represent a three-dimensional object, but the sculpture depends, just as the object does, on lighting to show its form and texture.

Moore. *Pink and Green Sleepers.*
(1898–   ; English.)
Chalk, pen, and water-color, 16″ × 22″.
*Reproduced by courtesy of the Trustees
of the Tate Gallery, London.*
Fig. 8–9.

Moore uses the texture of the bronze to remind us of similar textures found in other places: the repeated folds of cloth when it is draped around a body, the rough marks of the scraping of clay or stone when it is exposed to weather. In this figure the texture of the bronze calls up all of these textured forms and relates the experiences of them to each other. This is to a large extent due to the fact that the piece looks like both a human figure and two rocks, while it is also clearly a bronze cast of a modeled material.

THE ARTIST LOOKS AT ART

The rough texture of the *Two-Piece Reclining Figure* causes the light reflected from the sculpture to be broken by many small, shadowed indentations. This gives the piece an active surface unlike the earlier figure (Fig. 8–2) on which the light seems to flow easily over the smooth forms. The roughness and the activity of the skin of the two-piece sculpture give it a harsher look, because the form beneath the surface is heavy and massive. A sculpture on which the reflected light is broken up has a lightness, and a sense of movement and instability, as it has in much of the sculpture of Giacometti (Fig. 9–8). This is not the case with Moore's work. His forms always hold too closely to the ground, or seem to be rooted in it; they never give a sense that they might turn and disappear.

The impulse to touch and to stroke the later sculpture is much less strong than with the earlier piece which seems to encourage this tactile response. This is one of the sources of the feeling that much of Moore's sculpture has become less intimate; the viewer can no longer feel close to it. This is not, however, true of all his most recent sculpture, and the development has gone on slowly since the war. For example, *Interior–Exterior* of 1951 (Fig. 2–1), as far as the qualities discussed here are concerned, is much closer to the earlier reclining figure. *Interior–Exterior* suggests another source of this feeling in the way the forms are handled. In the two-piece figure note the squareness of the knees and the post-like head, and compare them with the rounded and egg-like forms of both the *Recumbent Figure* and the standing sculpture. In the first there is an abruptness and harshness which is not present in the other two.

Conclusion

Moore's work has always had the monumental quality of appearing larger and heavier than it actually is. In the sculpture of the late 1950's and early 1960's distance and a sense of overbearing are also present. Intimacy has given away to authority, grace to vigor.

This is not to say that there are two very different Moores. There are in these two reclining figures more similarities and continuity than there are differences. The artist has changed in some ways, but he is still working within much the same field of subject and theme in which he started. In the *Two-Piece Reclining Figure* he has developed other aspects of the subject and its thematic core, the stability and weightiness of this posture. But the subject, and what are for Moore the essentials of the theme of the figure resting on its elbows, are present in the different versions.

This two-piece figure is one of the most mature and successful works by Henry Moore. He is able to pull together in it many of the interests he has had over more than thirty years of sculpture. This quality of maturity is one that is found in an artist's work at that point in his life when he is able to integrate all that he knows about his feelings and attitudes, and the materials he uses to realize them. Moore has spent most of his life discovering and developing a way of working which is both personal and traditional; but the tradition is neither contemporary nor derived from one particular time or place. He has found his tradition in the works of many different cultures and has given this tradition a unity by the force of his own personality. In the past, the unity of an artist's forms has been largely the result of the tradition within which he works. In the present century when the form that the tradition is taking is unclear, the individual has had to use his own individuality as the vehicle of development. Moore has been able to give his sculpture a unity deriving from his own personal attitudes, feelings, and abilities, and yet his work has never been limited in scope. He has neither resorted to the repetition of a manner nor lost a sense of continuity—two of the weaknesses which have hurt the work of many twentieth-century artists. Moore's success in continuing to develop as an artist, and as the individual of which the artist is a part, is one of his greatest achievements.

Suggestions for Further Reading

GROHMANN, WILL. *The Art of Henry Moore.* London: Thames and Hudson, 1960.

MOORE, HENRY, in collaboration with GEORGE RAINBIRD. *Heads, Figures, and Ideas.* London: George Rainbird, Ltd., 1938.

READ, SIR HERBERT. *Henry Moore, Sculpture and Drawings.* London: Lund Humphreys and Co., Ltd., 1949.

READ, SIR HERBERT. *The Art of Sculpture.* New York: Pantheon Books, 1956. (Bollingen Series XXXV.)

9. The Sculptor's Means

Sculpture Asks Special Things of Us

I<small>F</small> a painting is like a wall or a page, sculpture is like a chair or a piece of silverware. It frequently seems to ask to be held or climbed upon. Hence we are made very much aware of its size, its feel, and its weight. The sculptor who has worked on a given piece is even more vividly aware of these things since he has given this object its form and in the process has touched or carried it very often. He has also moved around it and seen how it looks in different kinds of light and different kinds of space. We all know what happens when we move the furniture about in a room; the furniture looks different and the room looks different. Both are in a very real way different because we have changed the space from which both take a part of their character.

Sculpture in a similar way is affected by and affects the space around it. It is also affected by the light which exposes its form, and at least in one way, it affects the light by attracting our attention to the quality of light as it falls on the piece. Many people seem to realize fully the special quality of light in Greece only when they first see the bright sunlight falling on Greek sculpture and architecture. But these remarks are for the most part only relevant to sculpture which is fairly large, say half the size of a human being. What about small sculpture? What has been said about light is still true although it is of less importance. The quality which seems more important in most small sculpture is the way it has of asking to be held and touched.

231

The gratification which can come from holding things is one which often is too much ignored. How little we speak of how good a well-made, well-balanced tool feels in the hand, entirely apart from its practical use; or the texture of a wooden spoon, or the weight and sound of a good glass, or the form of a weathered stone. Think of feeling around in a pocket or a purse without looking for anything there, or of touching your own wrist or hand. These experiences are close to some of those of the sculptor both in the act of doing his work and in the appeals to experience which he embodies in his work.

The quality of tactility does not hold for all small pieces, especially for gold and inlaid work. These have more the qualities of a jewel or flower, and appeal to us in a similar way. This is the lure of the thing that glitters, that seems to be all radiance, color, and light. Many works of this kind of artistry make us not want to touch them for fear we will crush them like a flower, or because we do not want to cover their radiance with our hands.

Sculpture can give us intensified experience and awareness of space, of reflected light, and of various kinds of touching and holding. In these latter two experiences especially, the material of which, or from which, the piece is made has a large part to play. Whether the surface is shiny and smooth, as metal and glazed pieces, or dull and comparatively rough in texture as many wood and stone pieces, will affect the way in which the sculpture reflects light, and the way it feels to the touch. It should also be noted that the smoothness of a glazed terra cotta feels very different under the hand from the surface of polished wood, while the different ways in which light is reflected from various kinds of stone and from bronze and other metals are also very noticeable. It is in this area of experience that more and more subtle differences occur, for instance, in bronze casts from different foundries. These qualities are hard to find unless one is looking at the actual work. The sculptor usually spends much more time choosing the right piece of stone or the right foundry for the kind of work he is doing than he does in deciding whether the work will be in stone, wood, bronze, or some other material. It is in these concrete and particular distinctions and the attention and awareness that go with them that the individual must explore for himself. One way is to confront directly the work of art and to see its own specific qualities in its own specific context. This is especially important with sculpture which is permanently fixed to a building or other position where its maker intended it to be seen, because the kind of light, the relation of the position of the piece to the spectator, and whatever is close to the sculpture all are integral parts of it and inform its meaning.

The Sculptor's Materials and Methods of Working Them

Stone and wood are the two most frequently used materials of the sculptor who carves, or takes away from a larger shape to form his piece. He will use various kinds of tools to chip or cut or rasp down the block of wood or stone to the shape he wants. Many sculptors who work in this way say that much of the form of the finished piece is suggested to them by the material itself as they work on it. This is a useful and interesting remark if we do not take it to mean that the material tells them everything. There are other factors like the artist's own personality or the art of his time, which affect the finished form of the work more than does the material in which it is executed. But if we consider that these things are not so much up to him as is the specific handling of a particular piece of material at a particular time, we can understand something of what is meant. Making a piece of sculpture consists among other things of a series of reflections and decisions which add up to the finished work. While he is carving, the sculptor takes, or at least considers, the suggestions given him by the things which surround and interest him. Prominent in his attention is the material he is working on, and from it he picks up many clues as to the form the piece will take. He also learns from his use of materials which clues he as an individual can use and which he cannot.

Some of the qualities shared by wood and stone are grain, hardness, and color. We tend to be much more aware of the grain in wood since it is so apparent and is one of the ways we most easily distinguish between one kind of wood and another. We have a strong tradition of admiring the swirls of growth of the grain. The pattern is never identical from one part of the wood to the next, and it seems almost alive at times. Within the great variety and vitality of the wood, there is a unity given by the repetitions of seasonal growth. Light seems to go beneath the surface, making the wood glow and giving the color luster and radiance. If the wood is not polished or carved smooth it records the movements of the artist and his tools as he works the surface of the block. These marks tell us something about the way the artist works and about the hardness and texture of the wood, and suggest ways in which it can be handled.

These remarks are equally applicable to stone and to the stone carver. We can often sense how hard or soft a piece of stone is by the marks left on it by the sculptor's tools; we can see how one kind of stone flakes off when it is worked in a certain way. It should not be concluded from this that it is the only possible way this stone can be handled. Given one artist and his particular dispositions and desires, a single work merely shows the form they took in this particular material.

The density and grain of the stone have an important part to play in the reflection of light from and, often, through it. Leaving aside any discussion of how rocks are formed, we see readily that some are grained like wood with veins and layers of different color, form, and texture; others are honey-combed and have no linear pattern; in others it seems impossible to see any differentiation in the surface. These compositions pick up light in different ways and the light seems to penetrate the surface to different depths and to be reflected from inside the stone in different ways.

While the kind of material to be carved has a strong effect on the resulting sculpture, there is an even more influential factor involved when one turns from the carving of wood or stone to the modeling of clay which is to be cast in bronze or plaster. The carver *takes away from a block* while the modeler *builds up the work out of his material.* The kind of planning, the kind of activity, and the kind of experience are very different in these two ways of working. Of course the sculptor who builds his work up often carves it down in the end to give it the form he wants; and the carver will sometimes add on pieces to his work, but this is not the way the work is usually begun nor the greater part of it executed. One might say that, in a rough way, one sculptor finds his piece in the block and the other constructs it in empty space.

The most common materials of the artist who builds up his sculpture are clay, plaster, and wax. Clay, or rather clays, are kinds of earth which have the characteristics of adhering together, of being plastic when wet, and of becoming very hard when subjected to high temperatures. The qualities which are relied upon by the sculptor, whether he is going to fire his clay or not, are those of plasticity and adhesiveness. The first is important because it allows him to work easily and swiftly; the second, because it keeps the clay together and on the armature, the system of supports which hold the clay up. Support is not always used, especially if the clay is to be fired, but to use an armature is common practice for most sculptors who are working on large pieces.

The ability of clay to be fired is one that we are most familiar with in relation to pottery. Also from pottery we are aware of the ability of clay to take a glaze, a glass-like finish which can be in any of a number of different colors. Much small sculpture is made in this way. Think of the knick-knack figures in many homes. They may be of doubtful quality, but they are often made of glazed, baked clay or, as this material is sometimes called, terra cotta. The T'ang pottery tomb figure (Fig. 9–1) is an example of this. It would be difficult to conceive of this figure as carved out of stone. In its strongly proprioceptive quality, it retains some of the plasticity and vitality of clay.

It is not easy to carve figures out of most metals, but it is not impossible. Occasionally artists have carved directly into metal; much of the finishing—the chasing—of a piece cast in metal amounts to direct carving. There is also the area of welded metal which is sufficiently different from either carving in stone or wood, or building up in clay, plaster, or wax to require separate discussion. But the traditional technique of arriving at a metal sculpture is to work first in another material and then, through a series of steps, to arrive at the finished piece in metal. The metal used most frequently is bronze. The small figure by Henry Moore (Fig. 2–1) is an example of this method. It exists not only in several examples of the one cast, but also in a larger version.

The materials that are used in the initial construction of the piece are usually wax, plaster, or clay. Wax when it is warmed is pliable, can be molded, and will, under normal conditions, not lose the shape it has been given. It will also retain fine drawing and give good reproduction of this drawing in bronze. For these reasons wax is often used as a modeling material even though it is somewhat less easy to manipulate than clay or plaster.

Plaster and clay have somewhat different properties which lead to their being the most common modeling materials. Both are easy to work with, simple to prepare, and not difficult to keep. Plaster has the particular quality of hardening, or "setting up," very quickly. After the plaster has hardened it can be carved and drawn into with sharp tools rather as a soft stone can be. This is one of the most important differences between clay and plaster for the sculptor. Clay becomes hard slowly and it is possible to keep it soft and plastic for longer periods of time by keeping it damp, so that the artist can work with the material under fairly constant conditions. Plaster, with its rapid change from liquid to solid, gives the artist a material which has constant and consistent changes in qualities.

The artist's choice of material in which to model for casting into a permanent material (there are permanent materials other than metal, such as cement or plastic) depends on a number of different needs, some practical, some personal, and some aesthetic. For the viewer

Pottery Tomb Figure.

T'ang Dynasty.
Clay, engraved and painted, H. 44½".
*Courtesy of the Trustees, The British
    Museum, London.*

Fig. 9–1.

of the finished piece it is often difficult to tell what the earlier material of the sculpture was, especially if the final form is a highly finished cast. In many ways it is not particularly important to know just how it was done, but it is important to realize that the piece is, so to speak, the last phase in a series: to realize that it has evolved through a number of different forms and each time the artist has been able to see it in a new light or in a new way, and to make changes as the material allows.

In the last fifty years another technique has become increasingly common for the sculptor. This is the use of different kinds of welding and the widespread use of steel in making sculpture. In addition to welding, forging metal for sculpture has also come into more frequent use. A piece by David Smith called *The History of LeRoy Borton* (Fig. 9–2) shows the welding and forging of steel. Much welded sculpture has taken this linear form rather than the enclosed shapes of so many bronze and stone sculptures.

Brancusi's *Adam and Eve*

Let us consider the sculptor Constantine Brancusi (Fig. 9–3), as an example of a carver in stone and wood. He is a fitting choice because he shows so well his awareness of the materials he works with, and a great sensitivity to one material in relation to another. His piece called *Adam and Eve* is made of two kinds of wood, old oak and chestnut, and limestone. Each of these materials takes its place in the "column" of the piece. Brancusi was very concerned with the way in which his sculpture was shown, and therefore devoted as much care to the base as he did to the piece itself—so much care, in fact, that it is almost impossible to consider the sculpture apart from the base it is standing on. Indeed, what is the base of this piece? Is it just the block of limestone, or does the whole composite from the top of the block of chestnut resting at the middle of the piece constitute the base? These questions are not especially important, since what we call the different "parts" of the *Adam and Eve* should not affect the wholeness.

If one starts from the limestone block at the bottom and moves up the piece he is struck by the way in which the look and feel of each material is heightened by its relation to the others. The limestone has a white, chalky, granular appearance, while the oak is stringy, checked, and rough, and the chestnut is silky and fine-grained. It also seems that the materials took their positions from their own relative weights. Of course they did not; the artist put

SMITH. *The History of LeRoy Borton.*

(1906–   ; American.)
Steel, H. 88¼″.
Collection, The Museum of Modern Art, New York.
Mrs. Simon Guggenheim Fund.

Fig. 9–2.

BRANCUSI. *Adam and Eve.*

(1876–1957; Rumanian-born American.)
Chestnut and old oak, H. 88½″.
The Solomon R. Guggenheim Museum
  Collection, New York.

Fig. 9–3.

them in this order just as he gave them the form they have, but the point is that he probably *felt* that this relationship was what he wanted because it seemed appropriate to the material.

Brancusi was apparently working for, among other things, a sense of inevitability, a sense that these parts had to be in this order and had to be worked in this way. This is not to say that the piece is absolutely stable, but, rather, that it is in the right balance.

BRANCUSI. *The Fish.*

(1876–1957; Rumanian-born American.)
Gray marble, L. 71″.

*Collection, The Museum of Modern Art,
    New York.*
*Acquired through the Lillie P. Bliss
    Bequest.*

Fig. 9–4.

Brancusi's *Fish*

This point can be made in a more dramatic way if we turn to his *Fish* (Fig. 9–4). It is of marble and limestone; the fish is carved out of marble, the large round base from limestone. The title reminds us of the silent, balanced immobility which a still fish has when we look through water at him. It seems poised but not rigid; it seems in complete equilibrium but neither immobilized nor stuck. The materials and the way in which they were handled are a part of this meaning. The sheen of the polished marble, which seems so thin and finely carved against the roughness and thickness of the limestone disc, attracts our attention to the figure and makes it a precisely placed object in a field. This recalls what has been said about Brancusi's concern with the context his work was to be placed in, and what led him, as far as he could, to create the field in which his work is seen.

Michelangelo's *Medici Tombs*

This interest in the situation of the artist's work is one we will notice in different forms in the work of two other sculptors—Michelangelo and Giacometti. In the time of Michelangelo, large sculpture, which is what most of his is, was still mainly commissioned for a particular place and designed for that place and for a specific purpose. It is interesting that Michelangelo was also an architect and in the case of the Medici tombs designed both the sculpture and the chapel in which they were to be placed (Fig. 9–5). Thus the two become very much a part of each other.

Of particular interest here is the tomb of Giuliano de' Medici (Figs. 9–6, 9–7). It faces the tomb of Lorenzo de' Medici, on the opposite side of the chapel; the sculptures on each tomb are fitted into identical architectural structures. The sculpture is roughly similar: in each case there are three figures, one clothed and seated in a niche, and two nude reclining figures. Because of the close similarity of the architecture of the two walls, the differences between the figures are more vivid than their similarities. And since the figures within themselves are not symmetrical while their placement in the framework of architecture is, they seem to be straining against regularity and repetition.

This feeling of the figures trying to break out of the grid of the plan, and the curving, irregular forms of their bodies make them centers of vitality on which the spectator focuses, and with which

MICHELANGELO. *Medici Chapel.*
(1475–1564; Italian.)
San Lorenzo, Florence.
Photo: Alinari-Art Reference Bureau.

Fig. 9–5.

he can feel a strong identification. The space within the building is one of the most expressive this writer has experienced, and the experience is more related to power than to pleasure. The building seems to dominate a person within it—certainly not a bad thing for a building of this kind to do. The figures become a kind of embodiment of the lack of repose which the building conveys to visitors.

MICHELANGELO. *The Tomb of Giuliano.*

(1475–1564; Italian.)
Medici Chapel, San Lorenzo, Florence.
Photo: Alinari-Art Reference Bureau.

Fig. 9–6.

MICHELANGELO. *Night.*

Detail of *The Tomb of Giuliano.*
Photo: Alinari-Art Reference Bureau.

Fig. 9–7.

The female figure at Giuliano's feet (Fig. 9–7) represents *Night*. The other three nudes are Dawn, Day, and Evening. The figure of *Night* is asleep, but she is not in repose. Her body is twisted; one arm is pulled behind her back, and she is heavy and muscular. The material of the piece is marble and it is informative to compare it with the marble fish of Brancusi (Fig. 9–4). Both are carved and finished to a polish, but the similarity in the use of the material seems to end there. Brancusi minimized any sense of the weight of the stone by balancing it on a small point. Michelangelo emphasizes its heaviness with the weight of the marble and the representation of the heavy body pulling it down, almost off the curved ledge on which the figure lies.

The "sculptor's means" in this instance were more than simply the materials and techniques he used to make his marble figures. Michelangelo's means extended to the setting of the stage on which the figures could express what he wished them to. The figure of *Night* if it is seen apart from the building is difficult to grasp. She is too heavy, too muscular to fit into the long tradition of reclining nudes. But within the building and the experience of its space and light it is possible to understand the piece as a representation of the physical discomfort that is a part of the experience of the building, and, it might be added, a part of the common human lot.

Giacometti's *Composition with Three Figures and a Head*

The relationships of men to light and space and their bodily experience are also a theme with which the contemporary Swiss artist, Alberto Giacometti, is involved. In Giacometti's work it is less the pressure of inside space which surrounds and limits human beings than it is the way in which space separates them, and the way light seems to break up the edges of a form. *Composition with Three Figures and a Head* (*The Sand*) (Fig. 9–8) shows something of what is meant here. The parenthetical title—*The Sand*—suggests that this piece of sculpture reminded the artist of people on a beach standing at various distances from him. The figures are tall and thin like shadows in the early morning or late afternoon. The relative scale of the figures is not consistent with the space of the base, but they are consistent with the scale of human figures as they come toward us through an open space.

The piece is of cast bronze; it was first modeled in plaster over an armature. The bronze reproduces much of the look of the wet

GIACOMETTI. *Composition with Three Figures and a Head (The Sand).*

(1901–   ; Swiss.)
Bronze, H. 22″.
Pierre Matisse Gallery; Philip Johnson Collection.

Fig. 9–8.

plaster when it was buttered on, in the feet of the largest figure for instance, and the scraping and paring away of the dry plaster. This is most clearly evident on the base.

The base is, as it was in a different way with Brancusi, a part of the piece. The flat, squarish plane is lifted a little by short legs. The figures can be seen as parts of this surface, like the raised areas on a relief map. If it is looked at in this way, the figures are points by which we can measure the space. This can be just as easily turned around; the space is also what gives the figures their size.

The work of Giacometti, like the work of so many artists, can open our thoughts and cause us to reflect on some very familiar sensory experiences by making us shift our point of view about space or light or size. The works of sculpture are not so much like the abstractions of the scientist or the philosopher as they are statements of "This is how it looks," or "That is how it feels." To quote Irwin Edman again, "The artist utters reality." Sculpture is an attempt to revitalize our own experience of these things.

Works of sculpture, like other works of art, can provoke us into seeing things in new ways. This is also in large part the excuse for writing about art. It is frequently thought that art discussions are statements of fact, but they are actually statements of persuasion. As such they work in various and often unexpected ways and frequently are confusing and difficult to understand.

The Sculptor as a Builder

The sculptor, in whatever material he works, makes objects. He is a builder who through his craft constructs things which have weight and occupy space. He is usually very much aware of the physical labor involved in his work. He is also often aware of his work as an objectification of an idea or emotion, of the work of art as a tool through which he can arrest a feeling and put the feeling at a distance from him. The forms which these objectifications take, the characteristics of the feeling, perception, or idea that is emphasized in the work, are a part of the sculptor's means. The selection of forms and qualities is dictated in part by the artist's personal attitudes and values, but it is also deeply marked by the time and place in which he lives and the materials he uses. His materials also represent a choice which is only limited by the context of his life.

The use of welded and forged steel as a material for sculpture can demonstrate the dialogue between the artist and his material, and between the artist and his times. The piece of sculpture by

David Smith (Fig. 9–2) is much more a pattern of heavy lines in three dimensions than it is an enclosed volume. Although it makes an appeal to touch (which, it is interesting to note, the linear sculpture of Giacometti does not), this appeal is not a surface thing. The impulse is not to run one's hand over the surface as one would like to with a Brancusi. It is more that one wants to grasp the rods and wrap one's fingers around them, and perhaps try to pick up the work to test its weight. These actions are close to the actions of the sculptor when he is constructing a piece like this. He must grasp and hold the metal as he forms it and welds it together. The notion of construction as we use it when we speak of constructing a sentence is revealing in this instance. The sculpture is made by tying together a number of discrete parts to make the whole. Most of these parts are discernible in the finished piece, for instance, the long rods in the central section, the legs, and the cluster of pieces of metal at the top. At the risk of pressing the analogy with language too far, we could compare the use of found objects—like the legs in this example—with the way poets use words. The parts are placed in a new context which allows us to see them in a new way.

Since the majority of welded steel pieces are not made up of solid volumes, the question is raised whether they are sculpture at all, or if it is simply necessary to enlarge our ideas about what constitutes sculpture. Traditionally, a piece of sculpture encloses volume and stands still. Work like that of Smith and like Alexander Calder's *Lobster Trap and Fish Tail* (Fig. 9–9) lacks both of these characteristics.

Much of Calder's sculpture is constructed of wire and sheet metal, and balanced and joined in such a way that the parts can move. The over-all configuration is not constant but is one of a changing relationship of constant parts. The changes are in no sense uncontrolled, or any less controlled than are the variables in other techniques. They certainly are of a different sort, the constants in Calder's sculpture being the parts, the manner of their joining, the way they are balanced. Rather than enclosing space, they occupy it by moving through it.

It is interesting that most sculpture based on balance and movement seems to change less from one viewing of it to the next than does sculpture which depends on other aesthetic means. This may be because the parts, sheet metal shapes and the wires which connect them, generally have such bold, simple, flat shapes that variations in lighting do little to change the appearance of the parts.

CALDER. *Lobster Trap and Fish Tail.*

(1898–   ; American.)
Steel wire and sheet aluminum, H. 8½'.
Collection, The Museum of Modern Art,
*   New York.*
Gift of the Advisory Committee.

Fig. 9–9.

To expand our notions of the kinds of things a sculptor (or any artist) does is useful both in opening up the idea of what sculpture is and in allowing us to look back on the more traditional ways of working from another point of view. The carver who shapes a block of wood or stone is involved in a kind of activity very different from that of a person shaping and balancing wire and steel. They both give form to materials, but how different is the structure and the act of structuring in Michelangelo's *Night* and Calder's mobile!

Conclusion

In a three-sided comparison of Calder's *Lobster Trap and Fish Tail*, Brancusi's *The Fish*, and Giacometti's *Composition with Three Figures and a Head*, the threads of similarity pull the works together as much as the force of difference pushes them apart. The precision and clarity of the shape of the fish by Brancusi are not unlike the shapes in Calder's piece, but how completely different is the sense of weight in the two. The figures by Giacometti measure and divide the space of a field, and the same can be said of the moving shapes in the mobile; but the notion of a field is not closely akin in the two. These parallels can be developed, and the reader should do so for himself. The areas of the relation of exteroceptive and of proprioceptive sensations have only been touched upon here; but perhaps, in the process, we have suggested the richness and variety of possibilities open to the sculptor and, therefore, to the viewer in addressing a piece of sculpture.

Suggestions for Further Reading

The following three books are of a critical and historical character. Good illustrations.

GIEDON-WELCKER, C. *Contemporary Sculpture.* New York: Wittenborn, 1955.

READ, SIR HERBERT. *The Art of Sculpture.* New York: Pantheon Books, 1956. (Bollingen Series XXXV.)

RITCHIE, ANDREW. *Sculpture of the 20th Century.* New York: Museum of Modern Art, 1952.

STRUPPECK, JULES. *The Creation of Sculpture.* New York: Holt, Rinehart and Winston, Inc., 1952.

10. Drawings and Prints

What are Drawings?

Drawings are frequently and in many senses the most personal documents of an artist's work. A line, which by the simplest definition is the mark left on a surface by a moving point, is also the direct record of a physical gesture made by the artist. It marks the path of his hand carrying an instrument—a pen, pencil, or crayon, for instance—as it moves under the direction of his mind. The medium interposes itself less between the artist and his work than in any other technique.

Drawings are also personal in that they frequently constitute a tentative formulation of a notion that will turn into a fuller statement in a later work, perhaps in another medium. A drawing may be simply a linear notation of something that catches the artist's attention and so goes into a notebook for possible future use; or it may be in the nature of a study of a motif or detail which is to be developed in a larger work. This latter type is exemplified by the sheet of drawings in which Michelangelo studied the pose of a female figure in preparation for *The Libyan Sybil* of the Sistine ceiling fresco (Fig. 10–1). It is of incidental interest to note that in his drawing the painter studied the effect of light and shadow across the naked back, apparently in order to understand fully what existed structurally beneath the clothing which he intended to use in the final painting (Fig. 10–2). One sees here the artist actually at work on a visual idea or image.

MICHELANGELO. Studies for
   The Libyan Sybil.

(1475–1564; Italian.)
Red chalk, 11⅜″ × 8½″.
The Metropolitan Museum of Art,
   New York.
Joseph Pulitzer Fund, 1924.

Fig. 10–1.

MICHELANGELO. *The Libyan Sybil.*

(1475–1564; Italian.)
Fresco, Sistine Chapel, The Vatican, Rome.

Photo: Alinari-Art Reference Bureau.

Fig. 10–2.

Poussin. *Massacre of the Innocents.*

(c. 1593–1665; French.)
Ink, 5⅞″ × 5½″.
Musée de Lille.

Fig. 10–3.

Another example of such a study for a painting may be seen in the Poussin drawing (Figs. 10–3, 10–4). Here one sees how the artist can let himself go in drawing. He lets his mind wander and through drawing he talks to himself. Because the scale is small and the medium simple to use, he does not need to make each drawing count the way a painting or a piece of sculpture must. He need not be serious or so earnest when he is drawing, and the result often gains in spontaneity what is lost in importance.

POUSSIN. *Massacre of the Innocents.*

(c. 1593–1665; French.)
Oil on canvas, 57¼″ × 67¼″.
Musée Condé, Chantilly.

Fig. 10–4.

GRIS. *Portrait of Max Jacob.*

(1887–1927; Spanish.)
Pencil, 14″ × 10¼″.

Collection, The Museum of Modern Art,
  New York.
Gift of James Thrall Soby.

Fig. 10–5.

It would be a mistake, however, to give the impression that all drawings are sketches. Many artists do finished drawings, quite complete in themselves and in no sense studies for painting or sculpture. The Gris portrait (Fig. 10–5) is one example; another is Van Gogh's *The Fountain in the Hospital Garden* (Fig. 10–10). In each the artist has furnished us with a very complete work which has been seen as an end in itself and as something to be publicly displayed.

Much of the training of the artist is in drawing. It is through drawing that he learns many of the skills he needs, perhaps first and foremost the essential coordination of hand and eye. But he also learns more subtle and equally basic skills like the placing of shapes within the rectangle of a page or similar format. Traditionally, the artist learns through drawing to render the human body and its various parts in action and in repose. In drawing many artists first "find themselves"; they discover some of the important constant characteristics of their own methods and the nature of their personal imagery—in a word, the forms that will constitute a personal style.

Let us turn now to a discussion of individual drawings. Compare the *Seated Nude* by Modigliani (Fig. 10–6) with the *Seated Woman* by Seurat (Fig. 10–7). Modigliani delineates the figure in the simplest kind of outline. A few faint lines suggest a background. He does not indicate the illumination of the figure; all he shows is the boundary of the form. The line also breaks up the white of the page, but only slightly creates an illusion of space. The page is patterned by the line, but its flatness is not greatly disturbed.

In Seurat's *Seated Woman* the closest he comes to a clear line is in the back of the dress. She is silhouetted against the light but not definitely outlined by it. The light coming from the other side of the figure, that is, directly toward us as we look at the drawing, creates the form. The drawing evokes a certain kind of pale light that makes the contour unclear, and makes it hard to find an edge. These drawings by Modigliani and Seurat are poles apart: in the first, the artist is especially concerned with the boundaries or outlines of things; in the second, he is interested in the way light affects form. The outline of Modigliani describes a form which is at least related to a mental image, while the tonal drawing describes a visual, direct image.

The line that describes a form and patterns a page is the result of the artist's gesture, marking the path of movement his hand makes with a tool. The tool may be a pen, a brush, or an engraver's burin, and the surface may be paper or a metal plate or a stone, but the

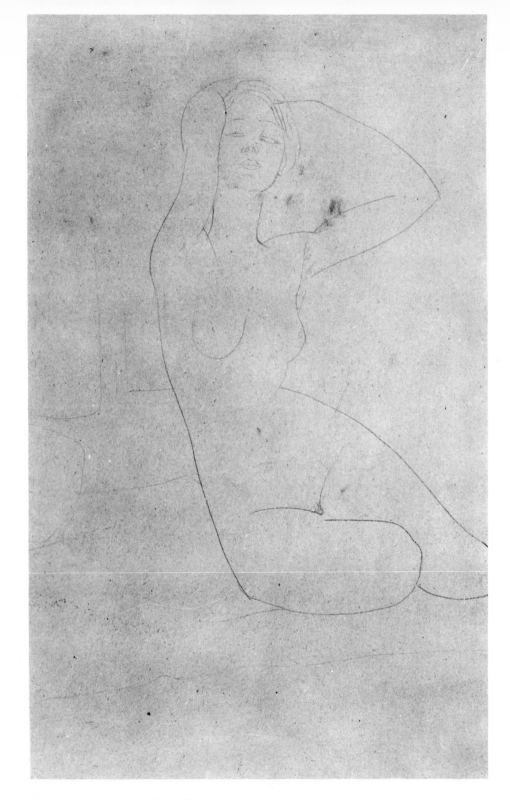

MODIGLIANI. *Seated Nude.*

(1884–1920; Italian.)
Pencil, 17⅜″ × 11″.
*Collection, The Museum of Modern Art,
New York.
Gift of Mrs. John D. Rockefeller, Jr.*

Fig. 10–6.

SEURAT. *Seated Woman.*

(1859–1891; French.)
Conte crayon, 18⅞″ × 12⅜″.
Collection, The Museum of Modern Art,
  New York.
Mrs. John D. Rockefeller, Jr., Bequest.

Fig. 10–7.

REMBRANDT. *Woman Carrying a Child Downstairs.*

(1606–1669; Dutch.)
Ink and wash, $7\frac{5}{16}'' \times 5\frac{1}{4}''$.
The Pierpont Morgan Library, New York.

Fig. 10–8.

marks on the surface are the record of a *particular* artist working with these materials in his own *particular* way. The line of the drawing is a kind of autograph; it is the personal gesture of the artist. In the drawing of the *Woman Carrying a Child Downstairs* (Fig. 10–8), Rembrandt's hand made quick, curving lines with his pen, constantly turning it and varying the pressure on the point. Modigliani, on the other hand, used his pencil with a kind of careful restraint; compared to his almost unbroken, wire-like lines, Rembrandt's line seems impetuous.

The artist finds his own mark by making it with his hand quite as much as he does by thinking about it. Drawing, like other forms of art, is a complex of working and looking, and the two are in constant interplay. In the drawing of the woman, Rembrandt also uses areas of wash to block in the shadows and, by contrast, to bring up the lights. This gives the figures and the space in the drawing a palpability, a certain weight and depth. He uses line to capture the general configuration of the drawing, and wash to give it weight and depth.

Light as it is seen and allows us to see is important in many wash drawings. These are usually done with a brush and ink applied in broad strokes and broken dabs rather than in lines. Pastel, chalk, and crayon are used in a similar way. Goya's *Two Prisoners in Irons* (Fig. 10–9) is such a wash drawing. The light he renders does two things: it exposes the form and, while making it visible, destroys most of its clear edges.

Both line and value are ways of abstracting, of editing appearances, of saying what is trivial and what is significant. In the *Two Prisoners in Irons,* Goya calls our attention to the dramatically dark shadows that are cast by figures standing on a light surface in bright light. We notice the contrasts between the dark and light of features which are recessed, like eyes, and features which stand out, like a nose; and the way in which brilliant, undiffused light gives us a sense of theatricality, a feeling of intense drama, of the pitiless degradation and helplessness of the human beings chained in blinding sunlight for all to see.

The selective emphasis of drawing is related to the selections and reductions made in other human activities. Drawings that deal with light and dark point up the drama of a scene or event as the theatre does; while line drawings often reduce a visual image to a diagram, or a schema of the significant characteristics, as we saw in the Egyptian painted, incised drawing (Fig. 4–35).

GOYA. *Two Prisoners in Irons.*

(1746–1828; Spanish.)
Ink wash, 8¹¹⁄₁₆″ × 5¾″.
The Metropolitan Museum of Art,
  New York.
Dick Fund, 1935.

Fig. 10–9.

Tools and Techniques of Drawing

The tools and techniques of drawing are simple. A drawing is made, usually, on paper with pen or brush and ink, or with a pencil, crayon, charcoal, or chalk. There are many possible combinations of these materials at the artist's disposal, but most drawings are done simply and directly. This is because drawing, as Ezra Pound said of poetry, is "piths and justs"; it is a record not only of what the artist found essential to communicate an image, if the drawing is representational, but also of what is necessary to make the page, the piece of paper and the marks on it, look "right."

Liquid materials—inks, water-color, and similar media—generally have a fluid look in the finished piece. In the Rembrandt (Fig. 10–8) the lines made by a pen with ink and the washes laid on by a brush are distinct. In both, the initial wetness of the material is retained in the finished drawing. The curls of the child's hair are written in with quickly flowing strokes, and the longer lines down his back to the woman's arm show by their darkness and apparently rapid application, the fluidity of ink and line that is typical of a certain kind of pen. The broad darks which are brushed in with wash—the ink here may have been diluted with water—show both the wetness of the full brush and what happens on paper with a rough surface or tooth at the end of a stroke when there is very little ink left in the brush. This is most obvious in the stroke down the woman's hip toward her foot. The brush mark starts quite dark and then breaks into an optical gray when the ink just catches on the highest parts of the paper.

The Van Gogh drawing (Fig. 10–10) reveals some other qualities of pen and ink. In this drawing a reed pen is used which makes angular, square-ended marks; the ink has dried with a range of values. The wetness and transparency of the ink are evident here as in the Rembrandt but they are realized through a different handling.

Chalk, like crayon, charcoal, and pencil, rests on the tooth of the paper just as the ink of a nearly dry brush does. In the Seurat (Fig. 10–7) and in Grünewald's *Crying Angel* (Fig. 10–13) it is possible to see this and also to note the different kinds of paper the artists have drawn on. The paper in Seurat's drawing has a much finer and more regular surface than has the paper which Grünewald used. The quality of the paper in each case is an important part of the over-all character of these drawings. The texture of the paper contributes to the very still, regular form and mood of the Seurat, just as the irregularly toothed paper used by Grünewald supports the activity and expressive posture of the angel's head.

VAN GOGH. *The Fountain in the Hospital Garden.*

(1853–1890; Dutch.)
Pen and ink, 18⅛″ × 17¹¹⁄₁₆″.
Collection of V. van Gogh, Laren.

Fig. 10–10.

Personal Styles of Drawing

A comparison of the Seurat and the Grünewald drawings indicates several of the possibilities available to the artist working with materials applied by abrasion; that is, where the drawing is made by rubbing a soft but solid substance on the surface of the paper. Grünewald worked mostly with line, but how different this line is from Rembrandt's made with pen and ink! Grünewald built up his dark areas with repeated strokes and with lines of varied thickness. Seurat on the other hand uses almost no lines; instead he fills in areas with his conte crayon and varies the heaviness of application.

Seurat and Grünewald deal in their own ways with the solidity and weight of the forms they render. Modigliani (Fig. 10–6), Ingres (Fig. 10–11), and Matisse (Fig. 10–12) treat their lines as the boundary of form and divide the page into a cluster of interlocking shapes. Each of these artists uses pencil for his drawing instrument but each uses it in a different way.

In the portrait drawing by Ingres of Madame Hayard, there is tremendous variety in the use of line. The head has a certain weight and tangibility, while the front of her dress is a pattern of lines with little suggestion of shading. Even in those areas where there is little or no shading to build up a sense of the roundness of the form, the overlapping of the material of the dress, and the perspective drawing of the woman's hands allow us to see the figure as occupying a three-dimensional space. It is also possible to ignore this dimension and delight simply in the beauty of the fine line and in its subtle variation.

The portrait of *Mlle. Yvonne Landsberg* by Matisse (Fig. 10–12) was done much more quickly and with a much coarser, thicker pencil than was the *Portrait of Madame Hayard*. The difference in rapidity of execution and coarseness of medium is consistent with the more general differences between the two drawings. There is descriptive grace about the Ingres drawing; it is more a report than it is a comment, and the report is made with ease and skill. Matisse, on the other hand, presents us with what is nearly a caricature of the sitter. He distorts and emphasizes her features, and places the drawing roughly to one side of the page. Consider for a moment the eyes of the two sitters. Madame Hayard looks out at us from eyes which are fairly precisely rendered. We can make out the pupil and iris, which are highlighted, and can distinguish the eyelid. Mlle. Landsberg's glance is away from the viewer, the eyes are not identical; they can be seen as supplying two different characteristics of the sitter's eyes; both must be almond-shaped like her right eye, and

INGRES. *Portrait of Madame Hayard.*

(1780–1867; French.)
Pencil on white paper, 10½″ × 7 1/16″.
Courtesy of The Fogg Museum of Art,
  Harvard University.
Meta and Paul J. Sachs Collection.

Fig. 10–11.

MATISSE. *Mlle. Yvonne Landsberg.*

(1869–1954; French.)
Pencil, 20¼″ × 16″.
Estate of the artist.

Fig. 10–12.

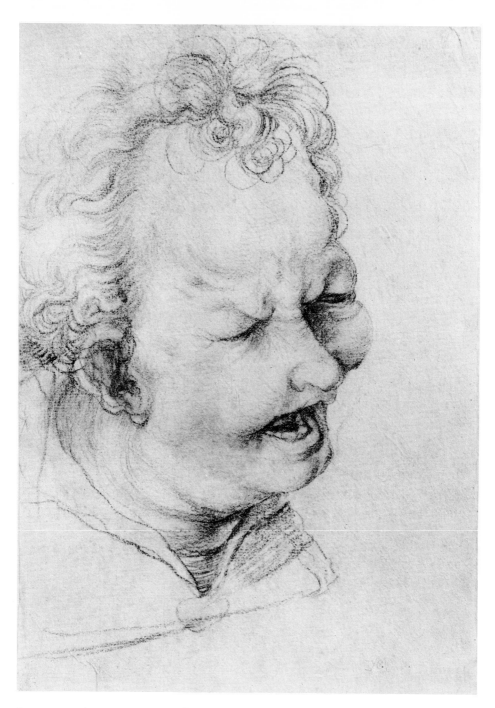

GRÜNEWALD. *Crying Angel.*

(c. 1470–1528; German.)
Black chalk, heightened with white,
  9⅝″ × 7⅞″.

Kupferstich-Kabinett, Berlin.

Fig. 10–13.

heavy lidded as is suggested by the left. The necessity the viewer is under to complete the face of the sitter, the artist's way of showing us just enough to allow us to fill out the face, is especially common in the present century. The use Matisse makes of the method here is interesting in contrast to the Ingres drawing. There is undeniably greater force, a feeling of verve and power in Matisse's drawing, and just as undeniably a roughness and grossness.

In both drawings the artist is completely consistent: in the way the material is used, in the pose of the model, in the placement of the drawing on the pages. Everything fits together closely, and everything contributes to the total character of the drawing.

It is possible to see something more about this wholeness and the integration of different aspects of the drawing by placing the Matisse portrait beside the *Crying Angel* of Grünewald (Fig. 10–13). Both artists express strongly overt feelings, and both place and posture their figures in unusual ways. Even the line often has similar curves and breaks in it. But the artists are not doing identical things. Their purposes, except in the general sense of communicating a strong emotion, are quite different. The Matisse portrait has the quality of a caricature: it selects and distorts individual features to the point of ugliness, twisting the face out of shape to point up its unique weaknesses. Grünewald distorts the features of the angel's face, describing the way in which all faces are distorted by emotion. The *Crying Angel* is not the image of an individual; it is a typical representation of a grief-stricken person.

Grünewald has left much less to the imagination of the viewer than has Matisse. The soft form of the lower jaw and neck is indicated with shading and we are shown explicitly how this form turns over the jaw. Mlle. Landsberg's face is only suggested by the curving of the side of her neck and the line that curls around her chin. But the smooth quality of skin sustained by fat is clearly suggested.

The difference between rendering and suggesting is an important one. No artist can either suggest everything (he must give us clues that describe something), or render everything (there are always things he must leave out because he cannot see them or because the medium does not allow for their representation). Some artists render much more of what they "know is there" and what they see than do others. When the artist is concerned with other than visual appearance he often plays down visual phenomena in order to play up other kinds. The drawing by Daumier (Fig. 10–14) is an excellent example of this kind of drawing. The subject is the pursuit of one horseman by another. Daumier indicates much more of the

DAUMIER. *Two Horsemen
Galloping.*
(1808–1879; French.)
Pen and ink, 5¾″ × 11″.
*Collection of Claude Roger-Marx,
Paris.*

Fig. 10–14.

speed and heat of the subject than he does the visual appearance
of two horsemen at a fast gallop. He does this by a kind of metaphor. He equates the movements of the horses with the movements
of his pen on the paper; the haste with which he draws is like the
haste with which they move.

The Nature and Uses of Line

It is frequently said that lines do not appear in nature, but this
limits the meaning of the word too sharply. What of the division
between the dark branch of a tree and the lighter sky against which
it is silhouetted? Or the edge of a white house against the green
foliage of trees? And what of the horizon marking the "meeting"
of earth and sky? In our visual experience of the outside world, lines
mark the limits of things; they delineate the shapes of things that
have little substance, like leaves. Line also traces the path of movement. The worm leaves a line in the soft clay over which it travels;
the skater cuts linear figure-eights in the surface of the ice; the
meteor leaves a trail of light across the sky.

THE ARTIST LOOKS AT ART

We have described line as the path of a gesture. It may be external to us, like that of a meteor which we perceive exteroceptively; or it may be in our own bodies, either an outward gesture, a wave of the hand, or an inward one like the "sinking" of the heart.

It is hardly necessary to point out that our gestures are always very personal to ourselves; one has only to compare handwriting to realize how personal these written gestures become. One knows also from experience that the character of handwriting varies with the mood of the writer, or responds to the relationship between the writer and the recipient of a letter. The reflection in line of psychological states can be even more vividly noted in the involuntary scribbles one makes on a telephone pad. Compare the absent-minded, meandering curly-cues and shaded triangles that occur during a leisurely telephone conversation, with the marks made during a midnight call to the doctor when the telephone rings and rings and there is no answer. In the latter, the sharp, jagged lines start and break off, abruptly change direction, are black and hard—the direct record of muscular and psychic tension.

A distinction has been made between rendering and suggesting. This can be carried a little further with reference to our perceptual experience. It may not be stretching the point to say that when, in our mind's eye, we have an image of something, we make a mental gesture around the object to separate it from nothingness, in effect "rendering" it as Matisse does in his portrait of Mlle. Landsberg. In Chapter 4 we saw that the mental image tends to be thus delineated, as in the child's "think" with a line drawn around it. But the direct, visual image presents us not with this abstraction of essentials but with a varied pattern of light and dark, of color and of movement, and these the artist suggests by a variety of technical means already touched upon, as in the form-drawing of Michelangelo's *Sybil*, or in the sharp and expressive contrasts of dark and light as in Goya's *Two Prisoners*.

It is, however, in the suggestion of movement that the artist finds line most essential to his purpose. The direct relation between the movements of Daumier's pen and the action of the horses he describes has been noted. Why is it that line is so effective a device for conveying the illusion of movement in a static image? Perhaps the answer lies first in the fact that a drawn or painted line is in itself the result of action and the association with this technical gesture endows the created image with movement. But there is also the tendency we have to follow with our eyes the direction and extension of lines. This makes our attention literally move through the painting or drawing or sculpture, and a sense of movement within the image is set up. The matter is more complex than this, but these two factors are basic.

In Rembrandt's drawing the curved line which describes the woman's left knee also describes its action as she steps down with her right leg. But there is one vertical line between the left knee and the little bag hanging from her waist that describes nothing. It simply expresses the downward movement, the pull of gravity that makes the child heavy to carry. Each of Rembrandt's lines—more than those of Michelangelo or Mantegna—has a life of its own. The heavy, downward strokes of the pen frequently end in loops or hooks, tiny records of manual gestures without descriptive function but serving to infuse into the drawing some of the artist's own vitality. A completely non-descriptive line descending in a series of loops from near the baby's foot is a kind of controlled "scribble" which adds to the general sense of the heaviness of the baby, the downward pull that pervades the figure of the mother as her foot gropes for the next step.

This method of drawing, which is descriptive in purpose and in the total result but abstract and non-descriptive in detail, is not peculiar to Rembrandt or to the Baroque and later periods of the European tradition. One finds it frequently in the Orient. Other examples are in the major masterpieces of the Carolingian Renaissance and in manuscripts deriving from the School of Rheims out of which the Utrecht Psalter came.

The Utrecht Psalter (Fig. 10–15) was probably written and illustrated in a monastery at Rheims. It is profusely illustrated with active little figures that move weightlessly about in a landscape among buildings and temples, rocks and streams—all suggested in a linear shorthand even more summarily than in the Rembrandt. Working, as he did, six hundred years after the decline of the ancient classical tradition of descriptive realism and some six centuries before the rise of the related style of the Renaissance, the draughtsman had no thought of representing objects or persons as they might appear to the eye under actual conditions of lighting; tactually felt solidity was no concern of his. But he had inherited from his northern ancestors the feeling for vitality that pervaded Celtic ornament (Fig. 10–16), and from Greco-Roman ancestors of his Carolingian culture the memories of a man-centered art.

In the illustration of the Twenty-third Psalm the Psalmist is shown seated at the right holding a cup in his left hand and grasping in his right a staff which an angel offers him. "Thy rod and thy

THE ARTIST LOOKS AT ART

The Twenty-Third Psalm.

Detail from *The Utrecht Psalter.*
(c. 820–832.)
Ink.
University Library of Utrecht.

Fig. 10–15.

staff they comfort me." He sits "beside the still waters" which rise in a hillside spring to his left and flow away across the picture beside the flocks and herds whose presence proclaims the "green pastures" of the psalm. A table is prepared in the "presence of (his) enemies" who are energetically letting fly their arrows and their spears in the direction of the Psalmist. These serve to remind us of the "valley of the shadow of death" through which the Psalmist walks "fearing no evil." The tabernacle or small building to the left represents the house of the Lord in which the Psalmist will dwell forever. The picture reads very clearly.

The "house of the Lord" is rendered in rather simple delineation with a minimum of shadow used quite arbitrarily without reference to a source of light, or even to the nature of the materials represented. The table also is very simply delineated, as is the single clump of grass in the pasture. The rising hills are suggested by great swirling and overlapping loops, the under-surfaces of which are darkened, and in the upper left corner of the picture one "loop" overlaps the figures of some goats who are climbing among the crevices of the rocky hillside. This overlap establishes, again by the merest suggestion, a spatial dimension in depth. The flow of the not-very-still waters is indicated by waving lines which taper off to

DRAWINGS AND PRINTS   273

Chi Rho Page, Book of Kells.

(c. 800.)
Tempera and ink, 13″ × 10″.
Trinity College, Dublin.

Fig. 10–16.

nothing. And finally, the actions of the angel as he bends solicitously over the Psalmist, "anointing (his) head with oil," and of the enemies as they attack, are expressed with a swift sureness of line that follows not the outlines but the inner movement of the bodies. They are essentially lines of direction though they serve a secondary, descriptive purpose as well. For instance, look at the second figure from the left in the group of enemies; a single line describes the left instep, the calf, the back of the thigh and the hem of the short tunic. This one stroke of the pen expresses also, and more emphatically, the backward pull of the man's body as he prepares to drive his spear. The man's weight, if he can be said to have weight, is supported on the right leg, where the lines are darker, perhaps to suggest strength.

The expressive vitality that pervades the illustration of the psalm is abstract-technical rather than descriptive. The Chi Rho page (Fig. 10–16) is of Celtic rather than Carolingian origin, an example of vitalistic calligraphy which (with a few exceptions) does not describe or suggest objects, but simply sets up a linear movement which has a throbbing life of its own. Human or beast heads occasionally terminate the seemingly endless meander, and, on this page, two cats confront each other near the base of the illuminated initial. These may perhaps be read as mental images, symbols, of the vitality which is the theme of the ornament.

What are Prints?

Prints and drawings are similar; both are often in black and white, are generally of a small size, and are on paper. A print is essentially a duplicable drawing, produced by means of a master block or plate, stone, or screen from which an edition of impressions can be printed. As we have seen, it is in the nature of art that the materials and the technical procedures should condition the artist's final work; and, when one has made the statement that "a print is a duplicable drawing," one must qualify it by pointing to the ways in which the nature of the process of reproduction affects the character of the resulting work of art.

The greatest difference between prints and drawings is that a print is made to be reproduced. There can be many copies of a single print, but any drawing is unique. For every print there is some kind of a master, a block, a plate, a stone, or a screen on which the artist sets his design and from which the impression is taken; whereas the drawing is usually done directly on the surface of the paper.

The major technical concern of a print-maker is that of making the master from which impressions can be printed. The problem is to prepare it for the kind of printing technique that will be used, drawing on or into the surface of the master in ways that are appropriate to the method of printing. The possibilities are roughly these: the print can be made from a raised surface, printed as type is printed; or it can be made by pulling ink out of lines sunk into the surface of the master as engraved cards and invitations are done; or it can be printed from the surface of a plate or stone by a method based on the fact that oil and water do not mix. The first of these possibilities includes woodcuts, wood engravings, and metal relief prints; the second, etching and engraving; and the third, the lithographic techniques.

Due to the more involved nature of the processes by which prints are made and to the excitement and beauty of these techniques, there is for some artists and for some viewers a great deal more interest in the print process than there is in that of drawing. Along with the drama and excitement, let us examine some of the stages that go into print-making.

Etching

Consider first the making of an etching. The artist will often start with a drawing which seems to him to have possibilities of development in this process, but he need not. He can begin work directly on the plate. The master from which etchings are made is usually a copper or zinc plate. Whether he works directly or from a drawing, the artist will first ground the plate with a wax substance which will resist the acids in which the plate will be immersed later. The whole surface is covered with ground either by painting or by rolling the ground on with a brayer. When the ground is dry, the artist will begin to draw through it to expose the metal. (There are ways of exposing the metal other than drawing through the ground, for instance a process known as lift ground, but we discuss here only the simplest and most common method.) After he has done as much drawing as he considers desirable, he places the plate in an acid bath, and the acid "bites" the metal where it is exposed; that is, the acid makes indentations in the surface of the plate following the lines of the drawing the artist has made with his needle in the wax ground.

Now he can remove the ground and ink and print the plate in order to see what he has on its surface. For some prints this is the

MATISSE. *The Swan.*

(1869–1954; French.)
Etching, 13″ × 9¾″.
Collection, The Museum of Modern Art,
  New York.
Mrs. John D. Rockefeller, Jr., Purchase
  Fund.

Fig. 10–17.

REMBRANDT. *Christ Crucified Between the Two Thieves* (Second State).

(1606–1669; Dutch.)
Etching, 14¼″ × 17⅝″.
The Metropolitan Museum of Art, New York.
Gift of Felix M. Warburg and his Family, 1941.

Fig. 10–18.

REMBRANDT. *Christ Crucified
    Between the Two Thieves*
    (Fourth State).

(1606–1669; Dutch.)
Etching, 14¼″ × 17⅝″.
*The Metropolitan Museum of Art,
    New York.*
*Gift of Felix M. Warburg and his
    Family, 1941.*

Fig. 10–19.

end of the process except for printing the edition; for others this is just the beginning of a long series of trial proofs and of more work on the plate between the proofs. *The Swan* by Matisse (Fig. 10–17) is an example of an etching executed with only one biting by the acid and only one stage of drawing on the plate. This kind of etching is more like drawing with a pen than are those that go through many stages of biting, printing, and redrawing. Rembrandt's *Christ Crucified Between the Two Thieves* (Figs. 10–18, 10–19) is a superb example of the second process. In this, not only was etching used, but the plate was also scratched directly with a sharp etching needle. Lines made in this way on the plate have a burr that gives the printed line a fuzzy warmth the etched line lacks.

Inking and printing are done in the following way: a heavy, oily ink is rubbed all over the plate and pushed into the etched line with a piece of rolled felt. When the lines have been filled, the excess ink is wiped off the plate with a cloth. One must be careful not to pull the ink out of the lines in the process of cleaning the unetched surface. The final wiping is sometimes done with the palm of the hand to keep from disturbing the ink which is to be used in printing, and to get the right plate tone. The plate is often kept warm during the inking so that the ink will be looser and will flow into the lines more easily.

The plate is then ready for printing. A press is used which exerts tremendous pressure on the plate, and the paper is dampened in order that it may be flexible enough to be pressed into the lines and to pull out the ink. After the plate and paper have passed through the press, the felt blankets that cushion the roller under which the plate passes are lifted. The paper is removed from the plate, and the artist can see how his print looks. He will often clean his plate of ink and go through the whole process again, adding new drawing and scraping out old in order to obtain a more satisfying result.

In the Rembrandt there were at least four states, of which two are shown here (Figs. 10–18, 10–19) to illustrate some of the changes the plate went through. Look at the group of men and horses at the foot of the cross to the left of Christ in the second state (Fig. 10–18). In that area almost nothing has been left in the fourth state that was in the second. Horses have been turned around, some figures have been taken out and new ones added. Even greater changes were made in the sky, and in the way the light strikes the figures.

For many print-makers the range of possible changes, the possibility of working and reworking the plate, is a source of great satisfaction. This is especially true of etching, engraving, and lithography since one can erase the unwanted marks in or on the surface. It is less true of woodcutting because new wood must be inlaid in order to reconstruct the surface.

Woodcutting

Another source of satisfaction—and this is especially true of engraving and woodcutting—lies in the carving out of a resistant material. In both engraving and woodcutting, the artist cuts away the material of the master with a tool; he literally carves it out. The signal difference here is that the engraver uses his burin to incise the lines that will carry the ink and print black, while in a woodcut the artist carves away what he does not want to print, the areas that are to be white.

Much of the excitement of contemporary woodcuts stems from the rough, raw quality that many of them have. Beckmann's *Self-Portrait* (Fig. 10–20) shows something of the crude but powerful image often obtained by the contemporary woodcutter. The printed blacks are broader and more angular than those of an etching or an engraving. The tools used are larger, because soft wood does not take the fine carving that metal will take and the softness of the wood makes it possible to work very rapidly.

There are also many woodcuts of harder and finer grained woods —often the wood of fruit trees—that lend themselves to much finer cutting. In the color woodcut by Utamaro of a woman and child, *Yamauba and Kintoki* (Fig. 10–21), it is possible to see this finer cutting and several different kinds of line. The strong black drawing around the edges and fold of the woman's garment is not unlike the drawing in Beckmann's print, although it shows fewer marks of the cutting tool. Enclosed in these black lines is an incised leaf pattern made by cutting away the wood. Then there is the very fine cutting of the lines of the woman's hair.

The blocks on which Utamaro's design was cut are of a much harder wood than the kind Beckmann used. This allows for a greater refinement in cutting, but it also makes the task of cutting more difficult.

The speed with which the print-maker can work is an important feature of his craft. The slower cutting of a harder wood makes the rhythm of the work rather like that of engraving a metal plate. Engraving in metal often has a slow, quiet pace and requires a great amount of control, a self-discipline which is less needed in woodcutting and etching.

BECKMANN. *Self-Portrait.*

(1884–1950; German.)
Woodcut, 8¾″ × 6⅛″.
Collection, The Museum of Modern Art,
 New York.

Fig. 10–20.

UTAMARO. *Yamauba and Kintoki.*

(1754–1806; Japanese.)
Woodcut, 9½″ × 15″.

Fig. 10–21.

Engraving

The engraver works with steel tools on copper or zinc. He uses
his tools to cut lines into the surface which will hold ink as etched
lines do, and the engraved master is printed in the same way as
is the etched plate. An engraved line is cleaner and more precise
than an etched line. This is due to the difference between the way
the metal is cut into by a graver or burin and the biting away of the
metal by acid. When the acid bites it leaves a slightly ragged, irreg-

Dürer. *Melencolia I.*

(1471–1528; German.)
Engraving, 9½″ × 7½″.
Photo: Marburg-Art Reference Bureau.

Fig. 10–22.

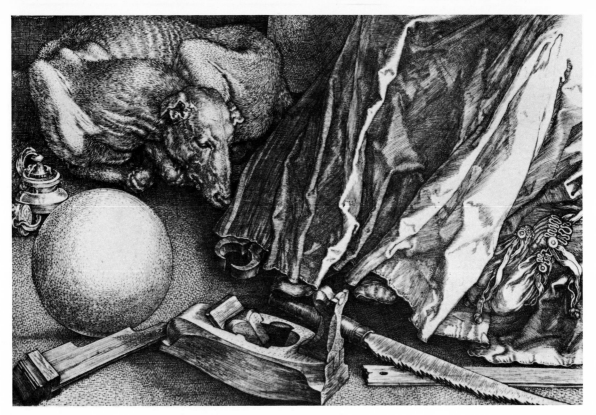

DÜRER. Detail of *Melencolia I.*
Photo: Marburg-Art Reference Bureau.
Fig. 10–23.

ular edge which gives the lines in an etching a slightly scratchy look, a little as though they were made by a slowly moving pen on a rough surface. An engraved line has none of this roughness; its precision is maintained throughout, since the pressure on the burin must be lessened in order for the tool to leave the metal without a rough spot.

The drama of the step-by-step procedure in etching is not present in the process of engraving. Each line is cut into the resistant surface of the metal, and the artist has a sense of making the print with physical effort. When an artist who has done engraving looks at an engraved print, he can almost feel the lines in his fingers, wrist, and shoulder. He has a sense of reliving the working of the plate that yields a real physical delight. The prints of Dürer's *Melencolia* (Fig. 10–22) are a store of the rich possibilities of the technique. In the detail illustrated (Fig. 10–23), one can see the various ways he used his graver in the ball, the plane, the saw, and the hem of the skirt. Each is very distinctive. Dürer's hand flicks and sweeps and curls about on the surface of the plate, cutting exactly the kind of line or the dot he wants.

Another masterpiece of the engraver's art is the *Mother and Child* by Mantegna (Fig. 1–6), which was discussed in the first chapter. To apprehend this print fully, imagine yourself groping over the whole with your hands, the sense of touch supplementing that of sight. Only in this way does one discover the relation between contour and volume, and between edge (as of the mother's cloak) and contour (as of the baby's head). Mantegna draws the pair with a simple, all-embracing contour which serves to establish the firm pyramidal group, but the outline is not continuous. It consists of a series of contours which constantly suggest the roundness of the forms contained within them. Follow the line that describes the shape of the mother's head; note that the lines of the hood and of the finer folds of her veil echo one another. Then notice that the outermost line comes in to the right of the throat, changes its direction, and marks the limit of the shoulder. It then descends along the upper arm and is lost behind a turned-back fold of the cloak. The line of the fold then takes up the boundary giving way presently to another drapery fold. This cooperation, or relay, continues around the whole figure.

In the hollows and valleys between the folds are passages of finely spaced lines of varying width and blackness. These describe the shadows into which the light does not enter; and by reminding us of the appearance of solid objects lighted from the side they strengthen our sense of the firm substance of the forms presented, of the roundness of the mother's arms as she clasps the baby, of the lift of her knees as she makes of her lap a bed exactly fitted to his body. The technique of the engraving seems itself to express the theme of the print.

Lithography

If one were to choose a single quality that distinguishes printmakers, it would be their enjoyment of and pride in their craft: in the skills of their work, and the sensory pleasures that accompany it; the beauty of the curl of copper as it is cut from the plate; the smell of wood chips; the gestures of wiping and printing; even the spin of a brayer inking a stone or block is very much a part of a print-maker's life. The sensations which go along with producing a print mean very much to the artist and leave only the faintest traces in the finished work. However, this sense of craft is not, of course, limited to the print-maker. It is part of any artist's dealing with materials, and it is the facet of the work of art that is most difficult for the non-artist to feel or appreciate.

In reviewing the procedures of print-making of which this kind of pleasure is a part, one thinks of grinding stones or watching stone being ground down for lithography. This grinding is necessary in order to take off any old drawing on the stone and to give the stone the proper grain for printing-drawing. It is often done by using two lithographic stones with water and abrasive between them, the upper stone being moved in a figure-eight over the lower. An easy rhythm is established and the whole body of the person grinding down the stones moves with a slow grace.

This part of the process leaves no recognizable mark on the print and it is not necessary to know about it when you look at a lithograph. It is, however, a part of the way of work, and even of life, for a lithographer. It should be noted here that many print-makers do not grind their own stones or print their own prints, but the actual doing of these things is a part of the ambience of print-making.

The stone is ground to prepare it to take the drawing which is usually done with either a lithographic crayon or a greasy liquid called tusche. Almost any greasy liquid or solid can be used since the underlying principle of the technique is to make the surface oily where the ink is to be picked up. This is done in printing by keeping the stone covered with a film of water which rolls off the greasy areas.

The artist draws directly on the stone; in this way lithography is more like crayon or ink drawing than the other types of print-making. He can scrape and re-draw as he works. When the drawing is finished, the stone (or plate, since metal is often used) goes through a series of steps calculated to make the areas not drawn on—those that are to print white—more resistant to grease, and the greasy, drawn parts less resistant. Thus, when the stone is finally ready for printing with a greasy lithographic ink, it will only adhere to those areas prepared by the drawing.

Goya, in his lithographs of bull fights (see *The Divided Arena*, Fig. 10–24) used a crayon almost exclusively. He seems to have covered the whole surface with a gray and then drawn in his darks and scraped out his lights. This gives a depth of tone and space to the print.

GOYA. *The Divided Arena.*

(1746–1828; Spanish.)
Lithograph, 11¾″ × 16½″.
*The Metropolitan Museum of Art,
    New York.*
Rogers Fund, 1920.

Fig. 10–24.

Goya uses lithography to combine the virtues of painting and
drawing. He has worked slowly to build up his print through a
series of steps or a combination of parts. In a bolder use of the
technique, an artist may draw with a brush and tusche in decisive
strokes, then cut through this heavy drawing with acid to produce

THE ARTIST LOOKS AT ART

clear whites. He may seem to have produced his print almost at one blow. (The phrase "at one blow" is used deliberately since the look has something to do with the fact that all these prints are made by pressure and they are in some sense struck from the master.) Thus in lithography may be found the same scope of expression that is evident in comparisons of woodcuts by Beckmann and Utamaro or of etchings by Matisse and Rembrandt.

Conclusion

To summarize, a print is an impression of a master block, plate, or stone; it is not a surface that is drawn on directly. This quality of the image, having been impressed on and often into the sheet of paper, gives to prints much of their uniqueness and distinguishes them from drawings. A drawing will often have a freshness and a fragility that a print cannot match; a print will frequently have a solidity, power, and depth that is difficult to obtain in drawing.

Suggestions for Further Reading

HAYTER, S. W. *New Ways of Gravure*. New York: Pantheon Books, 1949.
    Of special interest to the technician.
HIND, A. M. *History of Engraving and Etching*. Boston: Houghton-Mifflin Co., 1923.
    Of special interest to the historian.
IVINS, W. M., JR. *Prints and Visual Communication*. Cambridge, Mass.: Harvard University Press, 1958.
IVINS, W. M., JR. *How Prints Look*. Boston: Beacon Press, 1957.
    Of general interest.
PETERDI, GABOR. *Printmaking: Methods Old and New*. New York: The Macmillan Co., 1959.
    Especially for the technician.
ROSENBERG, J. *Great Draughtsmen from Pisanello to Picasso*. Cambridge, Mass.: Harvard University Press, 1959.
    A picture book.
SACHS, PAUL J. *Modern Prints and Drawings*. New York: Alfred A. Knopf, Inc., 1954.
SACHS, PAUL J. *Pocketbook of Great Drawings*. New York: Washington Square, 1962.
    Both picture books.
ZIGROSSER, CARL. *Six Centuries of Fine Prints*. New York: Covici-Friede, 1937.
    Of interest to the historian.

Index

Numbers in roman type indicate page numbers; titles and figure numbers of illustrations are in italics.

Proverb, translated into visual imagery, 7–8

Purposes of art, 50–51, 155, 158–72; private and public, 158; classification of, into four major types, 158–59, 171–72

Recumbent Figure (Moore), *8–2*

Relationships: within a work of art, 20, 41, 44, 150, 205; between an artist and a work of art, 186; of a mural to building space and light source, 194–95

Relief, examples of, *4–36, 5–5, 5–6, 5–7, 5–8*

Rembrandt Harmenz van Rhyn (1606–1669), *3–4, 7–10, 10–8, 10–18, 10–19*

Rendering, as distinguished from suggesting, 269, 271

Renoir, Pierre Auguste (1841–1919), *2–14, 4–13*

Repetition: as the basis of all order, 33, 34, 35, 36, 41; example, in decoration of Greek wine cup, 37–38; in *Adoration of the Shepherds* (El Greco), 44; in *Last Supper* (Leonardo), 46; repetitive pattern in archaic Greek style, 143

Representation, 14

Response to a painting, 3–4, 175; objective approach, 3–4, 175–79; subjective approach, 180–82, 196

Revitalization of experience, 247

Rhythm, 30, 41, 44

Romanesque Capital, from the Cuxa Cloister, *5–13*

Rouault, Georges (1871–1958), *4–2*

Rouen Cathedral, West Facade, Sunlight (Monet), *4–18*

Rubens, Peter Paul (1577–1640), *1–7, 3–3, 4–31*

Sachs, Hans, 8

Salisbury Cathedral (Constable), *4–16*

Satire, in *Land of Cockaigne* (Bruegel), 9

Schema, 132, 133, 134, 135, 136, 138, 139, 142; *see also* Mental images

Sculpture: craft of, 221; sculptor's means, 231–50; constructed sculpture, 247–50

Seated Nude (Modigliani), *10–6*

Seated Woman (Seurat), *10–7*

Self-Portrait (Beckmann), *10–20*

Self-Portrait (Rembrandt), *7–10*

Sensory quality of the artist's images, 121–29

Sequence, 35; in decoration, 37–38

Seurat, Georges (1859–1891), *10–7*

Shape, 63, 134, 177, 190, 203, 224

Shriek, The (Munch), *3–5*

Signs and symbols, 155

Sistine Chapel, The Vatican, Rome, *4–22, 8–4, 10–2*

Sketching, 257; *see also* Drawings

Smith, David (1906–   ), *9–2*

Solidity, 63; and images of reality, 111

Space, 49, 63, 111–19, 137, 138, 153, 176, 191–92, 241–43, 245

Starry Night (Van Gogh), *4–20*

State, of a print, 278–79

Steel, 238, 249

Stein, Gertrude, 3

Still life, 97–102; *for examples, see 4–9, 4–10, 4–11, 4–12*

Still Life (Holbein), *4–9*

Still Life with Basket of Apples (Cézanne), *4–12*

Still Life with Goblet and Fruit (Chardin), *4–11*

Stone, 23, 217, 218, 240, 244–45

Structure: as the vehicle of satire, 9; and emotional expression, 39–51; in *Gilles* (Watteau), 177–78

Studies, as preparation for painting; *see* Drawings

Style, 51, 141–45; concept of, 141; imagery, 142; archaic, 143; classical, 143–54; and purpose, 155

Subject, 6, 46, 51, 55–56

Subjective imagery, 84–88

Swan, The (Matisse), *10–17*

Symbol, 49, 80; symbolic method of artistic expression, 89

Symmetry, 185

Sympathy, contrasted with empathy, 122–23